Georgia State Literary Studies

8
READER ENTRAPMENT IN
EIGHTEENTH-CENTURY LITERATURE

GEORGIA STATE LITERARY STUDIES: No. 8

General Editor Victor A. Kramer

ISSN: 0884–8696

Reader Entrapment
in
Eighteenth-Century
Literature

Edited by

CARL R. KROPF

AMS PRESS
New York

Library of Congress Cataloging-in-Publication Data

Reader entrapment in eighteenth-century literature/edited by Carl Kropf.
    (Georgia State literary studies. ISSN 0884-8696; no. 8)
    Includes eight essays which originally appeared in the fall 1988 issue
    of Studies in the Literary Imagination, and nine essays commis-
    sioned for the volume.
    Includes bibliographical references (p.   ) and index.
    ISBN 0-404-63208-4
    1. English literature—18th century—History and criticism.
    2. Reader-response criticism. I. Kropf, Carl. II. title: Reader entrap-
    ment in 18th-century literature. III. Series: Georgia State literary
    studies; v. 8.
    PR442.R38 1992
    820.9'005—dc20

AMS Press, Inc.
56 East 13th Street
New York, N.Y. 10003

MANUFACTURED IN THE UNITED STATES OF AMERICA

Contents

vi   Contents

Notes on Contributors

G. DOUGLAS ATKINS is Professor and Coordinator of Graduate Studies in English at the University of Kansas. He is the author of *Reading Deconstruction/Deconstructive Reading, Quests of Difference: Reading Pope's Poems* and the forthcoming *Geoffrey Hartman: Criticism as Answerable Style*. He is also the General Editor of a new series from the University Press of Kentucky entitled *Literary Theory: Pedagogy and Practice*.

LOUISE K. BARNETT is a member of the English Department and Associate Dean of the Faculty of Arts and Sciences at Rutgers University. She has published numerous articles about English, American, and Italian literature. Her books include *The Ignoble Savage: American Literary Racism 1790–1890* and *Swift's Poetic Worlds*.

WILLIAM J. BURLING, an associate professor of English at Southwest Missouri State University, is a specialist in eighteenth-century drama and has published many articles on this subject. He is preparing a book on summer theater in London from 1660 to 1800 and *A Checklist of New Plays and Entertainments on the London Stage, 1700–1737* (Farleigh Dickinson, Forthcoming).

JOHN R. CLARK is Professor of English at the University of South Florida in Tampa. He has published extensively on a variety of subjects, including a book on Swift, and has edited an anthology of satire.

KEVIN L. COPE is Associate Professor of English Literature at Louisiana State University. Author of *The Criteria of Certainty,* he has written numerous essays on Restoration and eighteenth-century topics, from Rochester's satire to Johnson's prayers. His current projects include a book on genre and generic innovation in the eighteenth century and collections of essays on allegory and dialogue.

A. B. ENGLAND teaches at the University of Victoria in British Columbia, Canada. He is the author of *Byron's Don Juan and Eighteenth-Century Literature* and *Energy and Order in the Poetry of Swift,* as well as numerous articles on eighteenth and nineteenth-century literature.

CHRISTOPHER FOX, Associate Professor of English at the University of Notre Dame, is the editor of several books, including *Psychology and Literature in the Eighteenth Century* and the recent *Teaching Eighteenth-Century Poetry.* He is the author of *Locke and the Scriblerians: Identity and Consciousness in Early Eighteenth-Century Britain.*

ANTHONY KAUFMAN is Associate Professor of English at the University of Illinois, Urbana-Champaign, where he teaches Restoration and eighteenth-century drama. He has published on Wycherley, Congreve, Southerne, and others.

MELINDA ALLIKER RABB is an Associate Professor of English at Brown University and has published articles on eighteenth-century novels, poetry, and satire.

FREDERIK N. SMITH is Professor of English at the University of North Carolina at Charlotte. He is the author of *Language and Reality in Swift's "A Tale of a Tub"* and editor of and contributor to *The Genres of "Gulliver's Travels"* (1990). He has published also on modern fiction and is currently writing a book titled *Beckett's Eighteenth Century*.

JAMES THOMPSON, Associate Professor of English at the University of North Carolina, Chapel Hill, is the author of *Between Self and World: The Novels of Jane Austen* and *Language in Wycherley's Plays*. He is presently at work on a study of the origins of political economy and the novel.

JOHN P. ZOMCHICK is an assistant professor of English at the University of Tennessee, Knoxville. His essays on the eighteenth-century English novel have appeared in *English Literary History, Studies in English Literature,* and *Eighteenth-Century Life*. He is currently at work on a study of law, family, and fictional character in six English novels of the eighteenth century.

Prefatory Note

The articles gathered here were planned as an extension of the work that formed the Spring, 1984, issue of *Studies in the Literary Imagination* for which various essays were selected as examples of "Reader Entrapment in Eighteenth-Century Literature." As is the case with all editors of books in the Georgia State Literary Studies Series, this volume's editor, Dr. Carl R. Kropf, has encouraged extensive revision of earlier essays and commissioned (or selected) appropriate new ones that will balance with the revised materials from the original *Studies* issue.

Above all, this new collection of scholarly articles demonstrates that contemporary literary critics are involved *both* in the reading of classic eighteenth-century literature, as well as in enthusiastic writing about their reading. My judgment is that it is thus a matter of personal *engagement*—more than anything else—which has strengthened a quality already apparent in the earlier journal collection.

Many of the original essays are expanded. Many new topics are introduced. Additional ways of reading (or reading about readers) are demonstrated. The book that has resulted from the revision, updating, and expansion upon the earlier topic is, therefore, a demonstration that reading eighteenth-century literature—essays, poetry, drama, fiction—continues to be an experience which will draw readers.

One of the contributors for this book alludes to Roland Barthes, whose *The Pleasure of the Text* meditates upon the engagement that any text provides, and which is a desirable ingredient in successful reading. In that book Barthes writes: "The writer is always on the blind spot of systems, adrift; he is the joker in the pack, a *mana,* a zero degree, the dummy in the bridge game: necessary to the meaning . . . but himself deprived of fixed meaning; his place, his (exchange) *value,* varies according to the movements of history, the tactical blows of the struggle: he is asked all and / or nothing" (35). Because of the engagement of critics such as those in this book, we now more fully realize that readers (students, critics, scholars) can never ever really finish a text; rather they return to it with more attention, care, and interest.

Victor A. Kramer
General Editor
Georgia State Literary Studies

Introduction

The study of entrapment is one variety of audience-oriented criticism and as such has a long and complex history. From the time that Aristotle analyzed the cathartic affects of tragedy until the most recent arguments about the possible damaging effects of pornography, critics have assumed that literature has some measurable impact, for better or worse, on its audience. During the middle decades of the twentieth century the New Critics condemned the "Affective Fallacy" and redirected critical attentions from the audience to the text, but since then Reader Response Criticism, as it is called, has enjoyed a resurgence of popularity among academic critics and theorists. In her "Introduction" to *The Reader in the Text* (1980), Susan Suleiman examines six theoretical models of reader response: Rhetorical; semiotic and structuralist; phenomenological; subjective and psychoanalytic; sociological and historical; and hermeneutic. All of these theoretical constructs and probably some others as well can be deployed as justification for the study of reader response of which reader entrapment is one subset.

Whatever his theoretical basis, the reader response critic singles out and deciphers the codes and conventions the author built into the text to elicit the reader's response. In doing so, the critic may demonstrate that the text is designed to complicate, simplify, or even frustrate the reader's response, but in any

event he works out of the assumption that the text is designed
to have some measurable impact or discernible meaning as defined in terms of the reader's response to the text. Perhaps the
clearest and best known explanation of this approach to the text
is to be found in the opening words of the chapter, "The Reading
Process" in Wolfgang Iser's *The Implied Reader*: "The phenomenological theory of art" Iser explains, "lays full stress on the
idea that, in considering a literary work, one must take into
account not only the actual text but also, and in equal measure,
the actions involved in responding to that text" (274). Thus,
every work has two poles, the artistic pole, the text created by
the author, and the aesthetic pole, the reader's "realization" of
the text, to use the phenomenologist's term. In the event that
the text frustrates the careful reader's attempts at realization,
or if the realization or possible realizations cause the reader
discomfort, by placing him in the role of a voyeur, for example,
then the work is said to entrap the reader.

In short, entrapment occurs when an author seems to force
his reader into choosing among unacceptable readings, forces
him into an unacceptable role, arouses expectations he does not
fulfill, or otherwise causes the reader significant discomfort. Entrapment, therefore, is not simply or exclusively a matter of
satire, irony, or offensive statement. Merely to ridicule or to
insult is not to entrap. Entrapment beguiles the reader into
consenting to a proposition or assuming a role that has painful
consequences in light of more mature reflection or of later developments in the text. Perhaps the most obvious example of audience entrapment is the notorious "clap-trap," a common strategy
among eighteenth-century dramatists. In modern usage the
term means something like bombast or insincere language. To
the eighteenth-century critic it meant a visual or semantic trick
to provoke applause from an unwilling audience. Extravagant
scenic affects, clever political allusions, or inside jokes designed
to provoke a favorable audience reaction but of dubious relevance to the play's plot or theme are examples.

Entrapment in written texts usually beguiles the reader
into consenting to a proposition that is uncomfortable, self-con-
tradictory, or turns out to have painful consequences. If I may
ruin a joke by explaining it, consider Swift's first sentence in his

"Preface of the Author" to *The Battle of the Books*: "Satire is a sort of *glass,* wherein beholders do generally discover everybody's face but their own; which is the chief reason for that kind of reception it meets in the world, and that so very few are offended with it." The reader readily consents to the major premise that (present company excepted, of course) people tend to find faults in others but to overlook those faults in themselves. He is also likely to consent to the minor premise that satire is a species of fault finding. Only after consenting to these cliches, however, does the reader perceive that he has just assented to and reenacted the very fault Swift is lamenting and that he is trapped and cannot escape without going back and rephrasing the premises at least to soften the self-incrimination.

An author can often lure the unsuspecting reader into accepting premises or unarticulated assumptions that can then be used to support conclusions the reader resists as unacceptable. In some cases the reader may come to the work with such assumptions already in place. In his essay in this volume, for example, Kevin L. Cope shows how the multitudes of subtexts already known to the reader operate in mock-Miltonic poems so that the texts self-deconstruct and their meaning disappears into a sort of Swiftian "abyss of things." G. Douglas Atkins argues that professional critics too often bring firmly entrenched critical presuppositions to texts, presuppositions that then trap them into "raping" rather than "reading" texts and responding in professional "plain-brown-wrapper" prose that often does more to obscure than to illuminate the issues. Later in this volume in his essay dealing with Swift's *A Description of the Morning* A. B. England illustrates precisely the point Atkins is arguing. England shows that several critics have denied the discontinuity that England takes as an essential feature of the poem and have tried to impose on it a meaning that the evidence in the text does not justify.

The essays in this volume are loosely arranged by genre. The first two, by G. Douglas Atkins and Kevin L. Cope, have already been mentioned. The next five essays deal with Swift, two with his poetry and three with *Gulliver's Travels*. That Swift is so heavily represented in this volume will come as no surprise to those familiar with his works and their criticism. In the opening pages of his essay on "The Danger of Reading Swift," Frederik N. Smith shows that as early as 1934 F. R. Leavis recognized that reader entrapment is a characteristic feature of Swift's irony. The essays by Louise K. Barnett and A. B. England treat Swift's poetry, especially the scatological poetry. Barnett's argument is that what is shocking about these notorious poems is not so much their content as it is the role of voyeur that they privilege and force the reader to assume. England's essay, mentioned earlier, deals with two poems that seem designed to entrap the reader eager to locate the kind of meaningful unity most of us automatically assume is fundamental to all works with some claim to literary esteem. *Strephon and Chloe,* he argues, offers an obvious thematic statement about problems of the flesh, but at the same time the text itself undercuts any such reductive treatment. *A Description of the Morning* offers no such obvious thematic purpose and therefore provokes the reader into over-interpretation.

The next three essays treat *Gulliver's Travels.* Christopher Fox argues that one of Swift's seemingly gratuitous sexual jokes in the opening paragraphs of the work introduces the theme of self-love and self-loathing that becomes increasingly important as the work progresses. Frederik N. Smith's essay on "The Danger of Reading Swift" demonstrates that Gulliver's straightforward style in contrast to the complex style of *A Tale of a Tub* is particularly well-calculated to camouflage the numerous traps, reversals, and double reversals of reader expectations. John R. Clark's essay on "The Swiftian Swindle" demonstrates how in the final book of *Gulliver's Travels* Swift repeatedly violates the implied reader/author contract.

The next three essays are on the drama. In "The Smiler with the Knife" Anthony Kaufman analyzes three epilogues for the way they go beyond the ritualistic, licensed audience abuse typical of the Restoration and, relying on the background provided by the play itself, reverse normal expectations and genuinely abuse the audience. James Thompson analyzes Wycherley's entire dramatic career as an expression of the general hostility that prevailed between playwrights and audiences during the Restoration. William J. Burling finds several examples of the way sight and sound subvert sense and thus entrap the audience in the drama from Congreve to Goldsmith with special emphasis on the famous proviso scene in *The Way of the World* and the marriage arrangements in *She Stoops to Conquer.* The final two essays are on narrative. John P. Zomchick traces the complex manner Smollett uses to emplot the reader in *Roderick Random* so that he identifies with Roderick's private, erotic world as he struggles against a brutal Hobbesian public world. In the final essay Melinda Alliker Rabb analyzes Fielding's last narrative, *Journal of a Voyage to Lisbon,* as a configuration of opposites so that in the reading process the reader himself is forced to experience the same frustrations, delays, and irritations that Fielding himself experienced during his voyage.

Taken as a group these essays suggest several conclusions. Entrapment clearly provides one useful and flexible way of understanding a broad variety of eighteenth-century genres and texts that seem to defy most standard approaches. As England's analysis of Swift's poems demonstrates, works that frustrate attempts to reduce them to purposeful thematic statements or to understand them in terms of teleological structure become amenable to analysis if we take that frustration itself as an expression of the implied author's purpose. Rabb's analysis of Fielding's *Voyage* is another persuasive argument that the way the narrator complicates any reader's response to the text reflects the narrator's own complicated feelings and response to his experiences. It is also clear that entrapment is not so much a theoretical model as it is an interpretative tool that can be derived from any number of theories. In the present volume Cope's theoretical model is deconstructionist, Thompson's is Marxist, Burling's is historical; yet all conclude that the texts they treat are examples of audience entrapment.

And finally this collection offers further evidence, were any needed, that Swift's works remain one of the richest bodies of work for interpretative exploration. His prose satires are the densest the language has to offer, and in spite of the large volume of criticism devoted to them within the past decade, his poems remain fresh, enigmatic and fascinating.

Carl R. Kropf

On the Critical Character: Reading and Writing in the Poststructuralist Age

G. Douglas Atkins

The original title of my essay was "Reading/Raping/Reaping," for I wanted to play on the similarities of sight and sound that link *reading* with *reaping* and *reaping* with *raping*. My concern was to focus on reading while noting the very real danger that it may become a violation. But a woman who read a draft of this essay rightly objected to the linking of reading and reaping through raping. She convinced me to change the title and look again at my assumptions. Although my original title was inappropriate, and indeed insensitive, we must acknowledge, even as we deplore it, that reading *can* be a drive towards mastery that in its violence could be at least figured by the far worse violence of rape. Instead, it *should* be gentle and generous,

This is a significantly altered version of an essay published in *New Orleans Review* 15 (1988).

above all welcome and solicited. My terms are sexual, but not offensively so, I hope. You don't have to be a Barthesian to appreciate the similarities between reading and love(making): in both, slow, careful nurture and cultivation lead to reaping untold pleasures.[1]

This essay, then, treats critical attitudes, tact, and skills in cultivation, focusing on the kind of relation that exists between reader and text as well as between reader and culture and society. It also concerns the form that the critic's response takes, for the critic's *writing* is important, probably far more so than we often assume. In short, the discussion will raise questions of critical tone and deportment–in other words, *critical character*. In this, I shall be following Pope, of course: "Nor in the *Critick* let the *Man* be lost!" he exclaims in *An Essay on Criticism* (523). He also contends that only those who write well themselves should instruct others in the art of writing (I accept the point while feeling its sting). So important is writing to Pope that he argues, quoting the Duke of Buckingham, that *"Nature's chief Master-piece is writing well"* (724). At any rate, we in the post-structuralist age are witnessing not the birth of the critic, obviously, but perhaps the critic's achieving majority. Critical character thus takes on considerable importance.

To begin, at last: The number of available, current, but different, competing, and not necessarily compatible theoretical orientations raises important questions. What *is* the relation of these theories one to another? And what is the reader to do with so many choices, in the face of so much wealth? Having recently wrestled with these issues in co-editing a textbook, which consists of separate discussions from twelve other theoretical positions, I am sensitive to the enormity of the questions. In introducing the essays in *Contemporary Literary Theory*, I distinguish between *a theory*, which more or less affects, via specific openings, strategies, or privileged questions, how we read texts, and *theory* itself, which Gerald Graff defines "not as a set of systematic principles, necessarily, or a founding philosophy, but simply as an inquiry into assumptions, premises, and legitimating principles and concepts."[2] A powerful mode of self-consciousness and self-reflexiveness, indeed of self-critique, theory allows us to understand how we are thinking, what we are including and excluding, losing and gaining, when we employ a particular theory. What I am doing here may be considered the work of theory.

Amid this God's plenty of theories, are we free to choose? And does it make any difference whether the "approach" we opt for is structuralist rather than Marxist, feminist, Bakhtinian, or deconstructionist? Obviously it does. A deconstructionist does close, intense, and rigorous reading, which may lead to exciting, occasionally surprising, even breathtaking *textual* discoveries. A Marxist, on the other hand, may produce a discussion in which the reading of specific texts pales in comparison but gains in the capacious questioning of basic values. Often, it seems, *readings* at least verge on formalism—at the expense of "extrinsic," or referential, concerns, which thus appear bracketed or ignored. "Activist" discussions, on the other hand, seem to slight the text, sometimes paying only lip-service to it in the rush to condemn or to take on large social issues—that is certainly the charge of hostile traditionalist reviewers of poststructuralist studies of Pope and other figures.

Though a deconstructionist need not neglect cultural and political questions any more than a Marxist need slight the text, the power theories have, each with its particular biases and inclinations, can hardly be doubted. In fact, the choice of a theory may not only color but actually determine the reading produced. That is, the Dryden, the Swift, or the Pope we have can be, and probably is, dependent on, and a creation of, the theoretical orientation with which we read. Come with a feminist theory, and the Richardson that emerges from your discussion will inevitably bear the marks of that theory. With theories like feminism, Marxism, and deconstruction, the situation is particularly complex, for you will—to use my favored terms—"read against the grain," proceeding contrary to, say, Pope's apparent intentions and producing an interpretation of him as different: depending on your choice of theory, as different from himself or different from the values you cherish and apply.[3] He will be strikingly different, in any case, from the complex craftsman, firmly in charge of his line and his meanings, the master of language, that rose, lavished with elegant praise, from the influential New Critical readings of Maynard Mack, Aubrey Williams, Reuben Brower, and others. These critics and others—Earl Wasserman comes to mind—produced stately and sometimes graceful readings that were consoling in the way they managed to *contain* Pope's complexities (the idea of *concordia discors* lay ready to hand). Now Pope, even Pope, has come apart, and God only knows whether he can be put back together again. The situation has thus changed radically from that Frederick M. Keener described in 1974: "Elegant, aloof, most modern criticism of Pope reads as if it emanated not from twentieth-century America or England but from some miraculously undisturbed eighteenth-century estate, what Hugh Kenner has called 'the professional Popeans' Natchez-Augustan manor' "—a house now not so much divided against itself or in need of repair as condemned (fairly or unfairly) and apparently destined for demolition.[4]

My intention here is neither to celebrate unproblematically the new order nor, I hope it is clear, lament the passing of the old, though I do think that with the advent—for example—of the poststructuralist Pope, figured in a number of recent studies,[5] we are experiencing losses as well as gains. Nor do I rejoice in our freedom to have (or make) any text we want. And I have no wish to bewail the impossibility of a theory-transcendent or theory-free practice. My remarks hereafter will, then, strike some as unduly cautious, therefore reactionary, and others as iconoclastic and extreme. Such is the power ideology can (does?) hold over us.

The relation of a theory to a produced reading is the structural equivalent of the relation of reader to text, which subsumes it, in fact. At issue remains power, control, even mastery: Who is on top? I hope I may be forgiven for repeating with some modifications my own earlier account of "the battle of wills" involved in every act of reading. To ask a question of a text, I claimed, represents an attempt to coerce a response; it is an attempt to make the respondent responsive, that is, willing to answer. But the response, I continue to believe, which is also will-ing (though not necessarily willing), is incomplete at best, and serves mainly to raise additional questions. Imposition occurs, and it comes from text and critic alike. In this battle of wills, disturbingly dramatized in Swift's *A Tale of a Tub*, exists a dialogue of questions that is a mutual coercion. Mutually dependent on language, critic and text question each other, read each other.

The single-minded drive towards mastery, even rape, can be transformed into a more complex relation. For even as they jockey for position, critic and text are locked—it is a fortunate fall—in a ceaseless oscillation in which neither acts as master to a slave-other.[6] The situation I describe is not merely ideal, therefore; it is the structural definition of the reading process, which the willing critic may, of course, in any single enactment of that process, violate. The relation of the reader to text is like Wordsworth's understanding of the relation of mind or imagination to nature: it is one of "mutual domination" and "interchangeable supremacy."[7]

This situation entails respect for, as well as engagement with, texts. Such respect leads not to idolatry, where the text becomes, willy-nilly, a quasi-sacred object of reverence and worship, before which the awed critic prostrates himself or herself in abject subordination. The critic, in short, faces the difficult task of being true to herself or himself *and* to the text, of achieving a balance between competing and willful forces with needs that must be respected. I see no way to avoid questions of tact: the critic must take responsibility.

The criticism I find most attractive and effective shuttles between a text, which it reads closely rather than quotes closely or paraphrases, and a particular idea or issue in theory, whether that be literary, philosophical, religious, political, or cultural. Without close attention to a text the work hardly deserves the name literary criticism; without concerned attention to extrinsic issues, the work is puerile, constituting exegesis or explication *in vacuo* and not mature criticism. In order to resist the temptation, still fairly strong, to idolize the text, without either slighting it or neglecting important external issues, the critic might, taking a cue from Blake, look *through* the text and not merely at it. Like nature as Wordsworth came to understand his "anchor," "the muse, / The guide, the guardian of [his] heart, and soul / Of all [his] moral being" (*Tintern Abbey* ll.109–ll), the text leads us beyond itself, in an interpreted act of considerable generosity; in some sense, it continues to "anchor" us even as we transcend it.

The critic's task involves more than achieving and maintaining balance on what must seem, from my description, a highly unstable and even dangerous teeter-totter. It requires interpretive skill, knowledge, and immersion in tradition, with its severe demands (what *is* the relation of the individual critical talent to both literary and critical tradition?). With a parochialism of culture, we have "operators," or processors of texts, rather than readers, and in such cases we inevitably produce impoverished readings, the consequence of methods that submit texts to the meat-grinder of a particular theory, from which they will come out, you can bet on it, as hamburger, at best eighty percent lean. It is not, after all, "the individual poem that determines the meaning of indeterminate phrases but the poem as part of an intertextual corpus which the skilled interpreter supplies."[8] Because it is necessarily intertextual, meaning emerges not from individual, isolated, autonomous texts, as the New Critics thought, but from the way one text is related to another; no text is an island complete unto itself. The skilled and knowledgeable interpreter, widely read and broadly cultured, supplies the "intertextual corpus" from which the individual poem or play or novel or essay acquires its meaning. Thus the critic's responsibility is indeed considerable.

All of this talk of respect, generosity, tact, and responsibility may sound well and good—and even appeal to traditionalists since it embraces the human values they profess to cherish and claim to defend against the nihilist barbarians poised at the gates. But is it possible? Is it not merely an ideal, perhaps devoutly to be wished, but only a pie-in-the-sky dream, reflecting the irreducible vanity of human wishes? I don't know for certain, of course, but I believe it possible, for example, despite the lure of security and strength promised by commitment to one theory or another, to resist such seductiveness and to break the frame of meaning we (inevitably) bring to the act of reading. Otherwise, theory as defined earlier is an impossible enterprise. I remain unconvinced that the notion of "interpretive communities" tells the whole story. They are not always or inevitably determining, and we can break out of them. After all, we change our critical allegiancies and move from one interpretive or theoretical community to another. I, for instance, have moved around quite a lot.

The self-critical effort advocated here partakes of the indeterminacy championed by deconstruction—though some distinctions are in order. As Geoffrey Hartman argues, "indeterminacy does not merely *delay* the determination of meaning, that is, suspend premature judgments and allow greater thoughtfulness. The delay is not heuristic alone, a device to slow reading till we appreciate . . . its complexity. The delay is intrinsic: from a certain point of view, it is thoughtfulness itself," akin, no doubt, to Keats's "negative capability": "that is," Keats explains, "when man is capable of being in uncertainties, Mysteries, doubts, without any irritable reaching after fact & reason." Indeterminacy is, then, "a labor that aims not to overcome the negative or indeterminate but to stay within it as long as is necessary."[9] Looking toward a "negative hermeneutics," that effort thus manifests "a structure of postponement; the doubting or delaying of closure, the insistence on remainders or of a return of the past."[10] There is always, it seems, something left over or neglected, another issue to be considered, another side of the question that forestalls a solution. I am suggesting here a "negative way" that allows for a more open and dialectical—a more generous—thinking than appears in the single-minded, almost totalitarian drive that marks both much poststructuralist writing and the iron-fisted polemics of many of its opponents. Increasingly, it seems, we are being pressured to choose decisively, to come down definitively on one side or another, feminist, Marxist, traditional-humanist. I prefer Walter Benjamin's position as it has recently been interpreted: "The one-dimensional progressive claims of conqueror or would-be conqueror are disabled by hermeneutic reflection."[11]

Ultimately, the question of style rears its not-so-ugly head; from one perspective, we have been discussing nothing else. I want to be quite specific and reflect on the critic's way of writing. That reveals a good bit, of course, about the felt relation to the text commented on as well as about the critical character. We want to know, among other things, what the critic wants. It matters whether his or her own writing matters to the critic and how much. The critic too should cultivate prose, not necessarily in hopes of producing a garden of delights but at least with the expectation of removing unsightly weeds that threaten to choke the growth of the seedlings.

I agree with Hartman: "the spectacle of the polite critic dealing with an extravagant literature, trying so hard to come to terms with it in his own tempered language, verges on the ludicrous."[12] Literature represents the writer's attempt to come to terms with an extra-ordinary *event*. How much does it matter whether we are considering the extra-ordinary *event* that Yeats represented in "Leda and the Swan" or that Pope depicted as "the rape" of Arabella Fermor's lock or the extra-ordinary *language-event* that such poems are? In both cases, primary and secondary, each involving reception and response, the extra-ordinary is what matters. Demanded, one might suppose, is an *answerable* style. Should we expect (to be able) to respond to *The Divine Comedy*, *Hamlet*, or *Clarissa* in a style measured, distant, and objective? The cool, accommodated prose of the scholarly article, the *sine qua non* of the profession, practiced by traditionalist and poststructuralist alike, may reflect a critical character potentially impoverished, perhaps repressing its artistic instincts, and not very interesting.

Critical *writing* matters, though too few poststructuralists seem to agree, which is ironic given all their attention to language and writing—*others'* language and writing. An absence of any such concern constitutes, for me, a failure as well as a strategic mistake that offers aid and comfort to "the enemy." Remedy lies, I suggest, in considering our work as literary and seeking to achieve in our criticism some of those artistic qualities we admire in "primary" texts but consider out of place in our "secondary" endeavors. I am not talking, therefore, simply about the clarity that poststructuralist writing would assuredly benefit from and that traditional scholars might value a little less highly, at least in relation to other qualities. Nor am I suggesting that we simply pepper our prose with metaphors or load it with the pyrotechnical devices characteristic of certain "unisex" experiments in "paracriticism." My concern is that we consider our work a craft and take pride in it, as old-fashioned as that sounds. I propose only (!) that we care about the shape and rhythm of our sentences, the movement of our paragraphs, the resonances that can so please a reader, the sound and feel of our language as it strikes against the ear—and perhaps the heart.

We need, I think, to recover the tradition of the *essay*. Unfortunately, we have lost (if we ever really had it) the distinction between the essay and the article. What constitutes an essay and how it differs from the form prized by the profession has recently and provocatively been described by the philosopher-novelist-essayist William H. Gass, writing spiritedly on "Emerson and the Essay." I am going to quote him at some length, though I don't agree with everything he says. The essayist, writes Gass,

> is an amateur, a Virginia Woolf who has merely done a little reading up; he is not out for profit (even when paid), or promotion (even if it occurs); but is interested solely in the essay's special *art*. Meditation is the essence of it; it measures meanings; makes maps; exfoliates. The essay is unhurried (although Bacon's aren't); it browses among books; it enjoys an idea like a fine wine; it thumbs through things. It turns round and round upon its topic, exposing this aspect and then that; proposing possibilities, reciting opinions, disposing of prejudices and even of the simple truth itself—as too undeveloped, not yet of an interesting age.

Well . . . yes and no. The image Gass projects of the essay recalls "the professional Popeans' Natchez-Augustan manor," and in my mind's eye I see the essayist enjoying the good life—with the obligatory mint julep—while those who make that leisure (and civilization) possible slave away. The essayist, in any case, need not be one who has "merely done a little reading up"; he or she may be a scholar—like Gass himself—who assumes a particular *critical character*. That character, I agree, *is* one who loves (an amateur in that sense, at least), who, meditative and reflective, cares very much about writing and the form in which he or she works, *journeying* toward understanding and enjoying the process of interpretive discovery, played out in the writing, fully as much as any destination reached.

To continue with Gass: his following remarks, on the article, seem to me closer to the mark, though still extreme. The essay, he writes,

> is obviously the opposite of that awful object, "the article," which, like items picked up in shops during one's lunch hour, represents itself as the latest cleverness, a novel consequence of thought, skill, labor, and free enterprise, but never as an activity—the process, the working, the wondering. As an article, it should be striking of course, original of course, important naturally, yet without possessing either grace or charm or elegance, since these qualities will interfere with the impression of seriousness which it wishes to maintain; rather its polish is like that of the scrubbed step; but it must appear complete and straightforward and footnoted and useful and certain and is very likely a veritable Michelin of misdirection; for the article pretends that everything is clear, that its argument is unassailable, that there are no illegitimate connections; it furnishes seals of approval and underwriters' guarantees; its manners are starched, stuffy, it would wear a dress suit to a barbecue, silk pajamas to the shower; it knows, with respect to every subject and point of view it is ever likely to entertain, what words to use, what form to follow, what authorities to respect; it is the careful product of a professional, and therefore it is written as only writing can be written, even if, at various times, versions have been given a dry dull voice at a conference, because, spoken aloud, it still sounds like writing written down, writing born for its immediate burial in a Journal. It is a relatively recent invention, this result of scholarly diligence, and its appearance is proof of the presence, nearby, of the Professor, the way one might, perceiving a certain sort of speckled egg, infer that its mother was a certain sort of speckled bird. It is, after all, like the essay, modest, avoiding the vices and commitments of the lengthy volume. Articles are to be worn; they make up one's dossier the way uniforms

make up a wardrobe, and it is not known—nor is it
clear about uniforms either—whether the article has
ever contained anything of lasting value.[13]

A strong desire of presence, as well as nostalgia, punctuates
these intemperate remarks. Still, the basic distinction deserves
our consideration. And I rather admire Gass's quirky style, in-
formal, highly metaphorical, with surprising twists, turns,
terms, and rhythms, tossed off in sentences longer than my own!
I would not want us to imitate Gass's style, on any grand scale,
nor do I wish to see us bound to the "silver mediocrity" of
"plainstyle criticism." The choice, I hope, is not either/or: either
a theoretically informed and sophisticated criticism offered in
careless brown prose or a perhaps impressionistic criticism vapid
in thought but oh, so well expressed.[14]

Despite a certain nostalgic wish of my own, I am not so naive
as to believe, or advocate, that, with the burden of knowledge we
now bear, literary criticism can simply return to the traditional
essay for its basic form. There is now no way to avoid technical
terms and difficult theoretical and philosophical ideas, many of
them foreign imports. Purity of style seems no more desirable
than an isolationism regarding ideas. The essay has, however,
always been a protean form, capacious enough to accommodate
almost anything. That from its beginnings it has been an instrument of deconstruction I find heartening in this regard. Such is
the (perhaps surprising) argument of W. Wolfgang Holdheim,
who claims that Montaigne, the acknowledged "father" of the
essay, "was engaged in an *Abbau* of his tradition. . . . It is an
active deconstruction in the genuine sense: a clearing away of
rubbish, of reified sedimentations, so that issues may once again
be laid bare in their concreteness." Montaigne's "radical presentation of discontinuity," Holdheim continues, "is very much a
reaction against uncritically accepted accumulations of continuity; his insistence on the uniquely diverse and particular is directed against too exclusive a concern with universals."[15]

With so much in common, the essay and poststructuralism
might work together rather than at cross purposes, as seems
mainly the case at the moment. The result would be a form at
once theoretical *and* artful, the familiar (essay) estranged. It

might fulfill Matthew Arnold's wish for a literature of "imaginative reason," perhaps exist as a kind of "intellectual poetry." Here, too, Pope provides both incentive and example: *An Essay on Criticism* is, of course, both criticism *and* poetry. In such literary criticism, as may (again) be in the works, the critic would appear more prominently than at present, not parading his or her wares or grandstanding, but acknowledging the personal involvement and risk in the criticism. As it recorded the play and movement of mind, charting "the course of interpretive discovery," the critical essay could bring theory to life.[16] It would still, of course, proceed from specific textual considerations, on which it would brood, and much of its interest would perhaps lie in the way it foregrounded the relation I described earlier as existing between reader and text. Readers would respond, then, not just to the power of the particular interpretation but also to the critic's engagement with texts and ideas, his or her passion and human-heartedness, those qualities we value in other forms of art and that help make up the critical character.

In the situation I have described, critics of eighteenth-century literature labor under a heavy burden, one that entails special opportunities as well as responsibilities. Not only have we inherited a distinguished tradition of scholarly and critical commentary, only a few of whose ablest practitioners I have mentioned here, but we are also stewards of important critical writing much of which deserves to be called literature. I mean not only Dryden's *Essay of Dramatick Poesy*, Pope's *Essay on Criticism*, and Johnson's *Lives of the Poets*, but also essays in the periodicals that dot the literary landscape of the period, as well as the work of Hume, Wieland, Lessing, Herder, and others. James Engell has recently shown just how "formative" much of this writing has been on the development of criticism and theory.[17]

In the hands of Dryden, Johnson, Lessing, and others, critical writing in the eighteenth century set a standard that shames those of us working in the late twentieth century. That earlier writing achieved a level of artistry rarely if ever reached since. Essayistic in character, it represents a passionate engagement with literature that is genuinely evaluative and critical and that, partly because of its involvement and stance, can attract a broad spectrum of readers. Then as now the best critical writing derives from both close and wide reading, but its appeal and its address are not limited to a narrow—and small—band of professionals. What attracts and holds interest is the displayed powerful and intimate effect of reading on the mind and the heart. In detailing the "adventures of the soul among master-pieces" (Anatole France), criticism records the process of such discovery and affect.

If, as I have suggested, writing and reading are activities best figured as inseparable, mutually dependent, interchangeably supreme, and therefore symbiotic, then crucial is the form assumed by the writing that stems from reading (and, as Hartman has contended, "the difference that writing makes is, most generally, writing").[18] As I understand it, reading means a fully human response to—I quote Milton—"the pretious life-blood of a master-spirit" that emerges as the great poem, story, essay, or play. The work of reading requires a form compatible with that artistry, an "answerable style," such as we have shunned in our professional embrace of the article ("the spectacle of the polite critic dealing with an extravagant literature, trying so hard to come to terms with it in his own tempered language, verges on the ludicrous"). I don't see how that desirable, and indeed necessary, form, that "answerable style," can be other than essayistic. The critical character *is* essayistic.

NOTES

1. I thank Cheryl B. Torsney, of West Virginia University, for her painstaking and thoughtful commentary on this essay. She provoked further thought in me and made me aware of much I only half-knew.
2. Gerald Graff, *Professing Literature: An Institutional History* (Chicago: University of Chicago Press, 1987), 252. *Contemporary Literary Theory*, eds. Laura Morrow and G. Douglas Atkins (Amherst: University of Massachusetts Press, 1988).
3. Unresolved in such perspectives is the relation of ideology and poetic value: Can we continue to praise the poetry while condemning the politics? What would be left of poetry shorn of ideology?
4. Frederick M. Keener, *An Essay on Pope* (New York: Columbia University Press, 1974), 5. Keener cites Hugh Kenner, "In the Wake of the Anarch," *Gnomon: Essays on Contemporary Literature* (New York: McDowell, Obolensky, 1958), 176.
5. Of eighteenth century writers Pope has probably benefited most from poststructuralist commentary. See, for example, Laura Brown, *Alexander*

Pope (Oxford: Basil Blackwell, 1985); Ellen Pollak, *The Poetics of Sexual Myth: Gender and Ideology in the Verse of Swift and Pope* (Chicago: University of Chicago Press, 1985), and (I immodestly add) my own *Quests of Difference: Reading Pope's Poems* (Lexington: University Press of Kentucky, 1986), as well as the special issue of *The New Orleans Review, Poststructural Pope*, ed. Ronald Schleifer, *New Orleans Review*, 15 (1988).

6. I take these remarks, slightly altered, from my *Reading Deconstruction/ Deconstructive Reading* (Lexington: University Press of Kentucky, 1983), 87–88.

7. By this point the influence of Geoffrey Hartman becomes clear. Having just completed a book on his "reader-responsibility criticism," I am flooded with his ideas. I want to acknowledge their presence, in small ways and large, throughout my argument, and not just in the few quotations I adduce. My book is forthcoming from Routledge.

8. Geoffrey H. Hartman, *The Unremarkable Wordsworth*, foreword Donald G. Marshall (Minneapolis: University of Minnesota Press, 1987), 34:213 of Theory and History of Literature.

9. Geoffrey H. Hartman, *Criticism in the Wilderness: The Study of Literature Today* (New Haven: Yale University Press, 1980), 270. Keats describes "negative capability" in a letter of 21–27(?) December 1817 to his brothers George and Thomas (*Selected Poems and Letters by John Keats*, ed. Douglas Bush [Boston: Houghton Mifflin, 1959], 261).

10. Hartman, *The Unremarkable Wordsworth*, 186.

11. Hartman, *Criticism in the Wilderness*, 75.

12. *Ibid.*, 155.

13. William H. Gass, *Habitations of the Word* (New York: Simon & Schuster, 1985), 25–26. At one point, at least, in the passage I quote, Gass parallels Paul de Man, who also discusses writers' various pretenses of continuity, completeness, and so forth; see his Foreword to Carol Jacobs, *The Dissimulating Harmony: The Image of Interpretation in Nietzsche, Rilke, Artaud, and Benjamin* (Baltimore: Johns Hopkins University Press, 1978), esp. xi.

14. See, in a similar regard, Mark Edmundson, "A Will to Cultural Power: Deconstructing the de Man Scandal," *Harper's* (July 1988): 67–71.

15. W. Wolfgang Holdheim, "Introduction: The Essay as Knowledge in Progress," *The Hermeneutic Mode: Essays on Time in Literature and Literary Theory* (Ithaca: Cornell University Press, 1984), 21.

16. Paul H. Fry, *The Reach of Criticism: Method and Perception in Literary Theory* (New Haven: Yale University Press, 1983), 21, discussing Hartman's "personable but philologically keen, densely allusive criticism, that takes *more* and more diverse cues from its text than is customary." Fry believes Hartman's is "the most *realistic* record we have of what literate reading is like."

17. James Engell, *Forming the Critical Mind: Dryden to Coleridge* (Cambridge, MA: Harvard University Press, 1989).

18. Hartman, *Criticism in the Wilderness*, 19.

When the Past Presses the Present: Shillings, Cyder, Malts, and Wine

Kevin L. Cope

Reader entrapment promotes reader emancipation. An alarming term like "entrapment" conjures up images of barbed wire, guard towers, and iron maidens. Yet literary entrapment, which allows readers to follow their habits and desires at no greater cost than embarrassed astonishment at their own perversity, coaxes its would-be prisoners out of their social and literary cages. As David Vieth has argued and Carl Kropf has affirmed, entrapping works are " 'open' rather than self-contained, kinetic rather than static, experiential rather than cognitive."[1] Ludic and only minimally mimetic, they free readers from the labor of learning lessons, respecting conventions, or obeying the rule of verisimilitude. Swift's scatological and "progress" poems have proved unusually successful at catching the attention of professional critical entrappers, for Swift, deconstructing Milton's God, grants his readers the freedom to choose wrongly.[2] Like the Earl of Rochester's poems, entrapping works open vast ranges of "experience," from philosophy to dirt; like Wycherley's or Butler's harsh productions, they give free reign to frightening passions and alarming ideas. Entrapment compels readers to be free, to engage literature in any way their nasty, lazy, and unpleasant personalities will permit.

Lest I be entrapped in entrapment itself, I shall devote this study to several poems in which readers are snared not in the usual way, in some humiliating psychic posture, attempt at voyeurism, or dangerous lust, but in that most suspicious of conditions, being happy. Canonical works of entrapment, like Swift's, lure readers with ambivalent bait—the perverse pleasure of watching a psychic or physical strip-tease, the naughty delight of drubbing fools—then mercilessly confront them with their concupiscence. The mock-Miltonic poetry of John Philips, John Gay, and their imitators defines a kinder and gentler entrapment. Granted, it entices readers with an equivocal lure, the pleasure of abusing the great Puritan poet. But rather than exposing, beguiling, or irritating its audience, this poetry trains readers to enjoy being trapped. Poems like *The Splendid Shilling, Cerealia, Cyder*, and *Wine* implement a bivalent program of entrapment in which readers are bagged in the classical, unpleasant ways, yet are also enlisted into the literary, psychic, political, and compositional history of the entrapping poems—into the production of those tricks and techniques by which they were snared. Entrapping readers in their propensity toward entrapment, Philips and his successors practice a meta-entrapment in which audiences delight in the achievement of their own captivity.

By attending to happy, intoxicating poems, I hope to improve the "must" of the contemporary critical *cru*. Discussion of historical or productive processes could lead into geyser-pock-marked *terra infirma* of new historicism. I aim to "problematize" new historicism by drawing attention to the psychic as well as the social complexity of marginalized *jeux d'esprit* and by suggesting that the psychic reconstruction of history contributes as much as do economic or social factors to the complex, unionist, incorporative, "open" or "entrapping," and most of all happy character of early eighteenth-century mock poems. Rather than "implicate" apple cider, I plan to add "happiness" to the academic *carte des vins*. Scholarship has yet to problematize the conclusion to "The Splendid Shilling," where Philips "sinks found'ring in the vast Abyss" of his falling trousers. I also want to re-direct attention to pleasantly perverse writers like John Gay or John Armstrong, writers who enjoy being oppressed, marginalized, dismissed, or entrapped. In the process, I shall suggest that there is such a thing as "writer" as well as "reader" entrapment.

The first decades of the eighteenth century left behind an oversupply of parodies, travesties, and burlesques in which authors, books, and societies are indicted but in which an unhesitating whimsicality problematizes the pretentious sobriety of 1980s criticism. Writers like Garth, Philips, Pope, D'Urfey, Swift, and Gay assault the corrupting effects of social and patronage systems, yet all affect a sassy, cheerful tone. When a writer like Laura Brown snoops for problems, she charges past Pope's "The Happy Life of a Country Parson" in order to root through *Windsor Forest*. Brown would have little patience with John Philips, whose chief occupations were having servants brush his hair while reading Milton and cavorting with that famous tatterdemalion, Edmund "Captain Rag" Smith.[3] Few critics, in any case, can muster much respect for poems about the rejection of seriousness. This reluctance to equate fun with business has culminated in a counter-marginalization of popular works in which readers' pleasurable psychic engagements overshadow, displace, or even justify their social deviltry. Philips's *The Splendid Shilling*, for example, was a box-office hit, both in its pirated (1701) and authorized (1705) versions.[4] Its appeal remained still strong in 1775, when Thomas Maurice issued "The School-Boy: A Poem in Imitation of Mr. Philips's Splendid Shilling," an ill-advised mock-Miltonic on the switching of bare-bottomed youngsters (and a precursor to his even less attractive "The Oxonian," a curiously collective imitation of all of Philips's poems).[5] "Philo-Milton" thought enough of Philips to launch a brutal reprisal, *Milton's Sublimity Asserted*.[6] Dr. Johnson rated *Cyder* as the equal of "Virgil's *Georgicks*," and Philips's panegyrical *Blenheim* scarcely seems comedy-club material.[7] This smashing popular and critical acclaim for Philips's work belies its critical legacy, a few spotty references in six synoptical stud-ies.[8] Dustin Griffin reduces *Cyder* to a second-order recreation of Milton's already nostalgic recreation of the terrestrial para-dise; yet mock poetry, I shall show, has a vitality of its own, a voracious liveliness that allows it to incorporate its serious antecedents—along with its beguiled readers.[9] While John Chalker may brood over *whether* Philips is serious or comic, the dichotomy implied by "whether" has little relevance to the first audience of a poem in which readers are asked to fuse the serious with the ridiculous in order to produce the parodic.[10]

Popular definitions of mock poetry turn on an austere, unin-teresting contrast between "trivial subjects" and "grand style."[11] In practice, the relation between form and substance in mock verse is much more sophisticated. In the eighteenth century, as now, "mockery" could mean either imitation or desecration.[12] The archetype of all mock poems (Addison deems it "the finest burlesque poem in the English language),[13] *The Splendid Shil-ling* advertises itself as an *imitation*, not as a mockery or trav-esty of Milton.[14] *Cerealia*, too, bruits its cordial relationship to the great poet, while *Cyder* features a cameo portrait of En-gland's regicidal bard, bringing the mocked writer directly into the mocking poem.

The propinquity of Milton to Philips's texts draws attention to the complex, temporal, and asymmetrical relation between an individual, mocking poet and the long literary history embed-ded in the mocked style and implied by the act of mockery. Is Milton from the same heroic past as Homer? Is Philips con-trasting epic form to trivial matter, or his work to Milton's? Is he imitating or burlesquing Milton, or both? Do either imitation, which implies similarity, or travesty, which implies deviation, fit a simple "contrast" model? For lack of intra-textual clues, the duty of choosing between these possibilities falls on the disori-ented reader, who, in order to read the poem at all, must commit to some approach and pursue it to its inadequate conclusions. As *imitations of* Milton, *The Splendid Shilling* and its successors deal with polyvalent author-reader-imitator-work relations. "Complex heroic" might therefore be a better term for Philips's poems than "mock heroic."

Philips's subtly-textured language provides a good example of this reader-dizzying process of complication. As Fielding cautions in *Joseph Andrews*, caricature exaggerates some features more than others. For Philips, being Miltonic means using inverted word-order. Early in *The Splendid Shilling*, he talks of a "Pun *ambiguous*" and a "*Conundrum* quaint" (12). Unlike Milton's, Philips's secondary adjectives provide little new information about the modified object. Could there be such a thing as an unambiguous pun? The linking of nouns with nearly synonymous adjectives opens and complicates a dialectic by seeming to resolve it. By postulating a difference between puns and ambiguity, Philips invites readers to differentiate ideas for affective rather than cognitive purposes—a process not unlike that by which critics have dialogized Philips's "imitation" into mock-heroic travesty. By absorbing nouns into the more compelling adjectives that follow them, this quasi-periphrastic redundancy diverts attention from topical substance to reader affect.

The Splendid Shilling leads readers into many linguistic and epistemological holes. Its story spins down from a concrete (if trivial) point, a coin, into a self-consumptive whirlpool of Miltonic rhetoric. The shilling recedes behind the splendor of Philips's discourse while pseudo-heroic language lures readers away from the numismatic topic. Meaningless apart from its titular, adjectival, and affective power, Philips's coin would never have become a topic without being "splendid," psychologically compelling. One couldn't imagine this same poem being written on a tarnished shilling, even though its theme, the miseries of poverty, has little to do with Tarn-exization of coins. Pushing substantive and descriptive apart from one another permits Philips to inject his reader's reconciling imagination into the opened space. Enzymes, for example, are denominated "cheese inhabitants" (*Cyder*, I: 357) as though they had taken up residence in the holes of Emmenthaler and were inviting readers in for a wine-tasting. Phrases like "alimental Streams," likewise, divide processes from vehicles.

Philips presents his rhetorically perforated poems as invitations to readers to fill them up with something. *The Splendid Shilling* begins in day, then crosses over to night, then terminates in the intervening openness of a metaphorical "Abyss" (as imaginatively enlarged by readers, for this "abyss" is only a hole in Philips's pants). Early on in the poem, the entire work is open-endedly exhaled in the smoke of "Mundungus," the cheapest of tobaccos that, in turn, fumes out of a "Tube as black / As Winter-Chimney, or well-polished Jet" / (19-22). One might say that Philips blows his poem and its insubstantial effects around his readers, who may flail and cough yet who cannot hope to clear the air of an atmospheric poem in which they occupy the center. The trigger on a smoking gun, *The Splendid Shilling* ignites a great deal of rhetorical, ratiocinative, emotional, and, in short, reader action, action that moves the reader more directly than the poem itself. Stuffing his verses into the black hole of a tobacconist's bargain-basement, Philips burns through any substantial objects obstructing the free-wheeling, adjective and effect-generating process of reader titillation.

Concealing their substance yet productive of striking effects, Philips's poems feature panoramas of provocative surfaces. These stimulating appearances demand aggressive readings, for they lead readers deeper and deeper into horrific interpretive fantasies. "Strait my bristling Hairs erect / Thrô sudden Fear; a chilly sweat bedews / My shud'ring Limbs, and (wonderful to tell!) / My Tongue forgets her Faculty of Speech; / So horrible he seems! (44–48), Philips remarks on the arrival of the dun. His visceral reactions to, and the external fact of, financial necessity converge on and appear through his skin and peripheries. His tongue bodies forth the mental power of speech. The dun, too, emerges from a collection of superficial gestures, bodily parts, and wearing apparel. Vesting the substance of his poems in their vestments, Philips turns the superficial lessons of experience into experience itself. Swift's "clothes philosophy" would come as no joke to our mocking poet.

As superficial imitations, mock poems displace, replace, or consume their archetypes. By commenting on poems, objects, and traditions that have vacated the scene, they clear away obstacles and allow readers and poets room in which to reconstitute the "real" foundations of works. This interpretive latitude enables the simultaneously serious and comic tone of mock poetry, for readers of these capacious poems have the necessary space in which to respond to superficialities in several equally valid ways. Philips's terror at the catchpole could entertain some readers with its absurdity or disturb others with its scrutiny of social ills. On the receiving side of a superficial poem that, paradoxically, draws attention to the ingenuity and psychology of its author, readers cannot get access to poets' minds, yet must, when faced with so vast, so dark, and so provocative a hermeneutic space, spin out—and get enmeshed in—a web of conjectural interpretations.[15]

* * *

In Philips's literary game, interpretation emerges as the topic of principal interest. Yet, like any topic, it suffocates in the mundungus-smoke of interpretation. The moment Philips's readers stop interpreting, they discover that interpretation has been their chief concern all along. They find they have been frantically cutting through an interpretive jungle that constantly closes behind them. Enclosed in a relentlessly significant world, Philips's works deal with the overflow from literally and epistemologically filling fluids. Money, ale, hard cider, and tobacco all *flow*. All are "directional"; all speed from point to point, hand to hand, sobriety to inebriation, or poem to interpretation. All move forward while being pursued by their own mobility. All mean something, or at least move toward meaning. All, as it were, allow the past to flow into the present and future, whether by treating ale-drinking as a prologue to tuneful rioting (*Cerealia*) or the history of an objective shilling as a segue to the present circulation of interpretation-rich rhetoric.

This pressing of past into present and interpretation into experience begins with the title page of Philips's first and most famous poem. Reduced to an italicized headnote, "*The Splendid Shilling*" recedes behind a bold roman blazon, "An Imitation of Milton." In the heading to the poem, the title disappears altogether, leaving only the subtitle. Imitation and imitated change places; derivativeness and interpretation become the topics of the work. The secondary replaces the primary as imitation; an activity that should follow original composition drives out Philips's original title. Philips himself is displaced by Milton; or, rather, Philips-the-imitating-author and Milton-the-original-author fuse. History is both recognized and reversed as Philips writes backward into self-identification with his predecessor. Assuming that imitation privileges the imitated poet, befuddled readers find that Philips has written himself into this venerable post—and into their veneration.

Philips's inversion of the historical process redefines authorship and author-reader relations in his precedent-saturated world. Imitators usually station themselves above or below their predecessors, as either the superior masters of a declining tradition or as the struggling denizens of an inferior modern age. Philips refuses to subordinate imitation to originality or reading to writing. Parodying parody, he confronts readers with their bogus belief that derivative works will confess their inferiority to their archetypes. Philips's "shilling," for one, is constructed in the poem, by the imitating process. Neither existing prior to his work nor appearing in Milton, it emerges as an extension of Philips's reading of his mentor. Like its Denhamian namesake, Philips's "Auburn" cider is pressed from his (or his reading of Denham's) description of it, not from farm-fresh fruits. Joyfully and confidently de-centered, Philips exults in his status as a misleading appearance. Having been pushed out and away from the Miltonic tradition, he deploys a more comprehensive mock mode, a mode that, by valuing and incorporating both imitations and exemplars, surrounds and traps those readers who lust after a central, archetypal work.

The displacement of big archetypes by small imitations opens space in which readers and writers may experience the "kinesis" and "process" of entrapping works. I say "readers and writers" because Philips, by replacing authors with imitators, turns "the author" into a subspecies of "the reader," "the deriver." Reading, after all, is precursory to imitating; it is a defining of the range in which an imitation may be identifiably "Miltonic." Philips himself wrote four quite distinct imitations of Milton. Entrapment again emancipates, for the *writing* Milton could only be Milton in one way, but the *reading* Philips can be "Miltonic" in dozens—as are some of his stranger imitators.[16]

The largeness of its imitative space encourages a pleasant casualness in mock poetry. Milton illustrates specific ideas with pointed allusions, but Philips exploits Miltonic allusiveness to extend the range and to lower the level of anxiety in his poems.

Philips's is a laid-back God. Rather than showing one God cannoning uniformly wayward angels, this poet shows us the divine spirit of English malt challenging an assortment of continental *crus*.

> Delicious *Tipple!* that in heav'nly Veins
> Assimilated, vig'rous ICHOR bred.
> Superior to *Frontiniac*, or *Bordeaux*,
> Or old *Falern*, *Campania's* best Increase.
> Or the more Dulcet Juice the happy Isles
> From *Palma*, or *Forteventura* send.
>
> (*Cerealia*, 53–58)

"Tipple" is earlier acknowledged to be the newest entrant in this potation derby, yet Philips affiliates it with the ancient gods, thereby expanding its credentials and drawing readers into the largest possible historical space. Rather than summarily shoving high martial discourse into low oenology, Philips settles comfortably into effete chat about wine. His relaxed perusal of great European vintages counterpoints a ferociously nationalistic panegyric to Churchill, with the result that readers are calmly drawn into a great gulf between vastly different styles, moods, and voices. "Tipple," the yeoman's rude libation, quietly ascends from low butt of mock-heroic to comrade and eventually conqueror of foreign vintages. By casually admitting Bud Lite into the same *cave* with its more delicate colleagues, Philips's easygoing readers are implicated in a strangely incorporative rout of outlandish libations.

> Then from beneath her *Tyrian* Vest she took
> The bearded Ears of Grain she most Admird,
> Which Gods call *Crithe*, in Terrestrial speech
> Eycleeped Barley. 'Tis to this, she cry'd,
> The *British Cohorts* owe their martial Fame.
>
> (72–76)

This sudden and unexpected turn from culinary criticism to modern British military exhortation might have taken Ceres's ancient Grecian audience by surprise, but there is plenty of room for such a move in the wide conceptual space of imitative discourse. Ranging from classical myth (the naming of barley) to aboriginal language ("Eycleeped"), Philips quietly seduces his audience into the casually imperialistic harangue that follows. Judging from *Cerealia*, critics must acknowledge the justness of Thomas Campbell's judgment that *Blenheim*, an account of Marlborough's bloody escapades, is "as completely a burlesque upon Milton as *The Splendid Shilling*, though it was written and read with gravity."[17] Few critics so well sum up the spirit of mock-heroism, the relaxed consent to an apparently friendly yet relentlessly appropriative, seriously imitative mode—a mode in which wide-ranging imitation accidentally forces everything original to become derivative.

* * *

The construction of a casually incorporative literary and historical space allows Philips to play down the contrasts while playing up the ameliorative powers of mockery. Philips so greatly extends his scale of judgment and so elaborately qualifies his contraries that his mockery ceases to affect his audience as a mode of contrast. Past and present do not seem like opposites when the scale of time reaches into mythic antiquity and visionary future. Readers find their rage for sarcasm reduced into a relaxed sobriety, their pointed nastiness blunted into a diffuse happiness, and their desire for an encounter between low triviality and high outrage dispersed into a peaceful respect for serious jokes.

> What Soil the Apple loves, what Care is due
> To Orchats, timeliest when to press the Fruits,
> Thy gift, *Pomona*, in *Miltonian* Verse
> Adventrous I presume to sing; of Verse
> Nor skill'd, nor studious: But my Native Soil
> Invites me, and the Theme as yet unsung.
> (*Cyder* I: 1–6)

Contrasting his clownish lays against his predecessor's hieratic song, Philips juxtaposes country gamboling against adventurous cosmogony. Yet he also associates his homely language with

Milton's style as a native Briton. He rids his poem of contrasts by insinuating that he, Milton, and apples, as different as they may be, all spring from the same all-surrounding soil. A serious joke, this conciliatory incorporation of high song, national culture, agriculture, and literary spoofery legitimizes mockery. Wondering whether they ought to do something to re-establish common-sense contradictions, Philips's readers find themselves entrapped in the psychological equivalent of protective custody, taking naughty fun seriously and didactically because categories like "naughtiness," "fun," and "didactic" define the middle, not the ends, of the spectrum of rhetorical possibilities. Philips is fond of setting opposites in neat antitheses, then pulling his parallelisms together with some provocative conjunction. Heat and cold, drought and flood, spring and fall, for example, all queue up alongside his favorite conjunction, "but" (*Cyder*, I: 137 ff). "But" redirects attention from the potentially conjoined elements to the conjoining act. In suggesting antithetical as well as conjunctive relationships, it throws responsibility for completing conjunctions onto readers, who can see a wider range of experiences than that most disjunctive of conjunctions, "but," reveals.

Cyder as a whole is a bifurcated, parallelized work. It splits its account of the otherwise seamless pastoral world into two books, if only to produce reader confusion and textual instability. Partitioning *Cyder* allows Philips to station his role-model, the honest countryman, at both the center and the end of his poem: at the conclusion to the first book but in the middle of the work. Readers, who expect exemplary portraits to arrive at the conclusions to poems (as they do in Rochester's *Satyr* or Pope's *Epistle to Dr. Arbuthnot*), must decide, like T. S. Eliot, whether to count the middle as the end. Emanative rather than climactic, *Cyder* emerges from the reader's response to this central, dialectic-interrupting figure. Philips traps himself in the role of the reader, for he turns over the core of his poem to a figure who is an imitation, a reading, and a copy of assorted pastoral fictions. He relinquishes his character as an original, didactical author, confesses his preference of the eccentric to the centric, and enjoys his marginality.

By injecting reader responses directly into his poems, Philips accomplishes another neat trick. Poems that could be mistaken for period pieces, for works reflecting one historical moment's misconception of another historical moment's literary conventions, spring into life as continuing, open-ended compositions. In the first book of *Cyder*, Philips interrupts his discourse on apples with an extended history of "Ariconium," a utopia swallowed by the earth. The effect of this injected history recalls that of a black hole in space. It pulls the poem into a hyperextended, hyperbolic, and hyper-real time, into a super-condensed, supercharged contraction of an enormous historical interval that is ready to surge into the present of the reading experience. So great and yet so immediate is the comparison between the real present and the mythic past that it goes beyond a simple contrast between recent and ancient history. Indeed, the contrast passes as an identity; Ariconium and Cotswold appear to the reader *ensemble*. Apparent contraries define a larger, less contradictory progress toward futurity in which readers, as citizens of Britain and successors to Ariconium, have a part. Near the end of *Cyder*, Philips draws a marxist-beguiling comparison *and* contrast between the happy life of contemporary English orchardists and the legendary, swashbuckling life of piracy, conquest, and empire (II: 645–69). Whatever differences obtain between "*Mauritanian*" "Kings" and "unmolested" "Swains," " . . . to the utmost Bounds of this / Wide Universe, *Silurian* Cyder borne / Shall please all Tastes, and triumph o'er the Vine." Cider and wine coopt every taste, modern and British as well as ancient and European. In *Cerealia*, similarly, ale *incorporates* wine. The poem could end early with the toast to Churchill (43–58). Ceres, however, rises with "Marks–of Latent Woe / Dim on her Visage" (61–62). Foiling "nectareous" happiness with cerealian woe, she transposes the poem from one genre to another, from Miltonic imitation to original debate over beverages. Raising the stakes of the contest, she jumps from scholastic dispute to military history (75 ff.) and thence into modern life. Sensitive to Philips's sense of conflicted but reconciling immensity, John Gay relies on a similar gambit. "Now Glasses clash with Glasses, (*charming sound*,) / And Glorious *ANNA*'s Health . . . " (*Wine*, 211–12). Peaceful conquest by vine entails a perpetual clash of wines, wines having tastes that disagree with one another but that when evaluated with regard to a more capacious standard (that of their power to please a variety of present imbibers) lose the aroma of contradiction.

The "contrasts" of mock heroic literature are, then, not so much essential features of some identifiable genre as means for escaping genre, for suggesting that readers may unexpectedly enter, be entrapped in, or revise poems at any time. "Imitation," after all, defies and historicizes taxonomy. "Original" and "imitation" can never be compared without the intervention of historical, psychic, and literary change. The popularity and character of mock poems during the early eighteenth century, their tendency to mock the regicide Milton rather than, say, Spenser or Homer, indexes their character as poems of succession, as replacements for as well as imitations of their predecessors. Bruiting their newness, mock poems advertise the fact that they appear after what went before, a claim fortified by their heavy use of historical digressions (the diatribe on Ariconium being one instance, the discussion of history in *Windsor Forest* being another, and Blackmore's Milton-improving history of creation being the *sine qua non*).

Historical, mock poetry is also entropic. It depletes authorial power and dumps incomplete, energy-starved poems into readers' laps. Gay follows his short *Wine* with his extended *The Fan* and later his immense *Trivia*. Readers of the later poems must do more psychic legwork (and extra reading) in order to decide whether Gay, as his career proceeds and his works enlarge, alludes to Milton or himself. As *The Splendid Shilling* grew into *Cyder*, Philips, too, wandered through ever-larger segments of social and literary history, forcing his readers to work even harder to find their way past his own work and back to the precedent-establishing Milton.

This sapping of reader energy affords another explanation for the frequency with which energy-consumptive chasms engulf Philips's and Gay's poems. The more energy readers invest, the more vigorously they seek classical or Miltonic precedents, the grander the historical sweep and the bigger the poem they create—and the more likely they are to sink into the black hole of an energy-hungry artifact. Ariconium is swallowed by the earth, sophomores fall into bottomless ditches, Philips sinks into the "chasm" *and* "Orifice" of his pantaloons, Gay's wine-drinkers stumble down staircases, Gay's trivial walker fears that side-walk-cracks will swallow him alive. In the pants-dropping scene, the associating of Philips's predicament with epic precedents demands continuous infusions of reader energy. As the plunge continues, verbs commandeer Philips's verse ("They stare, they lave, they pump, they pray"). Despite these heavy labors, "still the battering Waves rush in" and "The Ship sinks found'ring in the vast Abyss." Linking the poem to Milton and to Pliny suc-ceeds in linking it with stories about wasted efforts. This obses-sion with energy-consuming chasms was not lost on one imitator of Philips, John Armstrong, M. D., whose *The Oeconomy of Love*, of which "a more nauseous work could not easily be found," describes in pseudo-philipian mock-Miltonics the poet's regimen for stewarding sexual energies. Dilating on the dangers of mar-rying deflowered women, Armstrong falls into a mock-heroic non-encounter with a missing hymen, "a horrid Chasm" which "Yawns dreadful, waste and wild; like that thro' which / The wand'ring *Greek* and *Cytherea*'s Son / Diving, explor'd Hell's ever open Gates."[18]

* * *

One gaping chasm in mock poetry is that between original and imitating poets. Philips qualifies this would-be division by making imitators into authors, suggesting that original authors write in order to be imitated, and insinuating that imitators themselves often become imitable (as the work of John Arm-strong verifies). The author-imitator contrast is redrawn as a linear relation between an original work and the fun, open-ended, and yet non-teleological sequence of readings and imita-tions following from it. Philips and Gay establish the preemi-nence of the imitator—hence of the reader—by absenting them-selves, in their capacity as authors, from their poems, only to re-appear in some other role, often that of the reader. As readers, they compare themselves to what readers expect authors to be. Joining the audience, they explore the possibility of writer en-trapment. When the dun appears in *The Splendid Shilling*, for example, Philips-the-author retreats from the scene of the poem, taking refuge, as Philips-the-man and Philips-the-reader, in a cupboard. Present and not present, he lays aside his role as the author of a mock-heroic burlesque in order to peruse a narrative of his life. Inside his cabinet, he occupies himself with wide-ranging ruminations, drawing his audience into a closed but gothically expansive space in which nasty spiders maul pathetic flies. Following Philips into his armoire, readers watch his neurotically Miltonic imagination spread across not the expanses of heaven, but across a dirty, insect-infested corner. Continuing this humiliating transformation of free author into caged reader, he re-appears at the end of his poem in yet another, lesser role, that of a non-writing and non-reading rag-man caught in the shredder of pseudo-epic versification.

In *Cyder*, the foundation of the poem Ariconium, is, like the author, hastily excised. Announced in line 179, "Heav'nly Pow'rs" have "Decreed her final Doom" by line 186. The remainder of the poem amounts to a continuous invocation of reader sentiment, an attempt to fill the hole created in the poem by the elimination of its source and the subsequent rootlessness of its author. "The Name" of Ariconium "survives alone" (I: 235), everything else being the product of successive reconstructions, imitations, and burlesques. Philips leads source-hunting readers on a wild goose-chase through literary antiquity and into the non-evidentiary world of fancy and wit. Gay's *Wine* (40–62 and *passim*) opens with a direct, personal invocation to the god of wine, but Gay soon changes his tune, describing rather than addressing Bacchus's brew. Reporting on a thousand different effects of wine yet personally experiencing none of them, he speaks with the authority of the WCTU, expounding on bibulousness he has never known. Louise Barnett wonders about the propriety of admitting voyeurs, with their curiously detached sense of engagement, into poems featuring an omniscient, privacy-invading viewpoint.[19] This problem becomes acute in mock-heroic poetry, for Milton's withdrawn imitators look into not just one personal space, but into a vast range of feelings and behaviors, all the while exploiting their status as imitators in order to evade authorship of and participation in compromising scenes.

Popular definitions of mockery portray it as a literature of fact, a matter of set responses to set literary conventions. Mock poetry would be better characterized as a poetry of possibility and procedure, a means of recruiting readers into the construction not only of one poem, but of all possible versions, experiences, and histories of it. Philips has a way of describing objects not by their qualities or essences, but by their origin and produce, the termini of their whole history. Apples become "unprest Cyder" (*Cyder*, I: 415). Traversing from some unspecified original state to a specified product, Philips periphrastically opens the possibility of a variety of actions between the "unprest" raw materials and their nectareous destination. Apples disappear in the verbal and conceptual chasm between objectivity and productivity, while readers busily imagine the intervening history—a history that happens to be the subject of Philips's poem.

Philips outdoes any deconstructionist, for he knowingly and lovingly mobilizes fixed objects into fluxile meanings. Fascinated by ciders that "have by Art, or Age unlearn'd / Their genuine Relish," ciders that mock the taste of fine wines, he animates his juice into an elusively prosopopoeic counterfeiter (II: 298–307; 354–62). He relishes tales about the startling transformation of stable things into rampaging (and uninterpretable) juggernauts, his favorite stories begin those of the eruption at Ariconium (*Cyder*, I: 190 ff.) and of the moving hill at Marcle (I: 78–88).[20] Readers are invited to work the imaginative valley between successive appearances of these volcanic settlements. Philips always prefers flexible procedures to particular data.

> Nor will it nothing profit to observe
> The monthly Stars, their pow'rful Influence
> O'er planted Fields, what Vegetables reign
> Under each Sign. On our account has *Jove*
> Indulgent, to all Moons some succulent Plant
> Allotted, that poor, helpless Man might slack
> His present Thirst, and Matter find for Toil.
>   (*Cyder*, II: 194–200)

Juxtaposing Miltonic astronomy against Extension-Service Agronomy, Philips gives his reader a wider field than Milton's in which to carry out imaginative labors. General and procedural, his advice amounts to an exhortation to *observe* the interaction of *moving* plants and planets. Abdicating his authorial role, he transfers responsibility for the study of his fluctuating nature to observant readers—readers who can, at best, only offer up comic speculations because, like Philips, they plow the library more often than the field.

Philips's mobile advice usually applies to someone else. His encounter with the dun and the catchpole (*The Splendid Shilling*, 35–67) includes a description of the path these officers ought to take when *they* take Philips to debtor's prison. Philips, the object of the action, transfers the narrative to the beadles—that is, to readers who must chart their career and who end up doing the imaginative dirty work. *Cyder* begins as a personal "Monument" to Philips's "matchless friend" John Mostyn, but it promptly turns into a discussion of everyman's agricultural technique. The "Silurian" landscape may well be saturated with the personality of Philips's local Lycidas, yet this quick detour from immediate feeling into procedural advice leaves readers wondering whether they have been asked to supply the passion that Philips omits.

The suddenness of this transition from lament to textbook exemplifies the urgency of Philips's verse. Philips could compact Milton into the 150-odd lines of *The Splendid Shilling*; the more entropic *Cyder* runs only to 1,465. Entropy itself, getting the work quickly exhausted, is a species of urgency. Rushing history into modernity, rhetorical suddenness hurries the background, psychology, and production of poems into the foreground. If we read one of C. A. Patrides's books on Milton, we wonder, like St. Augustine, whether, after spending an eternity searching through the vast store of classical learning, Milton, God, or anyone else could ever have found the time to get to the present poem. Philips circumvents this problem by turning poem into procedure; the longer the poem goes on, the more it says about the immediate presence of past literature, about responding quickly to eruptive events, and about the preemptive powers of present readers. Philips's ruminations on sudden agricultural ills, from pests to hurricanes, keep reminding readers that imaginative pastures never stop producing, that mock poetry, its readers, and its writers should expect to exploit sudden opportunities. Milton, after all, appeared adventitiously; where would Philips have been if that remarkable contingency had not occurred? Would we have had the splendid shilling if Philips were not fond of *Milton à la coiffure*? In the aforementioned conclusion to *The Splendid Shilling* ("They stare, they lave, they pump, they swear, they pray"), Philips's language accelerates and escalates the action. Passive staring accedes to salvific works and finally to an appeal to heaven. The earlier, more ponderous parts of the poem come crashing into the foreground as the triviality of the preceding verses leaves readers asking whether they ought to re-read, reconstruct, or otherwise reinterpret the poem so as to prepare for this stunning, explosive conclusion. Philips slams his readers against an exclamation point ("Vain Efforts!"), rebounding them into the story preceding this conclusion and suggesting the vanity of trying to conclude his *magnum opus*. The point of the poem becomes the pointing to an unending series of sudden conclusions. Like the movie *Alien*, *The Splendid Shilling* ends with a seque to a sequel, a sudden ending leading back into a story. Everyone sinks, but no one is seen to perish. *Cerealia* goes further, rushing headlong into scatology.

> They Run, they Fly, till flying on Obscure,
> Night-founder'd in Town-Ditches stagnant Gurge,
> SOPH Rowls on SOPH Promiscuous—Caps a loof
> Quadrate and Circular confus'dly fly,
> The Sport of fierce *Norwegian* Tempests Roar
> Of loud *Euroclydon's* tumultuous Gusts.
>
> (192–98)

In the next line, the progress toward scatology is interrupted, not by stopping it outright but by transposing the riot to the heavens, where the gods will continue the sport. Combined with the rhetorical habit of suddenness, this interest in continuous procedures generates a quasi-allegorical, complexly "mock" poetry in which appearances lead to appearances and imitations lead to imitations. The reading of mock-heroic poems never ends, for their climax is the sudden, terminating discovery of their historicity and ongoingness.

Progressing from one sudden compression of history to another, mock poetry proceeds right past readers. One gag in the mock poet's bag of tricks is the leaving of the reader to follow behind the poem—to write its history while the poem moves out of sight. The moment Philips introduces the splendid shilling, he drifts away from his topic, sending his viewers sailing off "To *Juniper's, Magpye,* or *Town-Hall*" (6), there to enjoy conversation about the poem that just flew by. Sitting in the tavern, Philips devises the work before us while bypassing his projected ditty about the splendid shilling. The resulting surrogate poem concerns poverty—the *absence* of the splendid shilling!—rather than wealth. Philips dawdles over epic histories like those of Ariconium or Marlborough because these legends rival *Raiders of the Lost Ark* in their capacity to make an audience forget or find a substitute for a topic. Who could worry about the details of the Old Testament after watching the angels of the apocalypse vaporize a few Nazis? Who could recur to plain old Rome apples after a Pompeiian-style explosion? Detouring readers into their reveries, Philips's pastoral fantasies blunt both sharp mockery and clear-cutting technical manuals. Milton's dourness and the travestarian's arrogance accede to happiness as contented readers let the intended, nasty poem slip merrily by them. Rather than mock the old Milton, Philips prefers to build a new, derivative one in the reader's present, to take advantage of that elusive moment when original works turn one way and reader attention another.

* * *

Philips's imagery emerges from opportunities, missed or otherwise. Elsewhere I have commented on the susceptibility of eighteenth-century didactical poetry to a generative, iterative, and "fractal" analysis. I have no space here to reiterate my comments, but I would suggest that mock poetry, too, is about emerging, branching, and sudden, unpredictable torquing—turns that become intelligible only after they occur, to an audience that, unaided by any *a prioristic* model of genre, reviews more than it views—that imitates.[21] Grafting provides an image of a poetry in which fractured traditions branch, grow, and multiply in unpredictable ways.

Some think, the *Quince* and *Apple* wou'd combine
In happy Union; Others fitter deem
The *Sloe*-stem bearing *Sylvan* Plums austere.
Who knows but Both may thrive? Howe'er, what loss
To try the Pow'rs of Both, and search how far
Two different Natures may concur to mix
In close Embraces, and strange Off-Spring bear?
Thou'lt find that Plants will frequent Changes try,
Undamag'd, and their marriageable Arms
Conjoin with others. So *Silurian* Plants
Admit the *Peache's* odoriferous Globe,
And *Pears* of sundry Forms; at diff'rent times
Adopted *Plums* will aliene Branches grace;
And Men have gather'd from the *Hawthorn's* Branch
Large *Medlars*, imitating regal Crowns.

                         (*Cyder*, I: 297–311)

Grafted scions assert their original identities, yet, like Philips's verse, they also assert their mutability, their tendency to mock both themselves and audience expectations for them. An analogy emerges between grafting and unionist politics as intergrafted countries tap into and grow away from the trunk of the single, vital state.

Many of Philips's images could be described as "activated," as convergences of assorted forces or as reader provocations. Behold his wounded pheasant: " . . . the tow'ring, heavy Lead / O'er-takes their Speed; they leave their little Lives / Above the Clouds, praecipitant to Earth" (*Cyder*, II: 174–76). A vertex of vectored forces, an intersection of bullet and bird, Philips's pheasant lacks a stable identity. It is, rather, a productive process, a transformation that readers *follow* rather than see. The fixed, material "bird" is but a still life, a corporeal residue of the collision. Philips may well have conceived of his own *oeuvre* as such a progression of bypassings and surprisings. In *The Splendid Shilling* he is already talking about various beverages, juxtaposing wine against ale, using allusions he will later reiterate, and setting himself up for both his own career and for those responses, like Gay's or Philo-Milton's, that emerged from it.

Forcing their readers to re-enact their compositional and reconstruct their literary history, mock-heroic poems trap readers into becoming their writers. A master at disabling teleology

and at sliding from masterpiece to masterjoke, Philips draws
readers into making, following, and rushing through chronolo-
gies that aren't really there. In *The Splendid Shilling*, I have
already said, Philips moves spastically between dark and day-
light. But his metaphor implies an intermediate, twilight zone,
a yet-to-be-completed series of intervening events. At the break
between halves of his poem, Philips announces "So pass my
days" (93). But what precedes "so"? The preceding lines have
meted out an array of analogies, but have offered no plan, sched-
ule, or chronologically extended narrative. "So" dupes readers
into equating sheer comparison, sheer "mock" contrast, with
smooth, linear, and uninterrupted progress. The next line (94)
envelopes the world in "nocturnal shades," as though readers
should fill out the metaphor by proceeding into total darkness
through a series of halftones. In *Cerealia*, too, Philips trots the
reader through a tortuous sequence of contrast-reducing, time-
enlarging similes. Beginning with a set of sheer comparisons,
the poem turns toward the discussion of current events, swings
back to comparison by contrasting ancient against contemporary
events, then ends in modernized mythology. "As . . . so . . . such
is . . . " discourses Philips, gradually moving closer to real history, yet also heightening the literary, simile-intense character
of his work.

Like most of Philips's works, *Cerealia* abounds with prepositions. Prepositions can generate complex spatio-temporal relations between unlike things. "Now from" the beginning of his
historical digression (23), Philips runs through the vast array of
things, events, and persons that relate to malt liquors. Insubstantial, prepositions lead readers to perceive the world in a
way mocking the very disorder that makes travesty possible.
Reconstructive, a preposition-rich history disables the conventional expectation of a teleological, forward-running, narrative
history. *Cyder* opens in the near present of Milton, but within
seventy-seven lines has regressed to Anglo-Saxon times. This
regress continues to a complex "now" in which an "Apple-Tree"
"improv'd" "by our Fore-fathers Blood" incorporates both the
mythic, Edenic past and the concerns of contemporary botany
(I: 245–47). Philips's readers are pushed into more and more

remote areas—back to Eden, out to Marcle Hll—yet they somehow always end up back in his real *and* imaginative orchard,
an orchard that, as artifact and imitation, incorporates the process of reading and writing that led up to its production.

Philips's poems concern products—cider, ale, coins,
wine—that emerge from preceding processes. "Thus far of Trees;
The pleasing Task remains, / To sing of Wines" (*Cyder*, II:
31–32). Yet Philips subverts the expected eschatology of beverages. It is not the case that ciders and wines, being late developments and requiring intensive processing, are better than their
predecessors, grapes and apples. Fine champagne isn't necessarily better than Uncle Snuffy's quick-fix applejack. *Cerealia*, for
one, progresses and regresses along several axes at once. Ale
and the modern Britishness that Philips associates with it defeat
wine and its ancient champion Bacchus, yet ale, Philips knows,
is the more ancient drink. Old Bacchus, conversely, is trapped
into advocating modern *crus*. The present poem proves more
pleasing than any old drink. These complexities are epitomized
by the beginning of *Cerealia*, where Philips attends less to the
eternality of the Fates than to the fact that they recline on a
"*Divan*" (7). Resting on a modern sofa, they foresee the future
end of history while reclining on the modern products of a declining civilization. Old, they enjoy watching the "Young Actions"
of earlier times issue from their proleptically Cowperian couch.

All this decadence is not quite as comic as readers might
expect. The climax to *Cyder*, the modernized and centralized
portrait of the Virgilian farmer, is suddenly juxtaposed against
a brief, unexpected portrait of Milton (I: 730–96). Citing charges
he refuses to name, Philips throws his modern mentor into an
inexplicably awkward posture, splitting open the already dichot-
omous portrait of an ancient farmer in the modern English coun-
tryside and creating a troubling contrast between Milton and
the ancients from whom Milton drew. Lacking a proper historical place in this neo-georgic episode, stuck between past precedent and contemporary example, Milton becomes both a process,
a meteor shooting through the benighted modern world, and a
product, a ruined artifact of modern history. Like the fates on
their divan, he lacks the prestige normally associated with legendary characters. In virtue of its non-contrast with this not-so-
good Milton, *Cyder* suddenly strikes the reader as more serious

than it would have seemed had the reader expectation for a contrast between past and present poets been met.

> ... —However, let the Muse abstain,
> Nor blast his Fame, from whom she learnt to sing
> In much inferior Strains, grov'ling beneath
> Th' *Olympian* Hill.

Who knows how to react to this disclaimer from a self-confessed "grov'ling" poet who has learned how to be an inferior writer from a corrupt master, yet who seems to have the wisdom of Zeus? Philips refuses to specify an appropriate response, the only authorized reaction being vertigo over the defeat of proscriptive readings.

Most readers believe that writing will culminate in a poem, but Philips disables even this commonsensical teleological expectation. Rather than complete his works, he defines starting points from which readers may proceed with theirs. The principal virtue of ale is its power to "Excite / The Mind to Ditties blithe" (*Cerealia*, 164–63), to intoxicate the poet, do most of his work for him, and to stir the audience into further participation. Visitors to the John Harvard statue in the Harvard Yard know well the association between Puritans and tavern-keeping, an association not lost on Philips, who regards the imitation of Milton as a serious form of beer-hall singing, as the incitement of avid group vocalizing over nothing in particular.

General emotional states like happiness are therefore of paramount importance for Philips, who cultivates those moods that lead readers a good psychological distance away from their specific causes. Happiness, for example, influences a happy person's notion of experience, coloring, contradicting, or even creating the events that it allegedly registers.

> Happy the Man, who void of Cares and Strife,
> In Silken, or in Leathern Purse retains
> A *Splendid Shilling*.
>
> (1–3)

Opening with a mood, Philips works his way back from the mental process of happiness to its anterior condition, the possession of a shilling. This condition turns out to be his title as well as his topic; his poem constructs the occasion to which it responds. The imitative process likewise dupes readers into constructing an image of Miltonic verse that imitates Philips's as much as Milton's creations. History is reversed as Philips proceeds from open-ended mirthfulness, in which his leisured society has climaxed, back to the economic foundations from which it arose.

Many mock-heroic scenes portray the leading or pursuing of the audience from the present into dead-end historical reconstructions. Gay, for example, chases the reader of *Trivia* away from a pursuing football war and into the ruins of Arundel house. Philips runs his reader into ditches with college sophomores, flees from pursuing duns, reverse time-lapses from fruit to scion, and backslides from sobriety to drunkenness. Gay reflects that "in pensive *Hypoish* Mood / With slowest pace, the tedious Minuits Roll" (*Wine*, 38–39). An emotional state initiates a progress toward its foundations, not vice-versa; moods measure minutes, while minutes lead—crash—back into the present. Time regresses from a full-fledged roll to a retrogressive slowness. "Then solitary walk, or doze at home," advises Philips, as though vigorous perambulation and dreamy revery led into one another (*Splendid Shilling*, 17). In *Wine*, the mousse of champagne—a definitively mobile attribute of this beverage that restlessly rises willy-nilly into nothingness—explodes into a panegyric on Queen Anne's expanding empire. The more intense Gay's feeling, the greater his adoration for his monarch or for his city, the more likely he is to associate it with such a progression into conceptual nothingness but affective plenitude. His praise of Anna, after all, terminates in appeals to real, living persons and in the surprised mood of his reader. In stepping away from its foundations, mock poetry expands into a substantial, evocative imitation—if only of nothing.

*   *   *

The title of Gay's best-known poem, *Trivia*, alludes to the intersection of three Roman roadways. From a trivial point a modern writer may proceed in three ways—toward classicism, toward modernity, or toward mockery. Philips's poems, too, radiate from trivial points, whether circular coins or spherical apples. They *must* involve and incite readers, but they *may* do so in any of several ways. In straightforward imitation, antiquity determines modernity. What happened in the past limits the possibilities open to modern imitators. In mock poems, where the past presses the present, imitators create a sense of global contingency. As science-fiction buffs know, travel into the past can remake the future. Anything might happen; everything is built on no one thing. By refusing to say explicitly whether a poem like *Cyder* is to be taken seriously, comically, both, or neither, Philips conditions the effect of his genre on an array of extra-literary, reader-relevant factors. One of Philips's reader-entrapping gins is his frequent insinuation that any reader at any time might react differently to mock-heroic than any other at any other. Gay's *Wine* showcases the impaired condition of the reader. "When fumy Vapours cloud our loaded brows . . . " (16)—when various things happen, various readers and various poems behave variously. By eroding readers' security, Philips makes them work all the more frenetically to delimit his protean poems. Were a concordance made from Gay's mock poems, "if" would prove one of his favorite words, for he plays up possibility while downplaying literary determinism. Gay portrays his mentor, Philips, as sometimes "soaring" "*o're Blenheims* Field" but other times "floundring" "in *Ariconian* Bogs" (122–23). Who can tell how or when to react to him?

This stress on contingency empowers the tradition of mockery. A finished, determinate work may have only one effect. Indeterminate works can make all sorts of demands on all sorts of readers at all sorts of times. Gay warns that his trivial city "demands instructive song," that urban life itself may invoke or even compose didactical poetry. *Cyder* offers assorted hit-or-miss solutions for assorted problems in assorted real orchards. Mock-heroic works acquire an unusual vitality and autonomy, for works that only spoof or imitate Virgil never attain Virgilian authority, but works whose natures are contingent, which sometimes heed Virgil but sometimes don't, can absorb, manipulate, escape, and even transcend the Mantuan's—or Milton's—influence. Making the poem and its process more powerful than the reader or writer, mock-Miltonics seduce Miltonolatrous, grandiloquence-hungry readers into disavowing the authority of their sage and acquiescing to the irregularizing but originative power of mockery. Agriculture is the best of all topics for a reader-entrapping poem like *Cyder*, for it directs reader attention to the predictably unpredictable behavior of plants, conscripting readers into the open-ended work of balancing uncertainties.

> . . . The *Herefordian* Plant
> Caresses freely the contiguous *Peach*,
> *Hazel*, and weight-resisting *Palm*, and likes
> T' approach the *Quince*, and th' *Elder*'s pithy Stem;
> . . . Therefore, weigh the Habits well
> Of Plants, how they associate best, nor let
> Ill Neighbourhood corrupt thy hopeful Graffs.
>
> (I: 263–72)

The management of ever-contingent nature is interactively mocked—promoted and parodied—by the surprise-susceptible reader's response to it.

> . . . lo!
> Strange Forms arise, in each a little Plant
> Unfolds its Boughs; observe the slender Threads
> Of first-beginning Trees, their Roots, their Leaves,
> In narrow Seeds describ'd; Thou'lt wond'ring say,
> An inmate Orchat ev'ry Apple boasts.
>
> (I: 353–58)

Nature and mock poetry spring on their audiences. Both surprise readers by emerging in conventional, imitable, and yet unpredictable forms. Philips goes so far as to put conventionally surprised words in readers' mouths, letting them know what "wond'ring" they shall say. Philipian mock-heroic requires readers to expect irregularity; it tells them that, conventionally, they must enjoy revising—and snaring themselves in—the rules.

Musing over the multivariate possibilities of his mock-poetic universe, Gay exults in the "Millions of worlds" that "hang in the spacious air" (*Rural Sports*, 111). His mock-Leibnizian metaphor is nowhere more appropriate than in the critical evaluation of mock poetry, a form in which contingency and possibility open vast critical spaces between occasional, eccentric, complex, and sometimes stellar acts of imitation. The critical legacy of mock-heroic poetry is nearly a vacuum—a mock-blank dotted with occasional semi-satiric commentaries. Unable to sustain *too* lofty a song, this mode bars readers and critics from obtaining the sense of closure that so forthrightly derivative a poetry invites. Mock poetry demands a surrender to pleasure, a resolution to follow the prompts and enjoy the surprises in the verse while constructing an open-ended, mock-critical notion of it. A complex motion away from literary vacancy and into the very center of instructive mirth, it is a poetry in which critics of later ages are engulfed by their own desire for critical fun. It is a poetry that surprises us into *both* sin and sense, that laughs us into a real world where the language of the cottager—or apple picker—becomes, Coleridge notwithstanding, the language of Milton.

NOTES

1. See Carl Kropf's Editor's Comment in the issue of *Studies in the Literary Imagination* on reader entrapment (17.1[Spring, 1984]: 1–2).
2. See, for example, the selection of essays in *Studies in the Literary Imagination* 17.1(Spring, 1984).
3. *Dictionary of National Biography*, vol. 15, 1062.
4. See Samuel Johnson, *Lives of the English Poets*, ed. George Birkbeck Hill (New York: Octagon, 1967), 313. For an account of the publication of *The Splendid Shilling* see M. G. Lloyd-Thomas's "Introduction" to *The Poems of John Philips* (Oxford: Blackwell, 1927), xxi. Philips's fame was persistent; Johnson also reports on the "loud praises" accompanying the publication of *Cyder*.
5. Oxford: "Printed for the Author," 1775; Oxford: 1778. In "The Oxonian," for example, Maurice incorporates ideas from *The Splendid Shilling* (the discussion of tobacco smoke), from *Cerealia* (the panegyric on malt ales), and from *Cyder* (the discussion of wines):
   > Whether the grape's rich juice regales my soul,
   > Or from the potent bowl I quaff new life,
   > Abhorrent still, I loath the nauseous fumes
   > Of that detested weed, *Virginia* hight,
   > Which the sage *Don*, in spiral clouds exhales,
   > Frequent and full, as o'er drowsy malt
   > Gravely he nods.

   (13)

Many other passages in this odd poem condense Philips's expansive imitations into similarly kaleidoscopic collages.

6. London: 1709.
7. Johnson, 313, 319.
8. See Dustin Griffin, "The Bard of Cyder-Land: John Philips and Miltonic Imitation," *Studies in English Literature* 24 (1984): 441. Griffin's sources: Harko de Man, *The History of English Romanticism* (London: Milford, 1924), 138–59; Alexander Harrach, unpublished dissertation for the University of Leipzig; Raymond D. Haven, *The Influence of Milton on English Poetry* (Cambridge,: Harvard Univ. Press, 1922) (a mention only); R. P. Bond, *English Burlesque Poetry, 1700–1750* (Cambridge, MA: Harvard Univ. Press, 1932), 100–10; John Chalker, *The English Georgic* (Baltimore: Johns Hopkins Univ. Press, 1969), 36–46; and Pat Rogers, *The Augustan Vision* (London: Weidenfield and Nicholson, 1974), 113–15. Since Griffin's article, Margaret Doody has touched on Philips in her *The Daring Muse: Augustan Poetry Reconsidered* (Cambridge: Cambridge Univ. Press, 1985), but she has limited her excellent comments to a few paragraphs.
9. For a portrait of Philips as a recreating, derivative poet, see Griffin, 451–55.
10. Chalker, 40–41.
11. For examples of this austerity, see C. Hugh Holman, et al., *A Handbook to Literature* (Indianapolis: Bobbs-Merrill, 1980), 273; and Northrop Frye, et al., *The Harper Handbook* (New York: Harper and Row, 1985), 293.
12. The *OED* stresses the sense of derision, but a review of the historical sources for the definitions of the word shows that its meanings softened over the centuries. Mock poetry itself was doubtless an influence in the softening process.
13. *Tatler*, #249.
14. Title and first pages, *The Splendid Shilling*, in M. G. Lloyd Thomas, ed., *The Poems of John Philips* (Oxford: Blackwell, 1927). All subsequent quotations from Philips are drawn from this text.
15. As A. B. England has explained, works of entrapment invite "educated readers" "to take particularly active initiatives in the pursuit of meaning," even though these works may not intend to "turn interpreting readers into objects of satire" ("The Perils of Discontinuous Form: *A Description of the Morning* and some of its Readers," *Studies in the Literary Imagination*, 17 (Spring 1984): 9–10). England seems to be suggesting that, in order to maintain their characteristic openness, works of entrapment must be free of authorial designs, that authorial intention and intended meanings are not part of this paradigm. England is right, I submit, in dividing authorial intention from entrapping works, but would have been better to restrict this claim to those "teleological" intentions that demand a specific interpretation. Philips, unlike Swift, offers poems in which the author may intend that the reader not know all his intentions—or, alternatively, that the reader may know that he intends to generate varying conjectures about his intentions.

On the use of objects in works of entrapment as a means to conceal, displace, or otherwise encrypt the author's, reader's, or character's mind while also initiating a process of "imaginative elaboration," see Louise K.

Barnett, "Voyeurism in Swift's Poetry," *Studies in the Literary Imagination*, 17.1 (Spring, 1984): 21–2.

16. John Armstrong, for example, thought that it was possible to wax Miltonic on the topic of social hygiene ("Nor would I urge, precise / A total Abstinence; this might unman / The genial Organs, unemploy'd so long / And quite extinguish the prolific Flame / Refrigerant") or while chronicling the discovery by newlyweds of each others' sexual organs ("Forthwith discover to her dazzled Sight / The stately Novelty, and to her Hand / Usher the new Acquaintance," a "tumid Wonder"). See his *The Oeconomy of Love: A Poetical Essay* (London: M. Cooper, 1768).

17. *Specimens of the British Poets with Biographical and Critical Notices* (London: 1841), cited in Lloyd Thomas, xxxix.

18. *The Oeconomy of Love: A Poetical Essay.* Armstrong expurgated his poem for the 1768 edition, which his biographer in the *DNB* (vol. 1, 566) allows to be somewhat less nauseating than its 1736 precursor.

19. Barnett, "Voyeurism in Swift's Poetry." 23–24.

20. Geological transformations and sudden natural events were just beginning, during Philips's time, to tease writers' imaginations. See Stephen Jay Gould, *Time's Arrow: Myth and Metaphor in the Discovery of Geological Time* (Cambridge: Harvard Univ. Press, 1987).

21. See my "A 'Roman-commonwealth of Knowledge: Fragments of Belief and the Disbelieving Power of Didactic," *SECC* 20 (1990): 3–25.

Voyeurism as Entrapment in Swift's Poetry

Louise K. Barnett

The arts that depend upon direct or recreated visual apprehension all have the power to represent voyeurism, the appropriation of someone's private experience without their knowledge. Through such representation the artist can satisfy both active and passive forms of the instinct divided by Freud into scopophilia and exhibitionism: "(a) Looking as an *activity* directed toward an extraneous object. (b) Giving up of the object and turning of the scopophilic instincts towards a part of the subject's own body; with this, transformation to passivity and setting up of a new aim—that of being looked at."[1] Active voyeurism becomes embedded in the artwork, and is then passively "exhibited" to the eyes of others as a substitute for the artist's body.

For the reader, voyeurism in a literary text entails a special kind of participation: like other symbolic behavior it "lacks the punishable properties of the unsymbolic counterpart but retains properties which are positively reinforcing."[2] Voyeurism is an activity of distance, and as a secondary voyeur the reader is once removed from the experience depicted and also distanced from it by the mediation of language.[3] Conveniently, the primary voyeur absorbs the opprobrium attached to forbidden looking while the reader appropriates the voyeuristic experience by guiltlessly looking at words. At the same time, by choosing to read and thus to recreate this experience, the reader becomes implicated in seeing what the text represents.

Regardless of what is seen, voyeurism is a powerful aesthetic strategy because it violates the taboo of privacy, denies what we take for granted as an entitlement. "Privacy," Charles Fried writes, "is control over knowledge about oneself."[4] Furthermore, he continues, "Privacy is not just an absence of information abroad about ourselves; it is a feeling of security in control over that information."[5] We expect, in other words, not to be observed without our knowledge in certain places, at certain times, doing certain things.[6] To observe someone behaving in a public fashion in private is still spying, then, because the person seen is unaware of having exchanged a private for a public context; but there is a connection more commonly made between a private space and behavior, however innocuous, that the individual does not want made public. As Erving Goffman observes, "We expect that some place will exist where privacy is ensured. Here, presumably, the individual can conduct himself in a manner that would discredit his standard poses were the facts known."[7] In spite of its neutral terminology Goffman's second sentence has sinister implications. The suggestion is inescapable that the individual's conduct in private would "discredit his standard poses," and that these poses constitute a public facade that is always susceptible of destruction, "were the facts known." In the face of voyeuristic intrusion, literary or otherwise, all of us stand to lose our credibility as members of respectable society.

What is this potentially damaging behavior that requires privacy? Discovering someone committing murder fits Goffman's description since it would surely invalidate any customary social persona, but privacy to commit crimes is neither a right nor a legitimate expectation. Privacy is a variable governed by social norms: provided what we want to do is not illegal, we are entitled to do it privately if we so choose; in addition, society mandates privacy for certain activities. Unlike those actions that are crimes wherever they are performed, these activities are the objects of voyeuristic interest and are illegal only when they occur in public. In Swift's poetry common subjects of voyeuristic interest such as women undressing or excreting are the rule, and there is longstanding agreement in Western societies that these activities deserve privacy.[8] Swift's texts fit Goffman's definition: transforming the private into the public destroys dignity as well as privacy by discrediting "standard poses." It shatters the social fiction of the unified self that assumes we are everywhere the same, not radically altered by the demands of different contexts.

Analysis shows that the outrage provoked by Swift's scatological poems arose as much from the privileging of voyeurism as from the particulars the poems' speakers revel in. What the poems dramatize—a pathetic streetwalker disrobing, a disordered dressing room and lavatory, a young woman on the toilet—is indecorous, but not truly extraordinary. The appropriation of this private experience and the poetic vindication of voyeurism are more so. Actual voyeurism is neither legitimate nor respectable whereas a poem *qua* poem is both. Placed around the activity of voyeurism, the frame of art legitimates and confers authority in and of itself, but, as Goffman rightly asks, "Does the 'removal' from actual events suffice to keep us all within the unkinetic world . . . ?"[9]

That art can make even the most objectionable material aesthetically pleasing is obviously a major manifestation of its powers of entrapment. Like other antisocial impulses given literary expression, voyeurism is stabilized and conventionalized by the rubric of art. When the looking that a text privileges forces the reader into an uncomfortable awareness of his own voyeuristic response, this awareness can transform itself into a moral response.[10] The reader can therefore neutralize his complicity by recognizing it as such; an actual voyeur cannot. While the reader's pleasure replicates the voyeur's appropriation of another's private experience, the former brings to this process the additional insight that aesthetic appropriation is sufficient: [11] he need not put on a raincoat, turn up the collar, and slink off to view real people through real windows. Nor need the reader invoke, as the authorial voice of Swift's poems so peculiarly does, a rationale of commonly acceptable purpose to mask a subversive activity.

I

For the satirist, voyeurism would seem to be a natural technique for revealing a damaging truth ordinarily concealed by a public facade.[12] The kind of investigative reporting that brings about exposure in other instances, the penetration of layers of deception and calculated defenses, is unnecessary here: the target is off guard, unaware of being observed; the only activity required of the observer seems to be the passive one of looking. Swift's scatological poems present voyeurism as no more than a strategy, a means to a higher end—a means not even regarded as shabby but offered either neutrally or triumphantly. This spying is all in the service of satiric condemnation and some sort of moral about cleanliness and decency or the illusions that surround them. Whatever the moral extracted, the text never perceives voyeurism itself as an issue. It never acknowledges what it so obviously is: the poetic subject and the source of the poem's energy and power. This displacement creates tension between such dichotomies as means and ends, proper and improper behavior, and comic and serious treatment. In part because the texts in question do not confront these issues, they are not resolved.[13]

Where voyeurism as a strategy of defamiliarization differs from satiric unmasking is in its subject matter, which may be a natural condition (nudity) or activity (excretion) rather than a vice. In the voyage to Brobdingnag, for example, Gulliver has an experience that is suggestive of, although it does not technically qualify as, voyeurism: he observes women in private, in states of undress, much in the manner that a sentient insect in the bedroom might observe them: "Their Skins appeared so coarse and uneven, so variously coloured when I saw them near, with a Mole here and there as broad as a Trencher, and Hairs hanging from it thicker than Pack-threads; to say nothing further concerning the rest of their Persons."[14] The women are aware of his presence, but since from their point of view Gulliver is a

minuscule creature of another species, and thus has no consequence as an observer, they relieve themselves in front of him
as well as exposing their bodies. The common elements of Swift's
genuinely voyeuristic poems all exist in this passage: Gulliver
reacts with "horror and disgust" rather than excitation and the
unadorned female flesh that he observes is repulsive, in this case
not because it is dirty or decaying, but because, like other aspects of the Brobdingnag episode, it is rendered grotesque
through magnification. There is a similar moment shortly before
this when Gulliver records "the most horrible Spectacles that
ever an *European* Eye beheld" (112). These turn out to be physical blemishes and deformities and the lice that feed upon them.
Of the three examples given, one is a man with wooden legs,
another a man with a "Wen in his Neck, larger than five Wool-
packs"; and the third, "a Woman with a Cancer in her Breast,
swelled to a monstrous Size, full of Holes, in two or three of
which I could have easily crept, and covered my whole Body"
(112–13).

While all of these sights might well be startling simply
because of their enormous size vis-a-vis Gulliver, the breast is
the most personally rendered and the most threatening, capable
of engulfing him in one of its lesions. In both of these scenes the
text violates a social prohibition to expose what is supposed to
remain concealed, the bodies of women in certain postures and
conditions. Gulliver and the reader share the same human perspective, which, in spite of the context, is voyeuristic, and there
is even a prurient teasing when Gulliver mentions the girl who
placed him on her nipple, "with many other Tricks, wherein
the Reader will excuse me for not being over particular" (119).
Because of special circumstances, the women do not mind Gulliver sharing their private activities and the reader probably
will not either—primarily because the text does not linger over
these briefly described moments.

A number of Swift's best known poems in some way make
use of the voyeuristic shattering of privacy: it is the implicit
poetic occasion of "Cassinus and Peter"; it takes the form of some
bizarre advice in "Strephon and Chloe"; and it structures "The
Lady's Dressing Room," "A Beautiful Young Nymph Going to
Bed," and "The Legion Club." Aside from "The Legion Club,"

these poems entrap the reader into a sexist objectification of women recognizable as the obverse of the equally sexist romantic objectification that Swift's writings so often castigate. The voyeur is a man; the person spied upon is a woman. What John Berger observes about the nude in European painting applies equally to the presentation of women in these poems: "Women are depicted in a quite different way from men—not because the feminine is different from the masculine—but because the 'ideal' spectator is always assumed to be male and the image of the woman is designed to flatter him."[15] In painting, the woman's nude body becomes a fetish or icon, a pleasing image for the gratification of male sexuality (just as the woman's clothed body reflects male wealth and thus flatters male economic power). In the poems the woman's body is displayed to male spectators as a repulsive image designed to curb desire, but one that equally confirms male dominance by asserting the power to violate the woman's privacy and destroy her public image. The painted nude of European pictorial tradition is more desirable than a clothed woman; the semantic nude of Swiftian poetic tradition demonstrates that women's sexual attractiveness is illusory. The grim dismembering of Corinna, for example, is a parodic burlesque routine with every step revealing less rather than more (literally) and discouraging rather than inflaming desire. The final revelation of her body is the visual antithesis of the voluptuous nude of European art.

The women represented in these poems are victims not only of an appropriating voyeuristic gaze but of a male discourse that further objectifies them. According to Margaret Homans, "Women's place in language, from the perspective of an androcentric literary tradition . . . is with the literal, the silent object of representation. . . . "[16] In all of these texts a male character intrudes upon a woman's privacy in order to expose her in some way. She is devastatingly literalized, reduced from divine status to the equally unrealistic extreme of definition by a single function. The hypothesis that this radical defamiliarization is simply a strategy to emphasize that women are natural beings like men and to imagine them otherwise is male folly would keep the satiric focus on the male mythmaking that (foolishly) rejects reality. But the reader's experience of the poems does not sustain this satiric logic. As Charles Fried writes, "In our culture the excretory functions are shielded by more or less absolute privacy, so much so that situations in which this privacy is violated are experienced as extremely distressing, as detracting from one's dignity and self-esteem."[17]

The same division between unacknowledged and openly espoused motives may be attributed to a curious pattern of behavior in Swift's meticulous apportioning of charity. He regularly patronized a number of old women who shared two characteristics: they were street vendors rather than out and out beggars, and they were all hideously deformed. As Patrick Delany writes, Swift sought "objects in all quarters of the town from which the bulk of mankind turn with loathing. . . . One of these mistresses wanted an eye; another a nose; a third an arm; a fourth, a foot. . . . "[18] Swift invented a nickname to reflect the special deformity of each: for example, Cancerina and Stumpanympha. As a moralist, Swift rewarded only the deserving poor, those who had some occupation, however marginal. Yet it seems equally clear from the anecdote that his interest in these women was not merely the exercise of Christian charity. The women Swift sought "in all quarters of the town" had to have some physical anomaly that disgusted most people, and they became through his naming personified conditions of deformity and disease. This practice is remarkable in itself, but it becomes even more so in the telling because Delany jokingly refers to these unfortunates as Swift's "mistresses," "amours," and "seraglio." These women, so afflicted that the common run of humanity avoid them, are objects of attraction for Swift and can thus be linguistically assimilated to love interests.

Such tastes are evidently common among libertines, at least those of the literary variety. The elderly General C. in Sade's masterpiece of voyeurism, *The 120 Days of Sodom,* has preferences similar to Swift's, if not a similarly charitable motive:

> The women he required had to be damaged either by
> Nature, by libertinage, or by the effects of the law; in
> a word, he accepted none who were not one-eyed or
> blind, lame, hunchbacked, legless cripples, or missing
> an arm or two, or toothless, or mutilated in their limbs,

or whipped and branded or clearly marked by some
other act of justice, and they always had to be of the
ripest old age.[19]

The world of General C. is one that a reader of Swift has no trouble
recognizing, but whereas the authorial voice in Sade is unambiguous, that of Swift's texts is highly problematic. However we may
respond to Sade, we know what he is saying; namely, that such
tastes, which society styles perversions, represent refinements of
lust and tokens of a higher sensibility. Moreover, they are part
of the text's encyclopedic treatment of its subject, evidence of the
imaginative scope of sexual possibility that the *120 Days* valo-
rizes. In reading Swift's scatological poems, however, we confront
the unresolved tension between the satiric rationale, the exposure and condemnation of some sort of improper behavior, and the
subtext of voyeurism in which readers—respectable citizens
all—must participate like the stereotypical peeping Tom, clan-
destinely and furtively. Since these poetic texts do not provide the
way of reconciling voyeurism with morality that I referred to earlier, or with aesthetic coherence, they have often been misread or
dismissed as unworthy of being read.

II

"The Progress of Beauty" succeeds where the scatological
poems fail in incorporating voyeurism into its aesthetic design.
Since the poem is structured by changes in perspective, voyeurism becomes one kind of vision contributing to the whole, the
private close-up posed briefly against the public distanced view.
As in the later poems, "The Progress of Beauty" exploits the
gulf between appearance and reality by claiming the voyeur's
privilege to violate private space, but there is a significant difference between the writer creating this scene and the obtrusion
of an actual Strephon into Celia's privacy:

To see her from her Pillow rise
All reeking in a cloudy steam,
Crackt Lips, foul Teeth, and gummy Eyes,
Poor Strephon, how would he blaspheme!

(13–16)[20]

Clearly, Celia has no desire to be seen in this unsavoury condition, her "natural"/truthful state, as the poem would have it, in opposition to the artifice/deception of her public appearance. However, the comically elegant diction ("When the Lilly skips / Into the Precincts of the Rose") and the shift to a less graphic generalizing mute the voyeuristic thrust of these lines. The damage to the flesh is neither as severe nor as vividly presented as that of "A Beautiful Young Nymph Going to Bed"; the fetishistic vision of the face as a work of art, an aesthetic triumph, quickly replaces the voyeuristic moment of repulsion.

Turning Celia into a vaguely rendered pattern figure and abandoning her entirely for abstract discussion of cosmetic artifice distances the remainder of the poem. The image apprehended only through voyeurism can finally be concealed no longer, but when the now ravaged figure of Celia reappears, it is not sharply realized: "No painting can restore a Nose, / Nor will her Teeth return again" (111–12). The expression of these banal ideas lacks the bite of the telling Swiftian detail, the devastatingly literal depiction of Corinna in "A Beautiful Young Nymph." The Celia of this poem does not have the reality of the Corinna who is an object of sustained voyeuristic gaze in the later poem because this text prefers other activities to watching her. Celia quickly slips out of focus while the text foregrounds a witty discussion of cosmetic paraphernalia. Where a similar brief moment of voyeurism disrupts "Strephon and Chloe," becoming the nucleus of a disturbing theory of masculine behavior toward women, the initial voyeuristic appropriation in "The Progress of Beauty" is necessary to the controlling analogy that quickly envelops it. Unlike its effect in the scatological poems, voyeurism in "The Progress of Beauty" is neither intrusive nor obtrusive—it remains contained within the poetic design, where it works effectively.

In "The Lady's Dressing Room" the lack of involvement of the voyeuristic stance lends itself to a certain kind of scientific, or more accurately, pseudo-scientific enumeration of what is seen. The poem offers a "strict survey" or "inventory" of objects discovered rather than invented, a method that justifies the text's excessive specificity and insinuates objectivity. Why describe Celia's combs as "fill'd up with Dirt so closely fixt, / No

Brush could force a way betwixt"? (21–22). Because this is exactly what Strephon saw, an item in his "strict Survey." Yet how could Strephon possibly know that the dirt was actually a mixture of five different things: "Sweat, Dandriff, Powder, Lead and Hair"? Almost all of the objects inventoried reveal a process of imaginative elaboration that is in keeping with the ultimate goal of voyeurism: not the mere sight of the subject but the sexually enabling fantasy that vision inspires. Here, as the long description of Celia's magnifying mirror illustrates, the intention is sexually disabling:

> When frighted *Strephon* cast his Eye on't
> It shew'd the Visage of a Gyant.
> A Glass that can to Sight disclose,
> The smallest Worm in *Celia's* Nose,
> And faithfully direct her Nail
> To squeeze it out from Head to Tail;
> For catch it nicely by the Head,
> It must come out alive or dead.
>
> (61–68)

Strephon's dramatic posture and the speaker's speculations transform this innocuous object, most likely used with the previously mentioned tweezers to pluck Celia's eyebrows, into an accessory to a disgustingly elaborate procedure. It is tempting to go through the poem stopping the cinematically fast moving narrative to discover each point where extravagant imagining converts an inert fact into an unpleasant fantasy. But the text does not invite a leisurely scrutiny of individual particulars. Such contemplation could establish the reader's complicity in dirtying towels, spitting in wash basins, and using handkerchiefs—in other words, complicity with the voyeuristic *object* rather than with the voyeur. The inventory cannot be probed because it is not "strict" at all; it is wonderfully gratuitous and fanciful, in short, artful. The controlling imagination, after all, belongs to that most active of voyeurs, Strephon, who can't resist groping in the bottom of Celia's excrement chest. He is a ridiculous and ridiculed figure throughout the poem, but the speaker is equally if not so obviously foolish. After embellishing Strephon's idiocy with such mocking verve and slyness, he then addresses

the reader with patently ludicrous advice. To assume that this
is historical Swift speaking directly would be to do that writer
a great disservice: tireless devotee of reason and truth that he
was, Swift would never have blessed anyone's "ravished sight"
or approved an order arising out of confusion. Rather than
allowing his own sight to be ravished, he repeatedly courted
the disfavor of his women friends by describing their faults too
enthusiastically.

If "The Lady's Dressing Room" is simply a Laurel and Hardy
routine where the second comic figure in pompously trying to
correct the mistakes of the first only blunders more laughably,
why has it been so critically elusive and troublesome? First of
all, the absence of an authoritative voice, or the discrediting of
a voice that we expect to be authoritative—that of the
speaker—creates a situation described by David M. Vieth as one
that "entraps a reader between two opposite extremes, with no
compromise or reconciliation possible between them."[21] The second and most critical problem of the poem is the untenable position that its taken-for-granted voyeurism imposes upon the
reader. The text transmutes the voyeur into the victim and laments that his discoveries in Celia's dressing room upset him.[22]
The reader may concur with the text in satirizing the condition
of the dressing room while feeling, uncomfortably, that if everyone is forced to relinquish the zone of privacy, who shall 'scape
whipping? As Roland Barthes writes, "The 'private life' is nothing but that zone of space, of time, where I am not an image, an
object."[23] Although Celia is absent, her scattered possessions
constitute a self-revelation that she has chosen not to display
publicly. Strephon's violation of this zone of privacy turns her
into a horrific image, an object of gross human functions possessing no humanity. The extravagantly comic treatment of
Strephon's exploration and disenchantment notwithstanding,
Celia is held accountable for disappointing male expectations:
"O may she better learn to keep / 'Those secrets of the hoary
deep'!" (97–98). This portrait is not offered as another partial
view to counterbalance the public portrait of Celia as goddess,
but as truth itself, knowledge that justifies the means used to
obtain it. The repulsiveness of the specifics discovered in the

dressing room ultimately does not shock so much as the ruth-
lessness or the attitude manifested in the poem's unapologetic
voyeurism.

While voyeurism dominates "The Lady's Dressing Room,"
it intrudes disruptively in "Strephon and Chloe." In the first
poem, Strephon sneaked into Celia's dressing room and as a
result of what he found there (the evidence of her bodily functions), became as cynical as he had formerly been idealistic. As
a character he is clearly confined within a comic world although
the materials of his new belief system are not discredited by the
poem's speaker but instead fashioned into a different yet equally
unrealistic position. Both the form—a mock sermon with an
exemplum followed by a moral—and the speaker's superior
stance set up the expectation that he will deliver a genuine
moral. When he does not, the reader has no textual means of
supplying an authoritative interpretation.[24] In "Strephon and
Chloe," Strephon only discovers on his wedding night that the
"goddess" Chloe excretes, a revelation that similarly ends romantic idealization but produces another, equally unsatisfactory
extreme: the utterly uninhibited pair now "find great Society in
Stinking" (210). The moral here is sexually differentiated: the
speaker cautions women to attempt to preserve the illusion that
they do not excrete:

> Since Husbands get behind the Scene,
> The Wife should study to be clean;
> Nor give the smallest Room to guess
> The Time when Wants of Nature press;
> But, after Marriage, practise more
> Decorum than she did before;
> To keep her Spouse deluded still,
> And make him fancy what she will.
>
> (137–44)

At the same time, the speaker laments that Strephon did not
spy on his future bride on the toilet and in this way arrive at
the benighted condition of Strephon in "The Lady's Dressing
Room": "Your Fancy then had always dwelt / On what you saw,
and what you smelt" (245–46). Women are thus given an impossible charge and men are instructed that voyeuristic spying is

the preferred remedy for idealizing women inappropriately.[25] Here, as in "The Lady's Dressing Room," the response seems both excessive and puzzling.

This problem is more acute in "A Beautiful Young Nymph Going to Bed" because instead of personal possessions, the object of voyeuristic appropriation is a vividly realized human being, and instead of the filth of "The Lady's Dressing Room" the poem particularizes the more serious effects of age and disease. Moreover, "A Beautiful Young Nymph" lacks the comic fiction of Strephon's "Grand Survey" presented within the mediating frame of an ambiguous narration. The unwinking and unfeeling voyeuristic gaze is the speaker's, and nothing in the text suggests any mitigation of his view. There are no obviously absurd responses like those of Strephon and the speaker, the polarized monsters of intolerance and tolerance in "The Lady's Dressing Room." Here an explicit attitude of mockery and contempt informs the systematic stripping bare of Corinna, the invasion of her dreams, and the destruction of the artificial aids that make it possible for her to appear in public.

The voyeurism in "A Beautiful Young Nymph" seems especially gratuitous since there is no occasioning fiction of masculine illusion in need of correction, and Corinna is a more vulnerable subject than Celia or Chloe. It is, after all, the potency of the woman-as-goddess myth that they embody that makes these latter women so threatening to the male figures of "The Lady's Dressing Room," "Strephon and Chloe," and "Cassinus and Peter." Corinna cannot be taken seriously in such a role; on the contrary, she is accessible without ceremony to all men and is readily mistreated by them. The poem can assume that as a streetwalker Corinna deserves condemnation and punishment, but she emerges more vividly as a victim—of the categories of men and institutions enumerated by the text, of the animal world that destroys her props, and of an authorial voice that treats her misery jokingly. The roll call of critics who wish to read the poem as a sympathetic treatment of Corinna suggests a persisting need for the text to somehow justify its voyeuristic exploitation of her.[26]

III

Although the viewing of lunatics for amusement was an acceptable practice in Swift's time, artistic rather than historical valorization accounts for the instructive difference between the effect of voyeurism in "The Legion Club" and the scatological poems. First of all, the controlling vision in "The Legion Club" belongs to a speaker who is credible as a satirist in a way that the various speakers in the scatological poems are not. This speaker has authority, and it would do no violence to historical Swift to equate the two. Here the strategy of voyeurism works as Swift might well have intended it to work on the more problematic terrain of the scatological poems: the voyeuristic objects are malefactors deserving of punishment, and the observation of them provokes no disruptive sense of sympathy or empathy. Unlike "The Lady's Dressing Room" and "A Beautiful Young Nymph," this narrative is offered as a fiction from the onset, not as directly presented experience. Whatever is unpleasant in it can be distanced as merely a punitive wish fulfillment fantasy. More importantly, the voyeurism of "The Legion Club" is inscribed within the text in a public, quasi-official way that confers some measure of respectability. The poem transforms one kind of public institution into another with all the rituals of legality and correct procedure:

> Since the House is like to last,
> Let a royal Grant be pass'd,
> That the Club have Right to dwell
> Each within his proper Cell;
> With a Passage left to creep in,
> And a Hole above for peeping.

> (41–46)

Peeping becomes an acknowledged part of the organization, not a lonely, surreptitious venture but an official guided tour that gains in dignity from its association with other celebrated literary tours.[27]

To see voyeurism as the controlling structure of "The Legion Club" is to appreciate more fully the text's artistry. The simple act of changing their context reveals the legislators' reality; the passive act of viewing them truly, as vicious lunatics, is the experience of the poem. As opposed to description, the dramatic strategy of voyeurism has satiric resources of its own, for as I have previously discussed, it objectifies its targets, appropriating their privacy and their very selves for its own purposes. In "The Legion Club" the circumstance that contrary to the ordinary paradigm of voyeurism the people so treated are men, and their humiliation is one customarily reserved for women, intensifies this act of dominance.

Yet compared to the specificity and immediacy of "The Lady's Dressing Room" and "A Beautiful Young Nymph," physicality is muted throughout "The Legion Club" and the indictments are notably abstract. This is due to a crucial difference in the attitude of each text toward its voyeurism. In the scatological poems the body is culpable and is punished by being revealed; in "The Legion Club" political behavior is culpable and is punished by humiliating the body. The bodies of the legislators are not "guilty" in the way that the bodies of Celia and Corinna are. In other words, the male body is a neutral space where punishment may be inflicted, while the physicality/sexuality of women is inherently guilty—not because of its pretensions, which voyeurism unmasks, but because of what is revealed underneath—its inescapable nature.

Because the text persuades that its subjects deserve satiric treatment, the reader is apt to countenance the privileging of voyeurism in "The Legion Club" more easily than in the scatological poems. The voyeurism of "Strephon and Chloe," "A Beautiful Young Nymph," and "The Lady's Dressing Room" destabilizes these texts because it is both powerful and subversive. Privileging the male's right to appropriate the private female world and use it as he sees fit both reduces and literalizes women with a vengeance. It leads to defining women in terms of the "gross and filthy" and closing off any sensible middle ground between romantic idealization and complete cynicism; for if women must conceal their bodily functions in order to please men, and yet are denied the private space in which to do so, there can be no satisfactory resolution. As a basis for human relations and as an instrument for satire, this excremental vision must finally seem inadequate: the attacks directed against illegitimate objectives disrupt and overwhelm the proceedings against legitimate satiric targets. Just as "most readers question the sheer concentration of filthy, disgusting imagery and the intensity of Swift's passion to rub their noses in it,"[28] so they are apt to find the voyeuristic strategy of these poems, and its validation, disturbing. The reader's entrapment by these texts is remarkably like real life entrapment in substituting an un-looked for and unpalatable experience for one that he believed would be otherwise. In "The Legion Club," on the other hand, voyeurism is a stabilizing force, openly acknowledged and justi-fied within the world of the text and consequently made accept-able to the reader.

NOTES

1. Sigmund Freud, *Instincts and their Vicissitudes* (1915), *The Standard Edi-tion of the Complete Psychological Works of Sigmund Freud*, ed. and trans. James Strachey, 24 vols. (London: Hogarth Press, 1957), XIV: 129.
2. B. F. Skinner, *Verbal Behavior* (New York: Appleton-Century-Crofts, 1957), 377.
3. This much is true of reading in general. But while the point of view of the omniscient author always contains the potential of exploring a character's private space, not all writers adopt a voyeuristic posture in order to do so, that is, do so in terms of a *violation* of privacy.
4. Charles Fried, "Privacy" [A Moral Analysis] in *Philosophical Dimensions of Privacy: An Anthology*, ed. Ferdinand David Schoeman (Cambridge: Cambridge Univ. Press, 1984), 210.
5. Ibid., 219.
6. Privacy, both in time and space, correlates with progress and standard of living. Less privacy has a high correlation with poverty and lack of development in Western culture; hence, stripping someone of privacy also reduces them in socioeconomic terms. Alan Westin writes, "Anthropologi-cal literature suggests that the movement from primitive to modern socie-ties increases both the physical and psychological opportunities for privacy by individuals and family units and converts these opportunities into choices of values in the socio-political realm"—"The Origins of Modern Claims to Privacy," *Philosophical Dimensions of Privacy*, 69.
7. Erving Goffman, *Frame Analysis: An Essay on the Organization of Experi-ence* (Cambridge, Harvard Univ. Press, 1974), 168.
8. Fried, "Privacy," 214.
9. Goffman, *Forms of Talk* (Philadelphia: University of Pennsylvania Press, 1981), 164.
10. I will refer to the reader as masculine throughout this essay because scopophilia is an exclusively male activity in Western culture and in the poems under discussion. While the reader may be of either sex, to read the poems is to recreate a voyeuristic, hence masculine, perspective.

11. This argument is adapted from Leo Bersani and Ulysses Dutoit's discussion of violence in "Merde Alors," *October*, 13 (1980), 32.

12. The paradigm of voyeurism that Laura Mulvey describes in her seminal article, "Visual Pleasure and Narrative Cinema," *Screen*, 16 (1975), 6–18, is clearly appropriate to satire: "Pleasure lies in ascertaining guilt . . . asserting control, and subjecting the guilty person through punishment or forgiveness" (14).

13. *Swift's Poetic Worlds* (Newark: Univ. of Delaware Press, 1981), 172–83. Here I argue that conflicting intentions of satire and tragedy account for "the tonal complexity and troubling ambiguities of so much of Swift's poetry of the body. . . . The principle of unity in the scatological poems is a justifiable satiric condemnation of vice, deception, and romantic illusion, but the expansion that occurs produces an unacknowledged subtext, the satirizing of bodily existence per se" (172).

14. Jonathan Swift, *Gulliver's Travels*, 1726, *The Prose Works of Jonathan Swift*, ed. Herbert Davis, 14 vols. (Oxford: Clarendon Press, 1937–68), XI: 119. Further references will be given in the text.

15. John Berger, *Ways of Seeing* (New York: Viking Press, 1973), 64.

16. Margaret Homans, *Bearing the Word: Language and Female Experience in Nineteenth-Century Women's Writing* (Chicago: Univ. of Chicago Press, 1986), 32.

17. Fried, "Privacy," 214.

18. Patrick Delany, *The Life of the Rev. Dr. Jonathan Swift, Dean of St. Patrick's Dublin*, 2nd ed. (London: J. F. & C. Rivington, et al., 1787), 393, 394.

19. The Marquis de Sade, *The 120 Days of Sodom and Other Writings*, trans. Austryn Wainhouse and Richard Seaver (New York: Grove Press, 1966), 329.

20. All quotations from Swift's poetry are taken from *The Poems of Jonathan Swift*, ed. Harold Williams, 3 vols., 2nd ed. (Oxford: Clarendon Press, 1958).

21. David M. Vieth, " 'Pleased with the Contradiction and the Sin': The Perverse Artistry of Rochester's Lyrics," *Tennessee Studies in Literature*, 25 (1980), 37. See also, C. J. Rawson, "The Nightmares of Strephon: Nymphs of the City in the Poems of Swift, Baudelaire, Eliot," *English Literature in the Age of Disguise*, ed. Maximillian E. Novak (Berkeley: Univ. of California Press, 1977), 69: "It is sentimental of the critics to say that Swift resolved the dilemma by some kind of "compromise or middle way; it is the fact that he never resolved it at all which gives his work its particular urgency and truth."

22. For all that the speaker patronizes Strephon because his solution is wrongheaded, he is sympathetic about the problem; cf. "The Progress of Beauty," 13–16, where the text implies that if Strephon were to spy on the unadorned matinal Celia, *she* would become responsible for his reaction of blasphemy. As Ellen Pollak observes, "Whether disfigurement or defecation is the most immediate theme, what these poems have in common is their demonstration of the condition of male distress when the magic of the fetish is removed, when the accessories of the female no longer rectify her 'failings' but are divested of the power to repair"—*The Poetics of Sexual Myth: Gender and Ideology in the Verse of Swift and Pope* (Chicago: Univ. of Chicago Press, 1985), 165.

23. Roland Barthes, *Camera Lucida*, trans. Richard Howard (New York: Hill and Wang, 1981), 15.
24. Cf., for example, Chaucer's *Pardoner's Tale*, where the exemplum leads to a moral that the speaker immediately and flagrantly disregards. Because the speaker has characterized himself so plainly, there is no source of confusion for the reader.
25. Cf. Ovid, *The Remedies for Love in The Art of Love, and Other Poems*, trans. J. H. Mozley, 2nd ed. rev. G. P. Goold, (Cambridge, Harvard Univ. Press, 1979), 207, 209: "What of him who lurked in hiding while the girl performed her obscenities, and saw what even custom forbids to see? Heaven forfend I should give anyone such counsel! though it may help, 'twere better not to use it."
26. The work of numerous commentators testifies to the difficulty in withholding sympathy from Corinna in spite of the poem's unsympathetic attitude. See, for example, Murray Krieger, *The Classic Vision* (Baltimore: Johns Hopkins Press, 1971), 264, 265; John M. Aden, "Those Gaudy Tulips: Swift's 'Unprintables,'" *Quick Springs of Sense*, ed. Larry S. Champion (Athens: Univ. of Georgia Press, 1974), 29; Thomas B. Gilmore, Jr., "The Comedy of Swift's Scatological Poems," *PMLA*, 91 (1976), 35, 42; Jean Hagstrum, *Sex and Sensibility: Ideal and Erotic Love from Milton to Mozart* (Chicago: Univ. of Chicago Press, 1980), 153–57; and Felicity Nussbaum, *The Brink of All We Hate: English Satires on Women 1660–1750* (Lexington: Univ. of Kentucky Press, 1984), 111.
27. Peter J. Schakel discusses the poem in terms of literary descents into the underworld in "Virgil and the Dean: Christian and Classical Allusion in *The Legion Club*," *Studies in Philology*, 70 (1973), 427–38.
28. Donald T. Siebert, "Swift's *Fiat Odor*: The Excremental Re-Vision," *Eighteenth-Century Studies*, 19 (1985), 21.

Quests for Order and the Perils of Discontinuity: Some Readings of *Strephon and Chloe* and *A Description of the Morning*

A. B. England

In the nineteen-sixties and seventies much of what literary critics wrote expressed a desire to find that the details of a literary work connected with one another so as to embody and stimulate ordered referential thought about the nature of a reality to which they alluded. This desire was not, of course, new, and it seems a fairly natural part of the process of reading literature. At any rate, during those decades two poems by Swift not only stimulated such a desire rather powerfully, but also led several readers acting upon that desire into situations that were compromising or awkward because they were at odds with certain discontinuities in the poem's movements. It seems to me that these engagements with Swift's texts, however much they may now appear to belong to a past phase of academic criticism, continue to tell us things about the poems in question and about a distinctive power that they have exerted upon the reading mind. *Strephon and Chloe*, the poem I want to discuss first, appears to have stimulated interpretive desire by offering so much, such an open-handed invitation to read it as a didactic text: by a form of overstimulation, it has caused readers to adopt closural stances based on the notion that its primary thrust is toward the making of a definitive ethical statement about the problems of the flesh. Such stances, however, are in danger of being exposed as reductive or even complacent by tendencies in the work that undermine the authority of its severe didactic frame. The second poem, *A Description of the Morning*, has also played provocatively on the impulse to read literature with a strong sense of thematic purpose, but in an almost opposite way. That is, instead of a commanding and imperative presence, there is now an obtrusive absence of apparent thematic design, and this absence has proven a most provocative form of deprivation. As if refusing to believe that the poem could be what it appears to be, readers have sought to erect thematic links, connections, and continuities that are more expressive of interpretive desire than of the actual movement of the poem's words. In both *Morning* and *Strephon and Chloe*, this desire appears to have been given special stimulus because the signs that thematic design is absent or present are rather noticeable and arresting, and tend to dominate the immediate reading-experiences generated by the poems: at the end of *Strephon and Chloe* the reader tends to feel rather strongly that he or she has been lectured, and at the end of *Morning* has been given no interpretive guidance at all.[1]

I

Although there are notorious examples in the history of published throught about *Strephon and Chloe* to suggest that reading the poem can be a turbulently emotional experience,[2] it became axiomatic in the sixties and seventies that one of the poem's dominant features is an order-bringing didactic argument. Only the briefest summary of its guiding fiction is necessary to show why the work should have evoked such a thought about itself. Strephon falls in love with a woman who seems both to him and his social group to embody a flawless ideal of beauty. When he marries her, he confronts the reality of the woman he has worshipped as a goddess. The crux of both the narrative and its didactic argument comes when Strephon realizes that Chloe must urinate, and he is unable to cope with that recognition. The imbalance of his initial romantic idealization is then replaced by its polar opposite as he and Chloe, instead of avoiding all acknowledgment of bodily functions, now decline into a graceless inurement to and, indeed, obsession with them. The poem ends with advice to the reader about the value of decency and the importance of understanding the need to stress spiritual rather than physical matters. In this way the dangers of romantic idealization appear to be encapsulated by an argument that is virtually diagrammatic in its clarity, that reaches conclusions, and makes claims to closure. Although the poem refers (rather fully and vividly, as we shall see) to experience that has traditionally been thought of as disturbing and problematic for human beings, it also pushes the reader forcefully towards the contemplation of a framework for dealing with that experience, for, in a sense, putting it in its place.

Denis Donoghue found the poem very amenable to his emphasis on the notion that Swift perpetually sought to "subdue" the unruly features of "experience" by "administrative pressure."[3] A typically Swiftean structure, he says, will be closed, rather than "capacious" or "liberal," ideally analogous to the "self-enclosed diagram in geometry" and constituting a "model of life which enables him to hold the essential forts." Donoghue argues that the primary motive for such stylistic responses is Swift's desire to "secure" and "protect" himself. And clearly, a similar kind of protection will be made available to the reader through his experience of "negotiating" the text. Peter Steele draws attention to this when he describes Swift as "a builder of shields and of shelters, for himself and others, in a beset world."[4] When Donoghue analyses *Strephon and Chloe,* he defines it as a successful act of self-protection.[5] Although in the scatological poems Swift experiences "difficulty" in holding certain emotions and impulses "in check," the subject matter of *Strephon and Chloe* is in the end "judiciously acknowledged." The key to his analysis is the notion of "reduction," which he defines as an available means of containment and self-defense: "God allows every man to secure himself, and puts the necessary means at his disposal. In Swift's case the necessary means were negation and reduction: difficulties were either repressed or melted down." In the case of *Strephon and Chloe*, he suggests, such reduction is achieved by an argument that teaches us the value of "modifying" or restraining our passions, and stresses the value of "limitation," "prudence," and "common sense."

Donald Greene also describes the poem as a successful act of reduction that diminishes the importance of those bodily functions that loom so large for Strephon.[6] This is achieved by the systematically balanced narrative, which first attributes to Strephon an "irrational state of illusion" and then logically plunges him into an equally "irrational state of despair when the illusion collapses." The second kind of unreason derives from the breakdown of the first, and the whole psychological sequence is determined by Strephon's over-reaction to the physical realities he confronts. According to this analysis, the "physiology of human excretion" is regarded as a "trivial matter" by a rational mind, and the poem manages to "discount" what deeply disturbs its hero. When Greene comes to the poem's concluding reflections, he describes them as being like a "sermon" that Swift the "Christian priest" might deliver. The poem thus achieves the closure of didactic resolution, and this closure is securely within the limits of ethical tradition; it is the "view of the orthodox Christian moralist."

Thomas B. Gilmore senses certain limitations in Greene's approach.[7] But while he shifts the balance by emphasizing "comic aspects" that he thinks have been neglected, he also strongly reinforces Greene's account of the poem's logical moralistic structure:

> It would seem, then, that in Swift's view Strephon's fixation on physical beauty logically degenerates into a fixation on physical filth once beauty is shorn of romance and its affinities with the physically gross are revealed. Because the disillusionment is as obsessive as the idealization preceding it, there is no escape. . . .

Gilmore also follows Greene when he suggests that the final stages of the poem offer a clarifying didactic "solution" to the problem posed by the narrative: the concluding paragraphs, he says, achieve "a transcendence of the scatological problem which always threatens so long as beauty is prized and the mask of decency may slip." This transcendence is offered through the recognition that beauty is "less important than such mental qualities as sense, wit, prudence, and good nature" and that "friendship" is the "most exalted, durable relationship of which human beings are capable."

Each of these readings is highly responsive to the strong formulaic and didactic vein in the poem's growth, and attributes considerable power to it: the poem achieves a "reduction," a "solution," and a "resolution" in its response to the experience it confronts. Although Donoghue implies that some struggle may be felt in Swift's adoption of such an authoritative posture, he does not question its ultimate force. Also, each analysis moves towards a recognition of the strength of great Augustan values such as "common sense" (Donoghue), "rationality" (Greene), and "good sense" (Gilmore). The poem thus enables each reader to engage in processes of thought that lead to coherent, summarizing statements about the nature of reality; it frequently engages in such processes itself, most notably in its concluding stage, and when it does so appears to encourage the reader to follow suit.

Elsewhere in the poem, as has often enough been noted, Swift's language works in ways quite other than that of the closing sequence. Whereas that sequence makes it possible for Gilmore to say that Swift achieves a "transcendence of the scatological problem," other sequences dwell protractedly on the details constituting that problem. They also, I would suggest, show an alarming power to embarrass or discomfort attempts at ratiocinative containment. Gilmore acknowledges the presence of some of these sequences when he argues for fuller recognition of neglected "comic elements," but the satiric-didactic framework exerts enough influence for him to continue to write about it as if its authority is not significantly undermined or threatened. An example of Swift's protracted and comic engagement with the problems of the flesh occurs at the heart of the didactic narrative, at the highly instructive moment when Strephon has just gotten into the same bed as Chloe, the woman he regards as a kind of goddess: at this critical juncture in the thematic diagram there occurs a digression from the narrative. It is a passage of about thirty lines (115–44), and although it is relevant in that it deals with crucial themes, it drastically interrupts the action, and when Swift returns to the narrative at l. 145 he feels the need to define it as a digression. It begins:

> Now, *Ponder well ye Parents dear*;
> Forbid your Daughters guzzling Beer;
> And make them ev'ry Afternoon
> Forbear their Tea, or drink it soon;
> That, e'er to Bed they venture up,
> They may discharge it ev'ry Sup;
> If not; they must in evil Plight
> Be often forc'd to rise at Night, ...[8]

This is not quite the tone that we would ordinarily associate with serious didactic literature. There is certainly an instructive stance, and the sequence begins with an emphatic stress on the importance of serious thought, but it develops into a kind of parody of instructional discourse—with the raucous vocabulary of the second line, the finicky precision of "ev'ry Sup," and the dire emphasis on the "evil" consequences of ignoring the advice. At the crucial juncture in the didactic plot, then, Swift begins to clown in the role of teacher. And a little later, instructions on how to avoid flatulence come to include a parenthesis that pokes fun at the relationship between "Sage" and "Disciples": "('Tis this the Sage of *Samos* means, / Forbidding his Disciples Beans)." The structures of such a relationship are imitated in the language of the sequence, but what the passage most vividly dramatizes is the farcical power of the operations of the flesh. In the next two lines about Moll and her "Art," there is a suggestion that it is possible for these operations to become fascinating. And Swift's own dwelling on the scatological "problem" reaches a climax in his reference to the ability of the bowels' "Blast" to utterly extinguish the fires of love (l. 136). This magnification of the body's force is quite other than Donoghue's mode of "reduction." And when, in the last eight lines of the digression, Swift instructs the reader about what must be done to counteract this force, his advice that wives cultivate "Nicety" and "study to be clean" is not couched in language that gives an immediate impression of strength. In fact there is a hint of desperation in the extreme (and seemingly impossible) degree of suppression recommended to the wife who must not even "give the smallest Room to guess / The Time when Wants of Nature press." This leads to a clear exposure of the fact that deceit must be resorted to when the narrator argues that the wife must keep her husband in a state of being "deluded" (1. 143). During the whole sequence two contrasting styles of representation come into a kind of collision: the didactic and rationalistic mode is at one point clearly mocked, and at the end considerably harrassed.

There are several other stages of the poem at which Swift's mode of representation is quite different from the moral-satiric definition that comes to dominate at the end and that informs the didactic plot. Fairly soon after the above digression, for example, Swift's approach to the narrative climax shows an anticipatory glee that clearly derives comic pleasure from the protracted dwelling on bodily functions: the "Nymph" has drunk no fewer than "TWELVE Cups of Tea, (with Grief I speak)," she is "opprest before, behind, / As Ships are Toss't by Waves and Wind," and she must reach for a "fair Utensil" as "smooth and white" as her own skin. At the climax itself, an exuberant, even child-like delight in the rendering of the moment appears not only in Strephon's cry of agony (" . . . ye Gods, what Sound is this? / Can *Chloe*, heav'nly *Chloe*—?") but also in his subsequent response (" . . . as he fill'd the reeking Vase, / Let fly a Rouzer in her Face"), and appears to have some power to distract the reader's attention from the somewhat bleak act of moral-satiric definition perpetrated at the heart of the sequence: "He found her, while the Scent increas'd / As *mortal* as himself at least" (185–86). Later, when the narrator has described the couple's subsequent decline into inurement and disillusion, he suddenly introduces an electrifying account of an experience that never occurred but that might have been salutary if it had: if only Strephon had seen Chloe on the lavatory, "In all the Postures of her Face, / Which Nature gives in such a Case," and had seen her "Distortions, Groanings, Strainings, Heavings," he might have realized the awful truth that in view of his present state he would have been better off to have "lickt her leavings" than to have married her (234–50).[9] In this sequence, the reality of bodily functions is transformed by a process of radical hyperbole into the appalling stuff of nightmare. And although Swift is clearly making an argumentative and thematic point, neither the point itself (which I shall return to) nor the mode of representation is one that commandingly puts excretion in its place by a process of reductive definition.

These shifts of mode are characteristic of what is a distinctly unstable poem. Each sequence I have mentioned contributes in some way to a sense that the poem's materials tend to be unmanageable, as does the discontinuity of the poem's development.[10] Thus, if we read the poem in such a way as to conclude that it transcends, reduces, or resolves the problem of human physicality, we run the risk that our reading will be exposed by the poem as an inadequate response to its exuberantly discontinuous life. The difficulty of reading is exacerbated, of course, by the fact that the forces causing the poem to be unstable tend to enhance the appeal of the ordered rationalistic argument and the "shelter" it provides. Indeed, in the course of literary history it may be seen that Swift's rendering of the problems posed by the flesh has actually caused a movement towards a concentration on the didactic frame, in that Donoghue's and Greene's accounts were in part reactions against such readers as Lawrence and Huxley, who were horrified by the passage about Chloe defecating.[11] But if we pursue the notion, as Greene does, that the poem is a kind of sermon on the problem of the flesh, we risk being placed in the awkward position of not seeming to have recognized that the speaker makes certain gestures that are peculiar for a preacher and that subvert the authoritative postures of his illustrative story and his ethical conclusions. These are gestures that turn the problem of flesh into the occasion for a snicker, a guffaw, a bawdy joke, or a horrible nightmare, and imply some awareness in the speaker that his didactic framework may provide only a fragile and partial resolution.

Other readers during the decades in question are less convinced by the didactic resolution the poem offers than are Donoghue, Greene, and Gilmore. A major example is Nora Crowe

Jaffe who finds a confusing "inconsistency" in the poem's growth.[12] This inconsistency does not derive from those shifts of representational mode that I have described, but from the shape of the poem's argument. Her reading is very much determined by the obtrusive presence of the didactic frame, but in giving this frame the close attention that it seems to demand Jaffe concludes that it is crucially flawed: Swift virtually contradicts himself because when he recommends "Decency" in marriage he endorses a mode of deception very similar to what he earlier ridiculed in Strephon, and thus appears to suggest that "romantic delusion is and is not reprehensible." This seems to me to tell an important truth about the poem, for its argument really is fissured, in a way that my earlier summary of it did not indicate. After the opening satire on Strephon's absurdly misleading process of idealization, the poem moves towards at least three potential solutions to his problem. One is that which modern readers might feel particular sympathetic to, namely an acceptance of physical reality somewhat along the lines of Shakespeare's sonnet, "My mistress' eyes are nothing like the sun." But we are given a kind of debased version of this in the couple's willing acquiescence in flesh, that Swift defines as vulgar and insensitive. The second is the solution that has a long and powerful tradition behind it, that is given great status in the poem, and that the readers I have described have particularly stressed: namely, the recognition that spiritual qualities are more important than physical ones. And the third is indeed what Jaffe says it is. When Swift stresses the value of "decency," he does recommend a process of concealment and delusion that has much in common with Strephon's initial state. What this "solution" implies is that the realities of the flesh are so disturbing that they must be suppressed or denied if a valuable relationship between human beings is to be sustained, and the structural "flaw" in the poem's argument is thus a sign of the radical unmanageability of the material it deals with.[13] It is this sense of how deeply disturbing the flesh is that leads to the nightmarish sequence about Chloe on the lavatory, where Swift argues that if Strephon had seen such a sight he would have been preserved from the dismaying contact with her body that marriage inevitably entails. One noticeable feature of Gilmore's reading of the poem is that when he describes a successful "transcendence" of the scatological problem he concentrates on the highly respectable argument about the need to place emphasis on spiritual matters. He says that the argument about the salutary lesson that might have been provided by the sight of Chloe defecating, an argument closely related to the stress on the value of decency, "staggers belief" (40). But this vein of feeling that leads to a high valuation of concealment, suppression, delusion, is nevertheless part of the poem's texture. Its relationship with the early part of the poem's argument is, as Jaffe says, uneasy and "confusing," and it is a sign that the didactic frame is subjected to considerable stress by the materials it seeks to contain. The poem may have begun by establishing the idea of a clear binary opposition between Strephon's irrational idealization on the one hand and a reasoning concern for spiritual matters and for decency on the other. But Swift's development of the "reasonable" solution(s) to Strephon's problem comes to include a desire for suppression consistent with a horror of the body verging on the hysterical. It turns out that the idealizing Strephon and the "decent" man (or woman) have something in common: thus, problem and solution seem to blur into each other,[14] and the clarity of the proposed opposition crumbles before our eyes. Jaffe responds to the "confusing" experience brought about by her close engagement with the didactic frame by counteracting it through a movement towards a decisive judgment of the poem's value: "Swift seems to have lost artistic distance here and introduced the inconsistencies of his personal attitudes," he has "entered the poem almost too completely," and has brought about its "disruption . . . as a work of art." In this way her own engagement with the didactic argument, though different from the others we have seen, leads her towards a closural response—in this case the closure of a decisive critical evaluation that defines the poem as a failure. By this, she is placed in the position of rejecting a feature of the poem that is crucial to the way in which it dramatizes the unruly life of its materials. And it would appear that a primary agent in causing such a response is the looming presence of the didactic frame itself, which stimulates the reader to feel that the defining tendency of the poem is an impulse towards ordering and definitive statement about the problems of the flesh, and that the poem seeks unreservedly to valorize such a mode of statement. Not surprisingly, the reader concludes that if such a statement is not achieved, the poem "fails" as a work of art. As I have tried to show, however, certain voices in the poem seem to say that if coherent debate in this context turns out to be difficult, that is only what we should expect from an attempt to deal rationally with such outrageously funny or horrifying material.

A perception that the poem does not achieve a logically ordered statement also dominates the accounts of their reading-experiences given by Peter Schakel and John M. Aden, and leads them to similarly conclusive judgments of the poem. Schakel draws attention to an "inconsistency" rather like that stressed by Jaffe when he says that the poem appears to imply both that men need to know about the reality of female defecation and that this reality needs to be "hidden" from them: he concludes that this inner confusion is a sign that Swift was "fallible" and "uncertain," and that the poem fails as a work of art.[15] Aden, too, believes that the concluding sequence of reflections is not adequately co-ordinated with the preceding narrative.[16] And he argues that this internal problem of logic is compounded by "redundancies" and "over-extension" that he finds "puzzling." This point is made particularly through his analysis of the poem's opening paragraph, where the aggregation of all the physical needs to which Chloe is supposedly immune is protracted to an extraordinary degree (8–24) and appears to endow her physicality with a radically pervasive life. In this sense the sequence is like certain others that I have described in that its representational mode is quite other than the "containing" definition that the plot and the concluding commentary would appear to suggest are possible. Aden's judgment is that this sequence typifies a poem "flawed" by "pointless repetition." Both he and Schakel, then, perceive some of the internal strains and discontinuities that give such awkward life to the poem's materials, but respond to the perception by seeking a decisive closural judgment about the poem's value. Once again, these reading-experiences illuminate the problems created by a poem that on the one hand encourages a process of judging it according to whether or not one finds its didactic argument to be sound, yet on the other shows itself eminently capable of exposing such judgments of itself as reductive.[17] And in the case of Aden's essay, we are made aware of one characteristic of Swift's art that will be particularly relevant to my account of *A Description of the Morning*: namely, that one source of the poem's subversive discontinuity is an interest in the seemingly "pointless" aggregation of physical particulars.

II

The manner in which *A Description of the Morning* has been problematic for several readers may be illuminated by a distinction that Stanley Fish drew at an early stage of his theorizing on the subject of reader-experience. Fish was interested in the reader's "primary or basic" encounter with a text, an encounter that he identified "more or less with perception itself."[18] It was this experience that, for him, brought into being and defined the literary text that was being read. And he argued that a typical literary-critical publication does not provide access to such an experience because in writing his analysis the critic will inevitably depart from it. What we get in the work of a critic is a "secondary or after-the-fact level" of experience (5), at which the reader engages in "an act of intellection, more or less equivalent with what we usually call interpretation." To make matters worse, "a reader who is also a critic will feel compelled to translate his experience into the vocabulary of the critical principles he self-consciously holds;" "he will . . . be reporting not on his immediate or basic response to a work but on his response (as dictated by his theoretical persuasion) to that response" (5–6). Fish saw these secondary acts of intellection as always and inevitably "distorting" because they carried the reader further and further away from that "primary or basic" experience consituting the identity of the text. One will not find this latter notion quite convincing if one holds to the traditional belief that responses occurring after Fish's "primary" experience continue to be able to tell us certain things about the identity of the text, as well as about its readers; and it is clear that the argument of this essay is largely dependent on such a belief. Fish's remarks, however, are extremely helpful to the process of clarifying a pattern that dominates the responses to *Morning* that I want to discuss. For in each of the essays I shall refer to there is a distinction between an initial experience of the work and a subsequent experience essentially determined by processes of "intellection." Moreover, although I believe that this secondary process of intellection is a crucial part of the "experience" generated by the poem and thus helps us to understand the nature of the text in question, it does also happen to be, in the case of this poem, "distorting." What it distorts, however, is not the "true" experience generated by the text, but the very structure of the text itself. And in saying this, I am expressing a belief that the text of *Morning* has an existence independent of the minds and reading-experiences of the critics I shall discuss, and that it is possible for the acts of description and interpretation practiced upon it to be inaccurate.

Fish has shown us, in his own case-history, that protracted self-examination can illuminate texts,[19] and I hope that a much more limited degree of similar self-examination might in my own case help to illuminate *Morning*. The first account of the poem that I want to consider is an essay of my own that appeared in 1966.[20] In that essay, I described a reading-experience that involved a high degree of discontinuity, a sense that the items referred to by the poem's words were not closely connected with one another. I said, "Swift enumerates a series of common sights and sounds with almost random unselectiveness, noting details without bringing them together" (43). These words define a sensation that has always been fundamental to my reading of the poem. But the qualifier in the phrase, "*almost* random unselectiveness," betrays a reluctance to accept it as the essential nature of the experience generated by a literary text. And indeed, I also argued that the seemingly miscellaneous items do actually connect so as to convey a satiric theme, and this led to statements like the following: "Swift's achievement in the poem is, without losing the fragmentary, confused effect of realism, also to attain a kind of thematic pattern" (41). It is now clear to me that my attempt to demonstrate the presence of this pattern is characterized by a considerable degree of falsity and artifice. I argued that, although the enumerated items are extremely various in kind, some being, for example, harmless and others criminal, "the flat, steady movement of the verse, the similarly unemphatic statement of each activity, suggest the uniform indifference with which they are all regarded" (41). The process of building an interpretation begins here with the assumption that because each item is enumerated in a "similarly unemphatic" way, or more accurately, with an absence of words that express strong judgmental attitudes or feelings toward what is being described, then the speaker in the poem necessarily feels "indifference"; such a conclusion, of course, is drawn as a consequence of hypothetical invention on the part of the reader, rather than as a consequence of pressure exerted by the words of the poem. Having thus invented a speaker of undiscriminating apathy, I went on to transform him into an emblem of eighteenth-century society, with the statement that, "A world which sees these incidents with equal unconcern has lost its sense of values" (41). The indifference attributed to an imaginary speaker is thus made to represent the moral confusion of a whole community, and the poem becomes an indirect and quite subtle satire on misplaced values; in other words, it is made to conform to certain expectations many readers hold about Swift and eighteenth-century literature.

In 1972 David Vieth published an essay that advanced a different interpretation of the poem, but in which certain features of what I think may be an archetypal pattern of reader-experience again appeared.[21] To begin with, Vieth recognized that initial sensation of discontinuity which tends to be created by the poem, and seemed to regard it as a feature of his own reading-experience; he wrote, "At the most literal level, nearly every reader of the poem has been struck by the drably realistic effect it achieves by cataloguing, in a flat, even tone, an apparently random selection of details from an urban dawn" (302–3). This comment refers to two of the distinctive qualities that are, as Vieth says, so often felt on a first reading of the poem: first, the lack of connection between the several items, and second, the absence of words that express attitudes or feelings towards the items described. However, Vieth takes a noticeably dismissive attitude toward the perception of these characteristics:

he describes it as characteristic of a reading that does not go
further than "the most literal level." In seeking to pass beyond
this level, and to achieve what he calls a "more comprehensive"
act of interpretation (302), Vieth says, "In *A Description of the
Morning* . . . meaningful order is so little evident that a full aesthetic response requires the reader to search for it. He is challenged, in the words of *The Lady's Dressing Room*, to find 'Such
Order from Confusion sprung' " (307). Thus, it is the apparent
absence of meaningful order that stimulates the reader to seek
that order, the evident lack of a thematic statement that chal-
lenges him to engage in a quest for such a statement. And as
Vieth builds his interpretation, the primary justification for creating it appears to lie in its power to bring order to the miscellaneous surface of the poem; as he puts it, "The reading of *A
Description of the Morning* as a parody of Creation, as depicting
a postlapsarian world of disorder and imperfection, is best supported by its consistent ability to explain the seemingly miscellaneous details in Swift's poem" (304–5). There is no suggestion
here that the poem's details themselves exert any pressure towards interpretation on the mind of the reader. But the essential
value of the thematic reading is felt to lie in its power and in
the power of the reader's mind to counteract the impression of
disorder initially given by the poem.[22] And once again, the act
of interpretation leads to certain moments that demonstrate the
fundamental recalcitrance of the text. Vieth argues that the
words of the poem do express certain quite strong attitudes toward the items they describe and that these attitudes cohere to
form a vision of "imperfection" and "disorder" in a fallen world.
But in order to establish this he is forced, for example, to claim
that when the speaker refers to Moll as whirling her mop with
"dext'rous Airs" he is communicating the critical implication
that she may not be intending to work with "genuine dexterity
and diligence" (305), and later on, that the oldness of the nails
that have fallen from passing vehicles and the "worn" condition
of the road-edges where they lie are symptoms of a postlapsarian
imperfection that the poem consistently, and with moral disapproval, defines. It seems to me that at these moments a noticeably forceful and assertive interpretive pressure is being

brought to bear on the text, and that as a consequence, a considerably degree of strain appears in the analysis.

A similar pattern of reader-experience appears again in the account of the poem by Nora Crow Jaffe.[23] She refers to the striking absence of close interrelatedness in the sequence of details when she says, "The vignettes in 'A Description of the Morning' are only very tenuously related to one another" (82). And she defines the lack of judgmental attitudes or emotions when she says, " . . . the reader hears no notes of rancor, censure, or judgment. The primary clue to the proper reception of the poem is simply the absence of any disparaging comment from Swift" (77–8). However, although she acknowledges these facts, Jaffe also insists on finding in the poem considerable degrees of both connectedness and disparagement. Her explanation of how this may occur focuses in a crucial way on the matter of reader-experience. She says, " . . . one will perceive complexity only as one moves further from the words themselves, only after the language has passed by, after the reading is finished and the book set aside. Then comes the struggle with the complexity of Swift's vision" (84). In this most illuminating sequence Jaffe suggests that the process of interpretation occurs at a stage of experience which is considerably removed from the reading of the words themselves, a moment in time when the actual language of the work has "passed by." What she says of her own experience is closely related to what Fish has said about the activities of literary critics, for whom "the act of interpretation is often so removed from the act of reading that the latter . . . is hardly remembered." As Jaffe introduces certain statements about the poem's theme, she does say that the process of arriving at them involves a degree of "struggle." And indeed, as in the two previous accounts of the poem, there are clear signs of this struggle in the interpretive analysis that she makes. The central theme of the poem now has to do with the "interplay of order and disorder," and with the omnipresent fact that the "figures responsible for preserving order" are simply failing to maintain it or are "actively engaged in disrupting it" (77). Perhaps the clearest sign of the obstacles that the poem presents to such an interpretive effort lies in Jaffe's treatment of the line, "Duns at his Lordships Gate began to meet." She comments, "His Lordship, who should be supervising the work of local sanitation, is hiding from his creditors" (77). From the words of the poem themselves, we cannot logically infer either that he neglects the matter of local sanitation or that he is hiding. Similarly, Moll is once again transformed by interpolation into an object of disparagement, this time because she is "prepared only for the entry and the stairs—the most visible and public parts, the avenues, into disorderly houses" (77). There is, of course, no evidence in the words of the poem that Moll is going to limit her activities *only* to the entry and the stairs, and we are told nothing of the condition of the house that lies beyond these avenues of approach.

In all of the above instances, then, the poem stimulates an initial experience that the readers feel to be in some sense unsatisfactory or incomplete, and this is followed by an act of interpretation that seeks to resist or oppose some of the sensations of that initial experience. The main reason for this happening seems to have to do with a perceived absence in the poem of certain characteristics that the readers expect to find. David Vieth is very clear about the fact that it is the apparent absence of meaningful connections that stimulates the reader to seek them. This quest that the poem induces then becomes a "struggle," as the text presents obstacles and difficulties. Eventually, each interpretive act arrives at moments that reveal it as an ultimately unsuccessful attempt to bring the poem's details to the desired order. And this is inevitable because the lack of thematic connection between the items is not merely apparent, but real. In other words, the same quality that induces the quest also ensures that it will be finally unsuccessful.

In trying to understand the poem, we need to pay close attention to the apparatus with which it was first presented to public view in Richard Steele's *Tatler*. Jaffe points out that Swift's relationship with Steele was very close at the time the poem was published, and she recognizes the possibility that he may have written the introduction himself (76). At any rate, given Swift's interest in this kind of introductory editorial apparatus, it is almost impossible to believe that he was unaware of it prior to publication. In a very deliberate way, the writer of this introduction seeks to divest the poem of general or representative significance; he says that the morning described in the poem is not only "in town," but in a certain part of town where the author lives "at present," thus suggesting that the details of the poem are determined by the particular aggregation of objects occurring in a particular place at a particular moment.[24] The writer goes on to forestall potential imitators, and gives an example of the kind of sequence that might appear in a poem imitative of this one. He says, " . . . I bar all descriptions of the evenings; as, a medley of verses signifying, grey peas are now cried warm: that wenches now begin to amble round the passages of the playhouse." Now although it could be possible with a little ingenuity to imagine a relationship between the grey peas and the wenches, it is clear that in this case such a relationship would be accidental, and that it is not the intention of the writer to move our minds toward a consideration of it. Rather, he seeks to move us toward an experience of random collocation "signifying" nothing. His whole point is that the kind of poem Swift has written does not work by means of logical or meaningful juxtapositions, but by the juxtaposition of items which may be adjacent to each other on the street but do not connect with each other in the manner of coherent discourse. That, it would appear, is intended to be crucial to the fun of this kind of poem, its studied departure from consecutiveness and logical order. The writer of the introduction further defines the poet's manner as a "way perfectly new," quite different from the predictable structures of what he calls "easy writing," and therefore likely to be disconcerting to readers who expect to encounter traditional and orthodox connections.

Swift was well aware of the human mind's impulse to find order in apparently random sequences, and he created an extreme and ludicrous image of it in his account of the academy of Lagado. But I do not wish to suggest that his purpose in this poem was to trick readers into inappropriate responses and thus make fools of them, or to turn interpreting readers into objects of satire. The poem simply does not seem to have designs on us in that way. And after all, Swift would no doubt feel that most of the interpretations that have been offered do their authors some moral, intellectual, or scholarly credit; there are obvious differences between these interpreters and the academicians of Lagado. We may, however, quite legitimately note certain effects that the poem has had on its readers, and that a fundamental pattern of experience has appeared in several of the writings about it. It is probably futile, in the absence of clear evidence, to speculate about what Swift's intentions with regard to his audience may have been. All we really have to go on is the *Tatler* introduction. But this does suggest the possibility that Swift regarded the poem as innovative, experimental, capable of disorienting readers who look for orthodox modes of literary organization. And this suggests the further possibility that he would not have been entirely surprised by a pattern of reader-experience that involves an insistent pursuit of clarifying and ordering lines of direction.

One reader who discusses the *Tatler* introduction at some length, only to decide that it is not a satisfactory guide to the true nature of the poem, is Roger Savage.[25] He does see that what the writer in *Tatler* stresses is a kind of "revolutionary realism" (181), but he does not seem to recognize the element of calculated discontinuity that is a feature of this "realism." And he soon leaves the introduction behind in his determination to show that Swift's poem expresses a highly coherent moral-satiric critique of a "fallen" city. His thematic account is different from those we have considered so far in that there is no real suggestion that part of his reading-experience was an initial sensation of discontinuity or disconnection. He perhaps makes a gesture towards such a possibility, only to dismiss it with some contempt, when he says that the poem's "realism is not simply the result of a walk through London at dawn with a camera" (176). And he moves rapidly to the notion that the poem's details cohere so as to communicate a satiric vision of contemporary civilization. His essay embodies a somewhat more extreme form of the rationalizing pressure brought to bear on the poem's details by the other critics. One can see the process vividly at work in the following, summarizing statement:

The crowd he points to is slipshod, raucous and none
too clean: and there are obviously as many moral wrinkles and deformities as physical. Along with the brick-
dust and coal, gutters and dirty doorsteps, there is Betty's whoring, his Lordship's profligacy, the prison system abused and the need for a secret police of watchful
bailiffs.

(183)

One may note here the neatly definitive moralistic structure of
Savage's statement. First, there is the use of the one word in the
poem that explicitly defines reprehensible behavior ("Slipshod"),
with the suggestion that it is capable of referring to a homogeneous "crowd" of items as well as the "Prentice" it does actually
describe. Savage's next phrase ("raucous and none too clean")
refers to the fact that some of the individuals make dissonant
noises and are dirty. After this, a linkage is made between these
physical characteristics and certain moral deficiencies that can
be sensed in some of the individuals: the colon reinforces the
idea of such a linkage, and it is further stressed by the details
and the structure of the sentence that follows. Savage's statement is thus very coherent, embodying a high degree of order
that he believes is capable of describing the development of
Swift's poem. But the problem is that some of the figures who
get physically dirty are in no way presented as morally reprehensible (e.g., the "Smallcoal-Man," the "Chimney-Sweep,"
"Brick-dust *Moll*"), and several other figures obviously do not
fit into a morally critical rubric (e.g., the "Youth with Broomy
stumps," the other "*Moll*," and the "School-Boys"). Similarly,
the arrangement of the two sentences in Savage's analysis implies that coal and gutters are examples of physical "wrinkles
and deformities," and to see them in this way surely requires
an extreme effort of the interpretive will. There is thus a real
discrepancy between the structure of the analytical statement
and the actual development of the poem that the critic is trying
to describe. The moralistic order of Savage's statement represents something that he is determined to see in the poem. But
in his pursuit of this order he ends up rather drastically distorting the text itself, and displaying an insensitivity to specific

detail that several other parts of his essay suggest is not characteristic of him.

Interpretive action may be performed in more sensitive and
graceful ways than this, as we can see in David Vieth's response
to the following lines:

> The Smallcoal-Man was heard with Cadence deep,
> 'Till drown'd in Shriller Notes of Chimney-Sweep,
> Duns at his Lordships Gate began to meet,
> And Brick-dust *Moll* had Scream'd through half the
> Street.

Three of these lines are connected in that they refer to sounds
made by human voices. One of these sounds is clearly defined as
unpleasant to listen to ("Scream'd"). Another is described by
a word that suggests it has a considerable potential to create
discomfort ("Shriller"). And the third would seem to be somewhat ironically described by a phrase suggestive of euphony
("Cadence deep"). So when Vieth attributes "dissonance" to the
subject-matter of these three lines (306) it does not seem that
an unduly high degree of creative interpolation is going on, although there is considerable variation in the strength and clarity with which Swift's lines are capable of communicating such
an impression. But when Vieth defines the relationship of the
third line to the other three, he seems to erect a structure of
meaning for which the text does not provide an adequate foundation: "Framed by this dissonance is the disarray of the nobleman's finances (13); the contrast in social levels merely under-
lines the common element of disorder" (306). The analysis is
clearly very elegant, and its satisfying order is most attractive to
the mind. But the interpretive alliteration of the critic provides a
harmony that is essentially remote from the nature of the poet's
text. For the crucial features of the second couplet are precisely
that absence of significant relationship and that abrupt shift
of context, tone and image that are cultivated in the *Tatler's*
juxtaposition of grey peas and wenches. The first line of the
couplet moves towards a definition of a particular social situation or problem, and it seems to involve a potentially thematic
or satiric comment on upper-class delinquency. The reasons for

the nobleman's financial straits are not given. But the mind naturally reaches for explanatory definition. We have seen that in the case of Nora Crow Jaffe the urge to develop and explain was so strong that the reader's mind went on to transform the line into a full-fledged satiric indictment of aristocratic irresponsibility. Such a thematic development is certainly not present in the text, though it is within the line's capability to stimulate a desire for or expectation of such a development. What happens in the text is that the words simply stop at an incompletely developed portrait of a social situation, and then shift abruptly to describe in sharply concrete terms the actions of an individual figure who is not only in a different social class from the nobleman, but exists in an utterly different context or situation, and exhibits a kind of behavior that is dramatically unrelated to that of the debt-collectors or the nobleman.

To recognize the nature of the reading processes that the poem has evoked should cause us to return with renewed attention to that way of perceiving the details of the poem that so many readers agree is a feature of their first or immediate response. One recent sign of this occurring is an essay by C.N. Manlove, who says that in *Morning* Swift shows "a predilection for describing things for their own sake"(466), that there is an "emphasis on the plainly physical," and that the poem "refuses 'meaningfulness' in any place" (467).[26] Indeed, the central principle of Swift's highly experimental poem is a mode of perception by which each successively presented object is seen in its separate individuality, rather than in its relationship to other objects or to general ideas, and without being placed in a context that causes it to serve an overriding moral or philosophical purpose. Swift celebrates such a mode of perception throughout the early stages of the *Journal to Stella,* and it was clearly a matter of great interest to him.[27] At the same time, the *Tatler* introduction suggests that he knew it would be disconcerting to readers of literature. And because the experience has been disconcerting, we have continued for some time to resist it in our reading of this poem. We have persistently been drawn by the poem to seek connections that we think may lead to a unifying interpretation. And what appears to have given energy to such quests has been the highly stimulating absence of those characteristics that would enable the quests to be successful.

NOTES

1. I have already written at some length about the two poems, and about some of the matters taken up in the following essay, in *Energy and Order in the Poetry of Swift* (Lewisburg: Bucknell Univ. Press; London and Toronto: Associated University Presses, 1980). But the argument of the present essay, I believe, goes sufficiently beyond what was said in the earlier context to justify my return to the poems. And I hope the reader will not feel that there is any undue repetition in what follows.
2. John Middleton Murry, *Jonathan Swift* (London: Jonathan Cape, 1954), 440. D.H. Lawrence, *Phoenix: The Posthumous Papers of D.H. Lawrence,* ed. Edward D. McDonald (London: William Heinemann, 1936), 281–82.
3. Denis Donoghue, *Jonathan Swift: A Critical Introduction* (London: Cambridge Univ. Press, 1969). Quotations are from 28, 30, 36 and 37.
4. Peter Steele, *Jonathan Swift: Preacher and Jester* (Oxford: Clarendon Press, 1978), 6.
5. *Jonathan Swift: A Critical Introduction,* 203, 210, 37, 211 and 214.
6. Donald Greene, "On Swift's Scatological Poems," *Sewanee Review,* 75 (1967), 672–89. Quotations are from 680–82, 688 and 685–86.
7. Thomas B. Gilmore, "The Comedy of Swift's Scatological Poems," *PMLA,* 91 (1976), 33–43. Quotations are from 33, 38 and 40.
8. Quotations are from *The Poems of Jonathan Swift,* ed. Harold Williams, Second edition, 3 Vols. (Oxford: Clarendon Press, 1958).
9. This was the sequence that particularly disturbed Murry and Lawrence.
10. Some comments by John J. Richetti are pertinent to what I am describing in this essay. He says that in eighteenth-century writing there is often a drive "toward compressed presentation of that which is extensive and more or less sprawling and unmanageable," but he also includes Swift among writers who "specialize in disrupting the world implied by the aphoristic," and argues that "such writing calls attention to its capacities for recasting conventional formulations, but at the same time by its stylistic energy and wit it tends to promote experience and to undercut the possibility of final formulation of any sort." *Philosophical Writing: Locke, Berkeley, Hume* (Cambridge,: Harvard Univ. Press, 1983), 31–32.
11. See Note 2.
12. Nora Crow Jaffe, *The Poet Swift* (Hanover, NH: University Press of New England, 1977). Quotations are from pp. 112, 115–17, and 109.
13. C. J. Rawson, one critic of the nineteen-seventies who was not drawn into misreading by the power of the didactic frame, comments as follows on this feature of the poem's argument:

> The ambiguity, or impasse, is characteristic. Between the civilized lie and the beastly truth, the middle way is hard to find. . . . Reality and artifice, in other words, are at their usual tug of war. We must in some sense face the reality of the flayed woman and the gutted beau, but decency and civilization demand that they also be kept out of sight. It is sentimental of

the critics to say that Swift resolved the dilemma by some kind of "compromise" or middle way; it is the fact that he never resolved it at all which gives his work its particular urgency and truth. "The Nightmares of Strephon: Nymphs of the City in the Poems of Swift, Baudelaire, Eliot," in *English Literature in the Age of Disguise*, ed. Maximilian E. Novak (Berkeley & Los Angeles: University of California Press, 1977), 68–69.

14. What I am describing here bears some relationship to what William Freedman has recently described as a "fusion" (486) of "Strephon" and the narrator, both in this poem and *The Lady's Dressing Room* in "Dynamic Identity and the Hazards of Satire in Swift," *Studies in English Literature*, 29 (1989), 473–87. It is also related to my earlier argument that Swift and "Strephon" appear to share certain attitudes, in *Energy and Order in the Poetry of Swift* (210 and 219–20).

15. Peter Schakel, "Swift's Remedy for Love: The 'Scatalogical' Poems," *Papers on Language and Literature*, 14 (1978), 137–47. Quotations are from 147 and 145.

16. John M. Aden, "Those Gaudy Tulips: Swift's 'Unprintables,' " in *Quick Springs of Sense*, ed. Larry S. Champion (Athens: University of Georgia Press, 1974), 15–32. Quotations are from 28, 26, and 23.

17. A possible way of describing the tendencies that collide in this poem, though not one that I feel able to pursue, is offered by Ruth Salvaggio. After expressing her opinion that "both a desire for order and an indulgence in disorder inform Swift's writing," she goes on to suggest "that we regard the Swift who creates and defends systems as the 'man' of classical satiric structure, and that we regard the Swift who writes so vivaciously and disruptively as the 'woman' who always seems to be hovering around his satiric systems" (79). She asks the question: "Can we understand the other side of Swift—the Swift of anarchy, flux, and disruption—as peculiarly feminine?" (80). This raises the thought that what readers have been over-directed by in *Strephon and Chloe* is the "masculine" didactic frame, which has suppressed the other, disruptive, "feminine" forces at work in the text, and that readers have been trapped into misreading by what Salvaggio (following Hélène Cixous) calls the "bisexual" quality of Swift's writing (81). *Enlightened Absence: Neoclassical Configurations of the Feminine* (Urbana and Chicago: Univ. of Illinois Press, 1988). Attempts to understand the sexual orientation of the text are complicated by Donald T. Siebert's notion of a "sexist bias" in the poem: in his argument the "bawdy" and "gaminess" (30) of the subversive sequences show Swift speaking "like a man to men" (37) in "traditionally masculine language" (38). "Swift's Fiat Odor: The Excremental Re-Vision," *Eighteenth-Century Studies*, 19 (Fall, 1985), 21–38.

18. Stanley Fish, *Is There a Text in This Class? The Authority of Interpretive Communities* (Cambridge, & Dondon: Harvard Univ. Press, 1980), 5.

19. Fish retrospectively examines his own earlier criticism at several stages of *Is There a Text in This Class?*

20. A. B. England, "World Without Order: Some Thoughts on the Poetry of Swift," *Essays in Criticism*, 16 (1966), 32–43.

21. David Vieth, "Fiat Lux: Logos Versus Chaos in Swift's 'A Description of the Morning,' " *Papers on Language and Literature*, 8 (1972), 302–07.

22. There are some interesting parallels between the process that I am describing here and what Stanley Fish has said about one of his early essays, "What It's Like to Read *L'Allegro* and *II Penseroso*," printed in *Is There a Text in This Class?* For example, Fish writes, " . . . in response to the curious discreteness that characterizes a reading of *L'Allegro*" several critics have been moved to "supply the unity by supplying connections more firm and delimiting than the connections available in the text" (6).

23. Nora Crow Jaffe, *The Poet Swift*, 75–84.

24. *The Tatler*, ed. George A. Aitken (London: Duckworth and Co., 1898), 4 Vols., I, 81–82 (No. 9, April 30, 1709).

25. Roger Savage, "Swift's Fallen City: *A Description of the Morning*," *The World of Jonathan Swift: Essays for the Tercentenary*, ed. Brian Vickers (Oxford: Basil Blackwell, 1968), 171–94.

26. C. N. Manlove, "Swift's Structures: 'A Description of the Morning' and Some Others," *Studies in English Literature*, 29 (1989), 463–72.

27. See A. B. England, "Private and Public Rhetoric in the *Journal to Stella*," *Essays in Criticism*, 22 (1972), 131–41.

The Myth of Narcissus in Swift's *Travels*

Christopher Fox

This essay begins with a question posed by the late Frank Brady in 1978 and (more recently) by William Kinsley in 1982. What do we make of Gulliver's apprenticeship, at the opening of the *Travels*, to "my good Master Bates"? Brady noted that it "is easy to find" such "jokes (errors? misstatements?) in *Gulliver*; what is difficult . . . is to determine whether they are (1) accidental, (2) incidental (local, restricted), or (3) significant?"[1]

Let us apply Brady's criteria to the "Master Bates" construct, developed in the opening three paragraphs of the work: in the first readers learn of Gulliver's apprenticeship to "Mr. James Bates" and later "Mr. Bates" who becomes, in the second paragraph, "my good Master Mr. Bates" or "Mr. Bates, my Master" and, in the third, simply "my good Master *Bates*."[2] To use

This is a modified version of an essay which appeared in 20 (Fall, 1986) *Eighteenth-Century Studies*. I wish to thank the editors and the American Society for Eighteenth-Century Studies for permission to reprint this essay as here revised.

Brady's first criterion, is this chain of references merely "accidental"? Pointing to Swift's use of "anticipatory variations" here and of "repetition and over-specification with a vengeance," Kinsley finds these elements alone convincing proof that the pun is deliberate,[3] and his contention is sound, though at least one objection remains: was the word "masturbation" even current *in Swift's day?* Milton Voigt, assessing Phyllis Greenacre's attempt to make the pun mean something, argues that it was not; and on the basis of the *OED*, which cites the earliest written use of the word in 1766, he is right. Brady tried to remove this objection by locating an earlier occurrence of the word, in Florio's Montaigne (1603).[4] But there were also some more current uses that (1) suggest the pun is not "accidental" and (2) supply, at the very least, an "incidental" context for the joke.

In *A Modest Defence of Publick Stews (1724),* published two years before the *Travels,* Bernard Mandeville relates that one of the "Ways by which lewd young Men destroy their natural Vigour, and render themselves impotent" is by "Manufriction, *alias* Masturbation." Dr. Mandeville then lists a host of ailments arising from this "lewd Trick" and argues that to "prevent young Men from Laying *violent Hands* upon themselves, we must have recourse to the *Publick Stews.*"[5] In advocating the brothel as a cure for those he calls the youthful *"Onanites,"* Mandeville was not alone. In *The Oeconomy of Love* (1736), another doctor, John Armstrong, counsels young men to "hie / To Bagnio lewd or Tavern, nightly where / Venereal Rites are done" rather than practice that "ungenerous, selfish, solitary Joy."[6] And earlier in the century, in his *Treatise of Venereal Disease* (1709), Dr. John Marten offers vivid case histories which seemingly support such claims. Here, we learn about "a very comely Gentleman . . . whose Case was lost *Erection*, by *Masturbation* in his Youth." Equally unfortunate, Marten adds, was a young student who, "deceiv'd by others, used daily *Masturbation,* as he [later said] lamenting and sorry, and thereby had contracted so great a weakness of his *Seminal Vessels* and *Testicles,* that although he lived afterwards continently, yet he was troubled with a *Gonorrhea* . . . and whereas he was before of a lively colour and strong, afterwards he grew pale, lean, weak, &c."[7] Along with the pre-*Gulliver* uses of the word "masturbation," the context of such remarks sheds light on the *Travels* in 1726. That context is the pervasive early eighteenth-century anti-masturbatory craze sparked, at least in part, by a pamphlet titled *ONANIA; OR, THE Heinous Sin of Self-Pollution, AND ALL its Frightful Consequences, in both SEXES, Considered, WITH Spiritual and Physical Advice to those, who have already injur'd themselves by this Abominable Practice* (London, c. 1709–1710).

Early in this pamphlet, the author confesses that to "expose a Sin so displeasing to God, so detrimental to the Publick, and so injurious to our selves, requires no Flights of Wit."[8] And the work that ensues—an often tedious compendium of moral and pseudo-medical advice (though not without a certain prurient appeal)—indicates that he is largely correct. In elucidating the frightful consequences of the "SIN OF SELF-POLLUTION" (among them, sterility, blindness, sloth, madness, gonorrhea, death, *"Lying," "Forswearing,"* and even *"*Murder*"*), *ONANIA* raised masturbation to the status of a "collosal bogey."[9] In a 1724 edition of the work, which advertises itself as "The Tenth EDITION/Above Fifteen Thousand of the former Editions . . . Sold," we discover that the secret sin has reached contagious proportions in Britain. Indeed, it "has now become almost as frequent amongst Girls, as Masturbation is amongst Boys." It is especially prevalent in the schools, where *"licentious Masturbators"* initiate unsuspecting youths into "that cursed School-Wickedness of Masturbation."[10] P.–G. Boucé notes that *ONANIA* enjoyed an "amazing success." Judging from the number of editions it ran through and the host of imitations it sparked, *ONANIA* (as Lawrence Stone adds) "clearly struck some hidden area of anxiety in early eighteenth-century Europe."[11] In the mid–1720s alone, for example, if the reader did not see *ONANIA* directly or, say, Mandeville's *Publick Stews,* he could consult *Eronania: On the Misusing of the Marriage-Bed by Er and Onan* (London, 1724). He could then move on, in the same year, to *The Crime of Onan (together with that of his brother Er, punished with sudden death): Or, the hainous Vice of Self defilement* (London, 1724). Four years later, he could read Joseph Cam's *A Practical Treatise on the Consequences of Venereal Disease* (London, 1728), the first part considering that dreaded specter, "onanism."

When Gulliver, in 1726, is apprenticed to "my good Master *Bates*" there are some historical reasons, therefore, for assuming that Swift's chain of references is far from "accidental." But is it only "incidental," that is, in Brady's terms, a "local" or a "restricted" joke? If so, we could end this essay here and simply say that, by introducing this pun—particularly within a larger discussion of Gulliver's schooling—Swift is playfully alluding to a context familiar to his readers.

Another Scriblerian work furnishes additional substance for investigation. In a book Swift contributed to—the *Memoirs of Scriblerus*—Martinus uses his "sagacity in discovering the distempers of the Mind" to solve the case of a young nobleman, who has cut himself off from others and "converses" with almost "none but *himself*." Martinus concludes that the young man must be "desperately in love"; and an interview with an aunt confirms the object of this "amorous inclination":

> Whom does he generally talk of? Himself, quoth the Aunt. Whose wit and breeding does he most commend? His own, quoth the Aunt. . . . Whom is he ogling yonder? Himself in his looking-glass. . . . Have you observ'd him to use Familiarities with any body? "With none but himself: he often embraces himself with folded arms, he claps his hand often upon his hip, nay sometimes thrusts it into—his breast."

The prognosis is poor. If the young man's self-love is not cured, we are told, he will be "condemn'd eternally to himself" and perhaps "run to the next pond to get rid of himself, the Fate of most violent Self-lovers."[12]

Important here is a cluster of associations linking masturbation to the "distemper" (i.e. madness) of self-love and to the greatest self-lover of them all. The young man's rejection of others, his fascination and "Familiarities" with his own body, his attempts to embrace himself, the closing evocation of the destructive pond—all suggest the story of Narcissus. Given this Scriblerian context, it is perhaps not surprising that a book which begins with its hero apprenticed to "Master *Bates*" ends with him "condemn'd eternally to himself" and with a vision that also evokes the tale of Narcissus: "When I happened to behold the Reflection of my own Form in a Lake or Fountain," Gulliver tells us near the end of *his* tale, "I turned away my Face in Horror and detestation of my self" (4.10). It is within this larger pattern, suggestive of Gulliver's Narcissistic movement from self-love to self-hatred, that the opening play on "Master *Bates*" becomes—in Brady's third criterion—"significant."

"Narcissism" in Swift's day did not necessarily mean what it means to us—the word itself was probably coined by a German in 1899.[13] It instead meant myth, specifically Ovidian myth,[14] and the traditional interpretations of the mythographers. He is known for the "hard pride" (*dura superbia*) with which he scorns the love of others.[15] He especially dislikes the company of women.[16] Despising all others in comparison with himself, he will not let others love him and tells all who attempt to do so, "embrace me not."[17] He who will not let others love him is doomed to a hopeless love himself; he gazes at the deceptive reflection, mistakes a shadow (*umbra*) for a substance, and blindly falls in love with an idealized vision of himself, a nothingness created by his own imagination: "*quod petis, est nusquam.*"[18] As he attempts to grasp the "adored image," it "ever elude[s] his Embraces." Transported "by selfe-love" and wasting away "with that madnesse," he spends the remainder of his days isolated from the world and attended by a few flatterers who reaffirm his delusion.[19] These traits (among others) were attributed to Narcissus by Ovid's commentators from the late sixteenth through the early eighteenth century. Many of the same characteristics appear, as well, in the Scriblerians' case of the young nobleman in the *Memoirs*—and in Swift's portrayal of Lemuel Gulliver.

We know from "Baucis and Philemon" or "The Fable of Midas" that Swift enjoyed playing with Ovidian types and themes.[20] The similarities between Gulliver and the Narcissus of the Ovidian tradition, and the evocation of the same myth in Book IV of the *Travels*, point to some larger transformations of the tale. Three Ovidian themes in particular, which link Gulliver to the Narcissus figure, shed light on his opening apprenticeship to 'Master *Bates*" and his closing rejection of self and species.

The first theme suggests itself in Gulliver's response to those who love him and his own experience with his beloved Houyhnhnms. This theme, the "frustrated love," had been seen for centuries as a central motif of the Narcissus tale.[21] The story in Ovid is not simply the story of Narcissus, but also of Echo and the others who tried to love him. At a key moment in Ovid's account, Echo sees Narcissus and, "inflamed with love," races up to "throw her arms around" him. He immediately "flees her approach," yelling "Hands off! embrace me not!" (*Metam.*, Bk. 3, line 390). In Book IV of the *Travels*, the same scene is comically re-enacted in Gulliver's encounter with the Yahoo woman who, "inflamed by Desire," came "running with all Speed" up to him and—his account continues—"embraced me after a most fulsome Manner; I roared as loud as I could . . . whereupon she quitted her Grasp, with the utmost Reluctancy, and leaped upon the opposite Bank, where she stood gazing and howling" (4.8).

This version of the "frustrated love"—with Gulliver playing Narcissus to a Yahoo Echo—is picked up later in a series of embrace scenes that are not as comic. When Gulliver arrives home, he tells us that "my Wife took me in her Arms, and kissed me; at which, having not been used to the Touch of that odious Animal for so many Years, I fell in a Swoon for almost an Hour" (4.11). As in his encounter with the Yahoo Echo, Gulliver's rejection here is explicitly sexual. During his association with "Master *Bates*," Gulliver had been advised "to alter my Condition" by marrying (1.1). Now, finally returning home, he laments that "by copulating with one of the *Yahoo*-Species, I had become a parent of more; it struck me with the utmost Shame, Confusion, and Horror" (4.11). He does not let this happen in the future and continues to scorn his wife's embraces right up to the time he writes the book; for Gulliver assures us that, in the five years he's been home, he has let no one in his family even "take me by the Hand" (4.11). Gulliver, in other words, commits himself at the end of the work to the Narcissistic isolation evoked at the opening, in his situation with "my good Master *Bates*." In Ovid's story, Narcissus shows his "hard pride" in rejecting not only Echo, but everyone else who attempts to love him. This theme also appears in another embrace scene in Book IV, this one with

Pedro de Mendez, who has treated Gulliver with great humanity. "He took kind Leave of me," Gulliver comments, "and embraced me at parting; which I bore as well as I could" (4.11). In
his proud rejection of Pedro de Mendez no less than of his wife,
Gulliver's posture is summed up by the boy's words in the tale:
"Hands off! embrace me not!"

The "frustrated love" works both ways. As Ovid and his
commentators remind us, he who will not let others love him is
doomed to a hopeless love himself, and to be tortured by the
"unattainability of an idealized self-image."[22] That image in the
Travels is embodied in Gulliver's "Love and Veneration" (4.7)
for the Houyhnhnms, who reject him just as he rejects the others.

Along with the "frustrated love," two other Ovidian motifs
are pertinent here. The first is the "reflection" theme, seen in
Narcissus's preoccupation with himself in the pond. In their ad-
aptation of the myth in the *Memoirs*, the Scriblerians connect
the "reflection" to the young man's masturbation and "Familiarities" with himself, to his absorption in the "looking-glass," and
ultimately, to a larger movement from self-love to self-hatred.

All these elements are at work in the *Travels*, where Swift
uses the same theme to suggest Gulliver's simultaneous fascination with, and rejection of, his own body—or, one-half of his
being. Indeed, the opening play on "Master *Bates*" is only the
first in a long series of references to Gulliver's "Familiarities"
with himself. Early in Book I, for example, Gulliver reports (1.3)
that when "some of the younger Officers" of the Lilliputian army
pass under his tattered breeches, they look up not simply with
"Laughter" but "Admiration." Elsewhere in the same book, he
vividly describes relieving himself and then feels the need to
apologize for it: "I would not have dwelt so long upon a Circumstance . . . if I had not thought it necessary to justify my Character in Point of Cleanliness to the World" (1.2). In a parallel
passage in Book II, he tells us about relieving himself again and
again asks the reader to "excuse me for dwelling on these and
the like Particulars; which however insignificant they may appear to grovelling vulgar Minds, yet will certainly help a Philos-
opher enlarge his Thoughts and Imagination" (2.1). How this is
so is unclear. What is clear is that Gulliver dwells "on these
and the like Particulars" throughout the entire work. And the

particulars he provides—his later defense, for example, of his own smell (2.5) or the "Shame" with which he views his sexual acts (4.11)—reveal a strange preoccupation with, and progressive hatred of, his own body. This same pattern suggests itself in the growing number of references to "mirrors," culminating in Gulliver's stark rejection of his human form in Book IV:

> When I happened to behold the Reflection of my own
> Form in a Lake or Fountain, I turned away my Face
> in Horror and detestation of my self; and could better
> endure the Sight of a common *Yahoo*, than of my own
> Person (4.10).

In a passage that directly evokes and also modifies the Narcissus myth, Gulliver—here as elsewhere[23]—tells us he hates his "Reflection" in mirrors. A similar modification of the myth appears in the *Fables* of La Fontaine (1621–95), where in "The Man and His Reflection" a Narcissus appears who avoids mirrors:

> Thinking himself one with whom none could compare,
> A man supposed himself the handsomest of mankind
> And found fault with every mirror anywhere,
> So that in time he had become morally blind. . . .
> What could our Narcissus do but stay away,
> In the kind of place in which he would be safe all day
> From any mirror that might catch him unaware?[24]

The reason this Narcissus avoids mirrors is that they show him he looks like everybody else and detract from his idealized self image. Gulliver has similar motivations. Mirrors reflect the human form he has now rejected, a rejection arising, in part, from the Narcissistic fascination with himself adumbrated throughout and in the opening play on masturbation.

Mirrors also detract from Gulliver's idea of what he wants to become. What he wants to become is a rational horse. (As Brady quipped, "Gulliver was not unusual among eighteenth-century squires in preferring his horses to his family, but his reasons for doing so seem unique."[25]) Thus, in the same passage in Book IV, Gulliver immediately turns away from his human "Reflection" to focus on another image—the Houyhnhnms—on

which he looks "with Delight" (4.10). When he first found himself "gazing" at that image "for some time" (4.1), he had won-
dered soon afterwards whether his "Brain was disturbed" and
had "rubbed my Eyes often" to see if "I might be in a Dream"
(4.2). But the "Truth" of this image—and the possibility of a
purely rational life—had since "appeared so amiable" to him
that he has "determined upon sacrificing everything to it" (4.7).
This is the image evoked again at the end of the *Travels*, where
we find Gulliver living "in great Amity" (4.11) with two "Stone-
Horses": stallions to most people, but to Gulliver idols of his
beloved Houyhnhnms. Gulliver's fixed obsession with this image
and his vain attempt to embrace it point to another theme, "illusion," which figures prominently in the Narcissus story.

In Ovid, Narcissus ignorantly (*inprudens*) mistakes an illusion for a reality and worships an insubstantial image that nonetheless "appears" to him "like a statue" (*Metam.*, Bk. 3, line
419). "What you seek is nowhere"—*quod petis, est nusquam*—the narrator laughs (Bk. 3, line 433). Because the illusion has no correspondence in reality, and cannot be attained,
the boy is destroyed. Later interpreters link Narcissus's illusion
to, among other things, the (a) folly of worshipping an image,
to the (b) blindness that arises from pride, and—from the late
sixteenth century onward—to a (c) self-pleasing delusion, a mental aberration created by his own imagination. The first two
threads are suggested, for instance, in Ben Jonson's *Cynthia's
Revels: Or, The Fountain of Self-Love* (1601), where Echo wishes
that Narcissus had picked a "truer Mirror" in which to view his
real self. "But self-love never yet could look on truth / But with
blear'd beams" (i.ii). The third—taking Narcissus's error as a
delusion—is prominent in La Fontaine's later Fable, where Narcissus avoids outward mirrors because they interfere with his
private vision of himself.

All these strands appear in Gulliver's worship of the Houyhnhnms. At the end of the work, we find Gulliver attempting
"to behold my Figure often in a Glass" in order "to Habituate
my self by Time to tolerate the Sight of a human Creature"
(4.12). But, like La Fontaine's Narcissus, Gulliver already has
an image of himself, a private mirror, he likes better. This is
the image he gazes at when he turns away from his human

reflection in a lake, or when he enters the stable with his groom to view those two "Stone-Horses." This image pleases him because it allows him to deny that human form he has rejected, and to dream the dream of a purely rational life. Just as important, it enables him to "pretend to some Superiority" over the rest of the human race (4.12). That the Houyhnhnm ideal is a delusion is strongly suggested by the disparity between what Gulliver wants to become and what he is. Attempting to escape his body, he ends up enmeshed in it, enjoying the fumes of his groom while unable to tolerate the smell of his own family. Attempting to live a life of pure reason, he loses it altogether. The references to madness abound. In short, like the boy in the story, Gulliver is deluded by a hopeless love for an unattainable image—in his case, the Houyhnhnms, who become an idealized projection of his own pride.

That Gulliver writes the book to convert *us* to this same image suggests another interpretation of Narcissus's "illusion," taking it as a mental aberration of a specific type. In a popular emblem book reprinted as late as 1784,[26] Andrea Alciati equates Narcissus with the proposer of "new doctrines," one who mistakes his own idea for truth (Figure 1). The image this Narcissus sees is an imaginary construct (*phantasias*) created by his own intellect, a construct he falls in love with and then attempts to impose on the rest of us.[27] Like Alciati's Narcissus, Gulliver has found what he takes to be *the* truth. And being (so he often claims) a lover of truth, he writes the book with the stated intent of teaching us this truth, learned among the Houyhnhnms (4.12). Like the man in the emblem, however, this "truth" is a delusion. Indeed, in his blind love for his delusion and his attempt to get us to embrace it as truth, Gulliver is yet another version of Alciati's Narcissus—and of the "projector" who pervades Swift's works, but with one difference, of course: Gulliver's project is the grandest one of all, no less than the immediate reformation of the entire human race. Whenever someone proposes a new system, Swift tells us in the *Tale of A Tub*, "the first Proselyte he makes, is Himself."[28] In Swift's projector Lemuel Gulliver, as in Alciati's Narcissus, the root of such proselytizing can be found in self-love.

This points to the larger eighteenth-century discussion of self-interest and also, perhaps, to another reason why Gulliver is apprenticed to "my good Master *Bates*." As a Christian and a moralist, Swift inherited a tradition that regarded self-love as a "main cause of psychological distortion," of "prejudice, misperception, misunderstanding, and worse, delusion, in one's thinking about oneself and everything else."[29] In the figure of Lemuel Gulliver, all of these are at work. As a satirist, Swift—like his favorite La Rochefoucauld or his contemporary, Mandeville—delighted in puncturing inflated claims to purely altruistic acts. As Frederick Keener points out in *The Chain of Becoming*, when Gulliver announces at the opening that he has fled "the corruption of fellow surgeons in London," he becomes one of a number of eighteenth-century heroes who "present themselves as extraordinarily selfless in motivation. . . . " But, Keener adds, "as quickly as these motives" are announced, the reader is set "thinking about the origins of such professions" (79).

Keener's insight can be extended, in Gulliver's case, to the act of writing itself. As we have seen, he consistently claims that he "*strictly adhere[s] to Truth*" (4.12). But the truth he adheres to is a Narcissistic delusion. Gulliver also says that he writes "for the noblest End" and that "my sole Intention was the *PUBLICK GOOD*" (4.12). This can be challenged, too. If Gulliver is so eager to share his truth, why does he wait so long to do it? Given the present mess in Gulliver's stable and the utter impossibility of becoming a rational horse, the reason is obvious: Gulliver has been unable to turn his own immediate world into a Houyhnhnm utopia, or to embrace the ideal himself. In these terms, the book becomes a futile attempt to adjust the outside world to his own private vision.[30] Modern psychologists would call this an exercise (among other things) in fantasy and wish-fulfillment. Augustinian Christians would call it the sin of similitude, evoked most memorably in Milton's allegory of Satan and the creation of Sin and Death. Like Satan—or Narcissus, for that matter—Gulliver is attempting here to replicate an image of himself. Thus, underlying a stated aim to serve the public is Gulliver's unstated desire to serve himself.

If, of course, Gulliver cannot embrace his idea in life, or alter the world to suit his fancy, he does have at least one outlet:

EMBLEMATA.　　　261

Φιλαυτία.

EMBLEMA LXIX.

QVOD *nimium tua forma tibi Narcisse placebat,*
  In florem, & noti est versa stuporis olus.
Ingenij est marcor, cladesq̃, Φιλαυτία, doctos
  Qua pessum plures datq̃, deditq̃ viros :
Qui veterum abiecta methodo, noua dogmata quærunt,
  Nilq̃ suas præter tradere phantasias.

FIGURE 1. From Andrea Alciatus, EMBLEMATA ... CVM COM-
MENTARIIS ... PER CLAVDIVM MINOEM (Antwerp, 1581).

to create another world that, while unattainable in life, can be found on the page, in language itself. A modern example of such an activity appears in the "villanelle" scene in Joyce's *Portrait of the Artist*, where Stephen imagines an ideal woman. Because he cannot embrace his ideal, he writes about it, in a process that metaphorically becomes an act of masturbation.

Theorists like Roland Barthes and Maurice Merleau-Ponty have also sensed a connection between *logos* and *eros*, suggesting (in the latter's words) that a "good part of eroticism is on paper."[31] To find writing imaged this way, we don't need to search for modern analogues, however. In Swift's *Mechanical Operation of the Spirit*, for example, the narrator coarsely describes the height ("*Orgasmus*") of the charismatics' rites, during which the spirit is said "to flag of a sudden" and the group is "forced to hasten to a Conclusion." Soon after this, the narrator himself abruptly ends the work with a sudden announcement—or, should we say, ejaculation: "the Post is just going, which forces me in great Haste to conclude." This conclusion is consistent with the rest of the work, which considers a process for "ejaculating the Soul"—a subject (the narrator boasts) "sparingly handled . . . by any Writer."[32] Swift evokes here what Pope would call "necessary Writing." For "there is hardly any human Creature past Childhood," Pope tells us in *The Art of Sinking* (1728), who hasn't had "some Poetical Evacuation" or enjoyed the "Discharge of the peccant Humour, in exceeding perulent Metre."[33] In these works, masturbation becomes a metaphor for writing that finds its sole basis in self. The same point suggests itself in Gulliver's apprenticeship to "Master *Bates*." Swift would certainly agree with Glanvill's assertion that "every man is naturally a Narcissus."[34] But he would also argue the need for the writer to go beyond this natural condition, to reach out and embrace the larger orders around him. It is Gulliver's failure to do this, to have intercourse (in any sense of the word) with the world around him, that leads him, in isolation, to fall in love with an idealized image of himself and to write this book.

In his study, *Literary Loneliness*, John Sitter has perceptively noted the gradual isolation, in the mid-eighteenth century, of the writer from his world.[35] Within this larger movement, it is perhaps significant that less than twenty years after the *Travels* Edward Young would invoke Narcissus as a *positive* ideal and compare virtue to

> the fabled self-enamour'd boy,
> Home-contemplation her supreme delight;
> She dreads an interruption from without,
> Smit with her own condition; and the more
> Intense she gazes, still it charms the more[36]

Swift seems to have foreseen this movement and in the *Travels* worked out some of its less charming implications. Indeed, as a type of Narcissus and a prototype of the Modern author, Lemuel Gulliver is apprenticed, from the very beginning of the work, to "my good Master *Bates*."

NOTES

1. Frank Brady, "Vexations and Diversions: Three Problems in *Gulliver's Travels*," *Modern Philology* 75 (1978), 350.
2. *The Prose Works of Jonathan Swift*, ed. Herbert David (Oxford: Basil Blackwell, 1939–1968), XI, 19–20. All further references are to this edition.
3. William Kinsley, "Gentle Readings: Recent Work on Swift," *Eighteenth-Century Studies*, 15 (Summer, 1982), 443. Irvin Ehrenpreis has also pointed to Swift's veritable "addiction to word-games." See *Dean Swift*, Vol. III of *Swift: The Man, His Works, and the Age* (Cambridge: Harvard Univ. Press, 1983), 141.
4. See Milton Voigt, *Swift and the Twentieth Century* (Detroit: Wayne State Univ. Press, 1964), 158; Phyllis Greenacre, *Swift and Carroll: A Psychoanalytic Study of Two Lives* (New York: International University Presses, 1955), 99–100, 115; and the *OED*, s.v. "masturbation." The *OED*, defining "masturbation" as "The practice of self-abuse," cites the earliest written occurrence of the word in *Onanism: Or a Treatise upon the Disorders produced by Masturbation* (1766), forty years after the publication of *Gulliver* in 1726. For the 1603 occurrence, see Brady, 350n.
5. [Bernard Mandeville,] *A Modest Defence of Publick Stews* (London, 1724; reprint ed., Los Angeles: Augustan Reprint Society, 1973, No. 162), 30–31. The *Defence* also went through a second edition, in 1725.
6. John Armstrong, *The Oeconomy of Love: A Poetical Essay* (London, 1736), 8–10.
7. John Marten, *A Treatise of all the Degrees and Symptoms of the Venereal Disease in both Sexes*, 6th ed., corrected and enlarged (London, c. 1709), 398–99. I thank P. –G. Boucé for calling this to my attention. Information on this book, which managed to get Marten prosecuted, is available in David Foxon's *Libertine Literature in England 1660–1745* (New Hyde Park, New York: University Books, 1965), 13.

8. *ONANIA; Or the Heinous Sin of Self-Pollution and All its Frightful Consequences* (London, 1724; reprint ed., Boston, 1724), 3. The author takes his title from the story of Onan in Genesis (38: 8–10) and is perhaps the first to use the term, "onanism." However, as often pointed out, both the title and the term are based on a probable misreading of the biblical text.

9. See Edward H. Hare, "Masturbatory Insanity: The History of an Idea," *The Journal of Mental Science*, 108 (1962), 2.

10. *Onania*, 1724, 16–17. For the same talk of *"licentious Masturbators"* and "that cursed School-Wickedness of Masturbation," also see the London, 1725 edition of *ONANIA*, 19–20. A 1756 edition of this work, owned by the Kinsey Institute, includes letters written by an "afflicted Onan" in "Dublin, Dec. 31, 1727" (24) who found *ONANIA* an inspiration; and from a similarly-troubled youth in "London, Dec. 31, 1729" who regrets his past involvement in what he calls "The Sin of Masturbation" (88). The letter from Ireland suggests *ONANIA's* presence there, as does the copy of the book in the personal library of a longterm Dublin associate of Swift's, John Putland, the stepson of Swift's friend and Dublin physician, Richard Helsham. (See item No. 1490 in Putland's manuscript list of his own library, *Bibliotheca Putlandia*, National Library of Ireland, MS 4186). Swift knew Putland well enough to loan him £1500; Putland also apparently ended up with several medical books owned by Swift and left to Helsham. See *The Account Books of Jonathan Swift*, eds. Paul V. Thompson and Dorothy Jay Thompson (Newark: Univ. of Delaware Press, 1984), cxxv, 310, 312, 313; and William LeFanu, *A Catalogue of Books Belonging to Dr. Jonathan Swift* (Cambridge: Cambridge Bibliographical Society, 1988), 2.

11. See P. –G. Boucé, "Aspects of Sexual Tolerance and Intolerance in XVIIIth-Century England," *British Journal of Eighteenth-Century Studies* 3 (1980), 176; and Lawrence Stone, *The Family, Sex and Marriage in England: 1500–1800* (New York: Harper and Row, 1977), 514. For more information, also see Robert H. MacDonald, "The Frightful Consequences of Onanism: Notes on the History of a Delusion," *Journal of the History of Ideas*, 28 (1967), 423–31; R. P. Neuman, "Masturbation, Madness, and The Modern Concepts of Childhood and Adolescence," *The Journal of Social History*, 8 (1975), 1–27; J. H. Plumb, "The New World of Children in 18th-Century England," *Past and Present*, 67 (1975), 64–93; Angus McLaren, *Birth Control in Nineteenth-Century England* (New York: Holmes and Meier, 1978), esp. 25–29; M. Foucault, *History of Sexuality*, trans. R. H. Hurley *(London: Penguin, 1978), vol. I., esp. 27–29;* Theodoré Tarczylo, *Sexe et Liberté au Siècle des Lumières* (Paris: Presses de la Renaissance, 1983); G. S. Rousseau's review of this work in *Eighteenth-Century Studies*, 19 (Fall, 1985), 116–20; and H. Tristram Engelhardt, Jr., "The Disease of Masturbation: Values and the Concept of Disease," in *Sickness and Health in America*, eds. Judith Walzer Leavitt and Ronald L. Numbers (Madison: Univ. of Wisconsin Press, 1985), 13–21. Such works are starting to confirm Jean Hagstrum's suspicion that fears of "onanism" and the like "haunted the mind of eighteenth-century man no less than the Victorians" (*Sex and Sensibility* [Chicago: Univ. of Chicago Press, 1980,] 224n.) There are several helpful collections of essays on the subject, including P. –G. Boucé's *Sexuality In Eighteenth-Century Britain* (Manchester: Manchester Univ. Press, 1982).

12. Jonathan Swift, et al., Memoirs of the Extraordinary Life, Works, and Discoveries of Martinus Scriblerus, ed. Charles Kerby-Miller (New Haven: Yale Univ. Press, 1950), 134–36.

13. Havelock Ellis, "The Conception of Narcissism," in Studies In The Psychology of Sex (New York: Random House, 1936), vol. I, 355–56. Though some similarities exist between eighteenth-century views of Narcissus and modern concepts of narcissism, I wish to differentiate the two, as much as possible. For an interesting exploration of Swift and "narcissism," in a modern sense of the term, see Thomas B. Gillmore, "Freud, Swift, and Narcissism: A Psychological Reading of 'Strephon and Chloe,' " in Contemporary Studies of Swift's Poetry, eds. John Irwin Fischer and Donald C. Mell (Newark: Univ. of Delaware Press, 1981), 159–68. On problems of applying modern, psychological terms to eighteenth-century texts, see Christopher Fox, "Defining Eighteenth-Century Psychology: Some Problems and Perspectives," in Psychology and Literature In the Eighteenth Century, ed. C. Fox (New York: AMS Studies In the Eighteenth Century, 1987), 1–22.

14. Though other classical accounts of Narcissus exist, the most influential appears in bk. 3 of Ovid's Metamorphoses, lines 339–510. All references are to Vol. I of F. J. Miller's translation (Cambridge: Harvard Univ. Press, 1936).

15. See Ovid, Metam., bk. 3, line 354 and Natalis Comes, Mythologiae (Venice, 1567; reprint ed., New York: Garland Press, 1976), 285–86.

16. See Henry Reynolds, MYTHOMYSTES . . . To which is annexed the Tale of Narcissus briefly mythologized (London, 1632): "Narcissus is fained to eschew and flye the companie of all women" (107).

17. See Ovid, Metam., bk. 3, lines 390–91; Marlowe's Hero and Leander (First Sest. 75–76), where Leander is compared to Narcissus who "despising many / Died ere he could enjoy the love of any"; and Bacon's Wisedome of the Ancients (London, 1619): "Narcissus was exceeding faire . . . but wonderful proud and disdainfull; wherefore dispising [sic] all others in respect of himselfe, hee leads a solitary life" (11).

18. See Ovid, Metam., bk. 3, lines 417, 433–34; George Sandys, Ovid's Metamorphosis Englished, Mythologized, and Represented in Figures, eds. K. K. Hulley and S. T. Vandersall (Lincoln: Univ. of Nebraska Press, 1970), 159; and Ben Jonson, Cynthia's Revels: Or The Fountain of Self-Love, The Works, ed. W. Gifford (London, 1816), vol. II, 236.

19. See Richard Steele's Spectator No. 238 (Dec. 3, 1711) in The Spectator, ed. D. F. Bond (Oxford: Clarendon Press, 1965), vol. II, 427; Sandys, 160; and Bacon's Wisedome, where we learn that those afflicted with the disease of Narcissus "leade for the most parte" a "private and obscure life, attended on with a fewe followers, and those such as will . . . like an Eccho [sic] flatter them in all their sayings" (12–13).

20. See The Poems of Jonathan Swift, ed. Harold Williams, 2nd. ed. (Oxford: Clarendon Press, 1958), vol. I, 110, 156. Narcissus is not the only Ovidian tale evoked in the Travels. For instance, the captain who rescues Gulliver at the end of bk. II compares him to "Phaeton"—"although," Gulliver tells us, "I did not much admire the Conceit" (2.8). Why Gulliver didn't is perhaps suggested by the title alone of an earlier work, by Thomas Hall: Phaeton's folly, or, the downfal of pride: being a translation of the second

book of Ovids Metamorphosis where is lively set forward the danger of
pride and rashness (1655) (1655). (See Douglas Bush, Mythology and the
Renaissance Tradition in English Poetry [New York: Norton, 1963,] 337).

21. See Louise Vinge, The Narcissus Theme in Western European Literature,
trans. R. Dewsnap and L. Grönlund (Lund: Gleerups, 1967), 15.

22. Frederick Goldin, The Mirror of Narcissus in The Courtly Love Lyric (Ithaca: Cornell Univ. Press, 1967), 68.

23. When, for instance, the Queen of Brobdingnag "used to place" Gulliver
"towards a Looking Glass, by which both our Persons appeared before me
in full View," he disliked it intensely (2.3). He subsequently tells us that
"I could never endure to look in a Glass after mine Eyes had been accus-
tomed to such prodigious Objects; because the Comparison gave me so
dispicable a Conceit of my self" (2.8). Mirrors here accentuate the littleness
of Gulliver's body and assault his pride. Later, he will reject that body
altogether. For other comments on the "mirror" in Gulliver, see, especially,
W. B. Carnochan, Lemuel Gulliver's Mirror For Man (Berkeley: Univ. of
California Press, 1968), 139–40, 175–81.

24. The Fables of La Fontaine, trans. Marianne Moore (New York: Viking
Press, 1952), 22–23. The Fables appear (as No. 502) in the sale catalogue
of Swift's books. See A CATALOGUE OF BOOKS, [IN] THE LIBRARY
of . . . Dr. SWIFT (Dublin, 1745), 13; reprinted in Harold Williams, Dean
Swift's Library (Cambridge: Cambridge Univ. Press, 1932).

25. Brady, 360.

26. For a publication history of Alciati's work, and his influence—both of
which are extensive—see Henry Green, Andrea Alciati and His Books of
Emblems: A Biographical and Bibliographical Study (London: Trübner
and Co., 1872); and Vinge, 177–78, 180, 204.

27. See Andrea Alciatus, Emblemata . . . CVM COMMENTARIIS . . . PER
CLAVDIVM MINOEM (Antwerp, 1581), 261–70; and Figure I. Vinge (141)
gives the following translation of Alciati's motto:
Too much comfort and joy did you find in your beauty, Nar-
cissus,
Therefore it turned to a flower and stuporous herb.
Self-love is death and decay of genius, and many a scholar
Such love brought to his fall; many men it still destroys;
Those who, rejecting the ways of their fathers, search for new
doctrines—
Then have nothing to give but their fanciful whims.

28. A Tale of A Tub. To which is added the Battle of the Books, and the
Mechanical Operation of the Spirit, eds. A. C. Guthkelch and David Nichol
Smith, 2nd ed., rev. (Oxford: Clarendon Press, 1958), 171.

29. Frederick M. Keener, The Chain of Becoming (New York: Columbia Univ.
Press, 1983), 79. Keener's chapter on self-love (55–85) and his analysis of
Gulliver (89–126) are both relevant to my discussion, as are considerations
in A. O. Hirschman, The Passions and the Interests (Princeton: Princeton
Univ. Press, 1977), 9–66; Anthony Levi, S. J., French Moralists: The Theory of the Passions (Oxford: Clarendon Press, 1964), esp. 215–33; Lester
Crocker, The Age of Crisis (Baltimore: Johns Hopkins Univ. Press, 1959),
202–17, 256–324; and A. O. Lovejoy, Reflections on Human Nature (Baltimore: Johns Hopkins Univ. Press, 1961), esp. 217–45.

30. That Swift is attempting here to evoke a private world may account for one enigma often noticed: that is, the *Travels'* seeming lack of *explicit* allusion. A related point is the connection Swift and others made between pride and madness. In his influential *Two Discourses concerning the Soul of Brutes* (Pordage trans., London, 1683), Thomas Willis, for instance, asserts that "Ambition, Pride, and Emulation, have made some mad" (203). In studying Swift's *Tale*, Michael DePorte has traced the importance of the madness/pride association, and its relation to a corresponding loss of self and assumption of a delusional identity. (See DePorte's "Vehicles of Delusion: Swift, Locke, and the Madhouse Poems of James Carkesse," in *Psychology and Literature In the Eighteenth Century*, ed. C. Fox [New York: AMS Studies In the Eighteenth Century, 1987,] 69–86). A similar case could be made for Gulliver as one who goes mad through pride, and loses his identity while attempting to become something he is not. In discussing the "manner of ravings" of the insane, Willis notes that "Fabulous antiquity scarce ever thought of so many *metamorphoses* of men, which some have not believed really of themselves"; some (Willis adds) have even "believed themselves to be Dogs or Wolves, and have imitated their ways and kind by barking and howling" (*Two Discourses*, 188). Near the end of bk. IV, Gulliver declares that by

> conversing with the *Houyhnhnms*, and looking upon them with Delight, I fell to imitate their Gait and Gesture, which is now grown into a Habit; and my Friends often tell me in a blunt way, that *I trot like a Horse*; which, however, I take for a great Compliment: Neither shall I disown, that in speaking, I am apt to fall into the Voice and manner of the *Houyhnhnms*, and hear my self ridiculed on that Account (4.10).

> When he first saw the Houyhnhnms, Gulliver thought they must be "Magicians" (presumably "men") who had "metamorphosed themselves" into horses (4.1). In Gulliver's subsequent attempt to make the same transformation, to neigh and trot like the horses and imitate "their ways and kind," could we be witnessing yet another "metamorphosis"—in Willis's sense of the term? I have explored this question in a forthcoming essay, "Of Logic and Lycarthropy: Gulliver and the Faculties of the Mind."

31. Maurice Merleau-Ponty, *Signs*, trans. R. C. McCleary (Evanston: Northwestern Univ. Press, 1964), 310. Also see Roland Barthes, *The Pleasure of the Text*, trans. Richard Miller (New York: Hill and Wang, 1975); and Jacques Derrida, *Of Grammatology*, trans. G. C. Spivak (Baltimore: Johns Hopkins Univ. Press, 1976). Derrida tells us that Rousseau's "masturbation . . . cannot be separated from his activity as a writer" (155). If this statement were applied to the narrator of the *Mechanical Operation*, Swift, I suspect, would agree.

32. *The Mechanical Operation of the Spirit*, in *A Tale*, 288–89, 267.

33. Alexander Pope, *The Art of Sinking in Poetry*, ed. Edna L. Steeves (1952; reprint ed., New York: Russell and Russell, 1968), 12–13.

34. Joseph Glanvill, *The Vanity of Dogmatizing* (London, 1661), 119.

35. See John Sitter, *Literary Loneliness in Mid-Eighteenth Century England* (Ithaca: Cornell Univ. Press, 1982).

36. Edward Young, *The Complaint; Or, Night Thoughts,* bk. 8 ("Virtue's Apology") in *The Poetical Works* (London: Aldine, n.d.), vol. I, 210. At about the same time Young was seeing Narcissus as a positive ideal, others, in a related move, were challenging the traditional view of pride, turning the first of the medieval sins into a modern virtue. "[N]othing," said Hume, "is more useful to us in the conduct of life, than a due degree of pride" (*A Treatise of Human Nature,* ed. L. A. Selby-Bigge, rev. P. H. Nidditch, 2nd ed. [Oxford: Clarendon Press, 1978], 596).

The Danger of Reading Swift: The Double Binds of *Gulliver's Travels*

Frederik N. Smith

In his introduction to a series of essays devoted to the subject of reader entrapment in Restoration and early eighteenth-century literature, David M. Vieth observes that critical interest in entrapment has been "in the air" at least since the mid-1960s.[1] According to Vieth, the starting-point would seem to be somewhere around the time when the entrenched, text-oriented New Criticism began to falter. In finally surrendering our belief in the existence of novelistic personae in eighteenth-century satire—first exposed by Irvin Ehrenpreis in 1963—we have shifted our interest from text to reader, and in admitting that personae tend to screen an author's creations from himself, and the author from the reader, we also open up the possibility that the reader alluded to in a text is closer to ourselves than perhaps we have been willing to acknowledge. But it is interesting that in the case of Swift—Vieth calls him "The all-time master of literary entrapment"—the beginnings of critical interest in this subject can be pushed back a good deal further than the mid-1960s. Indeed if entrapment is the demonstration to the reader that his usual procedures of understanding are debilitatingly naive, simplistic, complacent, inconsistent, or inadequate in some other way—then surely Swift's readers have felt this prior to our own generation.[2] We have of course only given a local habitation and a name to our shared bafflement or sense that we have been somehow ridiculed or punished by the author.

The history of discussions of Swiftian entrapment reads like one long rebuttal of Dr. Johnson's obtuse reference to Swift's "easy and safe conveyance of meaning,"[3] and is perhaps worth sketching out in order to establish a context for the present discussion. The landmark article would seem to be F. R. Leavis's "The Irony of Swift," first published in 1934 and widely reprinted. Swift's irony, says Leavis, "is essentially a means of surprise and negation; its function is to defeat habit, to intimidate and demoralize." Leavis is the first modern critic I know of to use the word "trap" to describe Swift's trick of catching the reader out.[4] Many years later, Henry W. Sams attempted to define this trait more broadly in his well-known account of "Swift's Satire of the Second Person," which appeared in 1959: "Let us suppose," said Sams, cautiously, "that at times the butt of Swift's satire may be his reader."[5] Less well-known is an essay by Oswald Johnston, published in 1962 and titled "Swift and the Common Reader," in which the point is made that in reading Swift's poetry, "The more one relies on the conventional attitude of reverence for the classics and for the moral values of poetry, the more one is likely to be made fun of."[6]

C. J. Rawson, referring both to Leavis and Sams, asserted in his 1968 article "Gulliver and the Gentle Reader" much the same thing as his predecessors, but more emphatically: "The aggressiveness toward the reader is what chiefly distinguishes Swift from the later writers to whom he can be compared, and who imitate him or are prefigured in his work."[7] While this was certainly not an altogether original idea, it was an idea whose time had come, and Rawson's forceful restatement of it made talk of Swift's aggressiveness toward his reader quite fashionable. Mentioning Leavis, John Traugott (1971) wrote that Swift "leaves us with the burden of anxiety that is his own"; praising

Rawson, Robert C. Elliott (1974) argued that often "the reader feels attacked—as though someone has hit him from a dark corner"; and Wayne Booth (1974) showed how the "controlled inconsistencies" of *A Modest Proposal* make every reader feel "to some degree duped."[8]

Beyond this general interest, some critics in the 1970s began to see Swift's entrapment of his reader as springing from his own deep-seated sense of "the problematical nature of meaning." Neil Schaeffer (1973), Rober Uphaus (1974), and Deborah Linderman (1979) each dealt in one way or another with what Linderman described as Swift's talent "for eluding the reader's efforts to attain a stability of meaning."[9] Alain Bony's "Call Me Gulliver," published in *Poétique* in 1973, demonstrated how Gulliver functions discomfortingly as both narrator and reader.[10] And in a 1979 essay tucked away in *Hungarian Studies in English*, John Fletcher refers to Swift's ability to "ensnare" his reader and, moreover, asks in his title: "From 'Gentle Reader' to 'Gentle Skimmer'; or, Does it Help to Read Swift as if he were Samuel Beckett?"[11] Fletcher is explicit about the implicit post-modern bias inherent in many recent readings of Swift.

In 1973 John N. Morris put the matter most succinctly: "Swift settles no questions; he unsettles readers."[12] Fueled by reader-response criticism, entrapment in Swift seems now to be a given. Critics over the past ten years have turned to refining our account of Swift's impact on his reader, as well as to describing how he accomplishes those effects. This new focus is represented by the essays on Swift that appear in special issues of two journals published in the 1980s: the articles by Brian McRea (on *A Tale of a Tub*), Donald C. Mell, Jr. (on the poetry), and Richard H. Rodino (an attempt to classify Swift's techniques) that appeared in the 1982 special issue of *Papers on Language and Literature*; and the earlier versions of three articles in the present volume by Louise K. Barnett, A. B. England, and Melinda Rabb that were published originally in 1984 in an issue of *Studies in the Literary Imagination*.[13] Finally, three essays in a collection published just last year demonstrate a continuing interest in this matter: Janet Aikins, " 'Reading with Conviction': Trial by Satire"; Louise K. Barnett, "Deconstructing *Gulliver's Travels*"; and my afterword to this volume titled "Style,

Swift's Reader, and the Genres of *Gulliver's Travels*."[14] Swift studies—like the study of literature in general—has adjusted its course away from the text *per se* and toward the reader's response to the text. As we have seen, however, in the case of Swift a recognition that his satire turns with a vengeance back upon its reader is not altogether new.

I

"The satirical energy in Swift's work," says Clive T. Probyn, "drives a paradox. It not only invites and involves the reader, it disorganizes him once he is involved."[15] This is true to different degrees for the reader of *A Tale of a Tub* and the reader of *Gulliver's Travels*; the latter work seems at first glance *not* to be in this mode, although a closer look reveals that the traps are only better camouflaged. In the *Tale* Swift creates a highly intense, pyrotechnically insane style, and he tells us in so many words that his paper-thin persona (if that is even the word to use here) once did time in Bedlam. We really don't get "involved." In *Gulliver*, however, Swift manages an objective, carefully unimpassioned style, and his more fully developed persona is a nononsense seaman, a meticulous story-teller, and a solid citizen of England and Europe. Gulliver speaks in terms of measurement, literal statement, and factual detail, and his travelogue is marked throughout by an unexceptional mildness of temper. The downright acceptability—even reasonableness—of the style makes the dynamics of reading *Gulliver's Travels* far more dangerous than reading the *Tale*. The Modern Author openly boasts that he drags his readers around by inciting their curiosity: "by this *Handle* it is, that an Author should seize his Readers; which as soon as he hath once compast, all Resistance and struggling are in vain; and they become his Prisoners as close as he pleases, till Weariness or Dullness force him to let go his Gripe."[16] On the contrary, Gulliver's consistently positive allusions to the "gentle Reader" and "my own dear Countrymen" make it more difficult for us to keep his text at a distance. Plainspokeness, courtesy, and flattery are difficult to ignore.

Swift's distinction in the *Tale* among three—really only two—types of readers is helpful. He mentions the superficial reader, the ignorant reader ("between whom and the former, the Distinction is extreamly nice"), and the learned reader ("for whose Benefit I wake, when others sleep").[17] Swift's essential division here lies between the superficial or ignorant reader on the one hand and the learned reader on the other. And it is interesting that this bifurcated readership pretty well matches the direction taken by contemporary criticism, which would appear to have located a useful distinction between what Daniel W. Nelson has termed the "characterized reader" and the "implied reader."[18] The "characterized reader" is a fictionalized reader who is directly addressed by the narrator or portrayed by him in one way or another—almost the way a character would be—in the text itself; the "implied reader" is that reader whom we can only infer from the text and for whom the author writes (not to be confused with any real reader, however, whom we can never know), and whose peculiar behavior, attitudes, and background are necessary for a proper understanding of the text. Nelson observes also that "readers to whom the narrator draws attention usually turn out to be negative foils, which help establish the implied reader's role but which differ from it."[19] This is precisely the rhetorical situation we encounter in *Gulliver's Travels*: most obviously present is Gulliver's characterized reader, directly addressed as "Reader" some sixty-two times (three more in the prefatory material) and who is one of the targets of the satire;[20] beyond him is Swift's implied reader, never mentioned, but for whom the satire was written.

Swift seems to be dealing ironically in the *Tale* and again in *Gulliver* with what Walter J. Ong once described as the "new fashionable intimacy" between author and reader that developed in the early eighteenth century. Ong refers in particular to Addison and Steele, who cast themselves as well as their readers in the role of coffee-house habitués.[21] In the *Tale* Swift alludes sarcastically to those "wonderful Civilities that have passed of late Years, between the Nation of *Authors*, and that of *Readers*," but we are not apt to be taken in.[22] We remain safely outside the satire. On the contrary, I believe that in *Gulliver's Travels* we are intended (I echo Probyn here) to experience the tug of a relationship with the narrator as well as the periodic disruption of that relationship. Thus Gulliver throughout assumes a Spectator-like acquaintanceship with his reader, almost always treating him with great deference. In addition to "gentle," his flattering epithets are "curious," "judicious," "courteous," "indulgent," and "candid."[23] Phraseology such as the following is common: "It would not be proper for some Reason, to trouble the Reader . . . ," "Let me deal so candidly with the Reader, as to confess . . . ," and "Upon this Occasion, I hope the Reader will pardon. . . . "

What portrait emerges from the sum total of Gulliver's direct as well as indirect references to his reader? What kind of person is he?[24] Of course he is English and European and patriotic to a fault. He is rather prudish and is (or at least pretends to be) shocked by talk of sex or bodily functions. He likes being flattered. He has read other travel books and knows well the conventions of the genre. Somewhat paradoxically, he has an insatiable thirst for factual detail yet wants to avoid tediousness. In some respects he seems to appreciate having things made easy for him; he has (or affects) an interest in truth above all else, but seems in fact to want to be shielded from complex realities, and is quite willing to overlook faults in his own country and contradictions in the text he's reading. Indeed he bears an uncanny resemblance to his author, Lemuel Gulliver, and accepts just about anything from him without question. For this reader at least, we can be sure that rational horses are an oddity but nonetheless exist, that Gulliver was right in viewing them as the perfection of nature, and that his expulsion from Houyhnhnmland was a real tragedy. "For a sentence [or indeed an entire text] to be properly ironic," says Jonathan Culler, "it must be possible to imagine some group of readers taking it quite literally."[25] In this respect, then, Gulliver's characterized reader—like Wotton in *A Tale of a Tub*—serves the important rhetorical purpose of bringing such a literal-minded reader into the text itself. There he can be held up to Swift's implied reader as a bad example.

In light of Swift's obvious concern in the *Tale* and *Gulliver* for the activities of reading as well as writing, it is surprising that more attention has not been paid to the image of Gulliver in Brobdingnag reading an oversized book from a scaffolding

devised for this purpose.[26] "Their Libraries are not very large,"
says Gulliver of the Brobdingnagians, with Swift punning over
his head. Nonetheless, in his customary detail, Gulliver goes on
to describe the operation of the wooden machine contrived by
the Queen's carpenter in order that he might read what books
there were in those libraries:

> I first mounted to the upper Step of the Ladder, and
> turning my Face towards the Book, began at the Top
> of the Page, and so walking to the Right and Left about
> eight or ten Paces according to the Length of the Lines,
> till I had gotten a little below the Level of mine Eyes;
> and then descending gradually till I came to the Bot-
> tom: After which I mounted again, and began the other
> Page in the same Manner, and so turned over the Leaf,
> which I could easily do with both my Hands. . . . [27]

Elsewhere Swift by magnification or diminution effectively focuses our attention on the sheer mechanics of walking, eating,
writing, or relieving ourselves; but in this instance, since the
reader of *Gulliver's Travels* is this minute engaged in the reading of a text, the description of Gulliver's mechanics of reading
takes on special significance as an example of how *not* to read.
Here there is no distortion of the physical process; in English
we do indeed read left to right, top to bottom, turning the pages
as we go. Deliberately left out of the description, however, is the
mental and imaginative engagement of the reader with the text
he is reading. How different is Swift's reference in *Thoughts on
Various Subjects* to his own experience: "When I am reading a
Book, whether wise or silly, it seemeth to me to be alive and
talking to me."[28] Like a play within a play, with its self-conscious framing of another performance before a fictional audience, the scene of a fictional reader reading a book inside the
book we are holding in our hands enables us momentarily to
step outside the act of reading. In this scene it is suggested that
Gulliver himself is a superficial or ignorant reader, while we on
the other hand are tacitly urged to be more involved readers.
    This occasion turns reading into performance and lets the
air out of the illusion that the text at least in part desires to

maintain; and *Gulliver's Travels* contains other such moments where Swift's actual reader finds himself suddenly on stage. In Lilliput, for example, after the Articles and Conditions are read to Gulliver it is demanded that he swear to them, which he readily does, and then introduces his own translation, "Word for Word, as near as I was able" (43). Gulliver appears more interested in impressing us with the accuracy of his translation and with giving us (as he says) "some Idea of the Style and Manner of Expression peculiar to that People," than with the *content* of the document. True enough, Gulliver's chains are removed, but he may not walk about without permission and is required to serve as messenger boy, as assistant to Lilliput's survey and construction crews, and as the empire's super weapon against Blefuscu. In thanks, Gulliver prostrates himself before the Emperor, who bids him rise, but adds that "he hoped I should prove a useful Servant" (44). The terminology escapes Gulliver's notice. His single question is how it was decided that his meat and drink should be equivalent to that of 1,728 Lilliputians. He shows himself to be a superficial reader, one with a gross insensitivity to the implications of words, with a seeming unawareness of what is *not* being said in the text he hoped would guarantee his freedom.

This same disturbing detachment in Gulliver's reading is demonstrated in his reaction to the Articles of Impeachment, wherein it is declared that he shall be blinded for his efforts to save the royal palace:

> Yet, as to myself, I must confess, having never been designed for a Courtier, either by my Birth or Education, I was so ill a Judge of Things, that I could not discover the *Lenity* and Favour of this Sentence; but conceived it (perhaps erroneously) rather to be rigorous than gentle. (72)

Gulliver's cautious, unoffended, ludicrously polite response to the Articles illustrates precisely the kind of passivity Swift works hard to avoid letting *his* readers exercise. The good captain may be clever with languages (as we are conveniently assured on page two), but in processing texts he scarcely gets past the understanding of a basal reader; although in both of the above examples Gulliver is in fact victimized by a text, he fails to comprehend this and seems incapable of grasping the personal relevance of the letters printed on the page. His would seem to be not a linguistic difficulty but a reading problem. Gerald Prince refers to such occasions: "Performed by an ignorant or ill-intentioned narrator, the readings put forth may really be misreadings."[29] Indeed Gulliver *is* a poor judge of things. And Swift's reader will likewise be a poor judge of things if he reads as superficially as Gulliver is shown to read the texts set before him in Parts 1 and 2.

I do not believe that I have merely substituted Gulliver as slow reader for that tired stereotype of the unreliable narrator; the self-consciousness thrust upon us in these and other passages about reading puts them in a not-altogether-neat category by themselves. Nonetheless I would be quick to admit that the difference between situations where Gulliver is literally depicted as a detached, rather comatose reader, and other situations, where Gulliver is shown to be lethargic in picking up cues in a non-reading situation, is relatively slight. In such a marvelously crafted passage as the following, the understandings of the Lilliputians, Gulliver, and the reader are challenged simultaneously. Indeed the similarity between this passage and a reading comprehension test is worth noting.

> About two or three Days before I was set at Liberty, as I was entertaining the Court with these Kinds of Feats, there arrived an Express to inform his Majesty, that some of his Subjects riding near the Place where I was first taken up, had seen a great black Substance lying on the Ground, very oddly shaped, extending its Edges round as wide as his Majesty's Bedchamber, and rising up in the Middle as high as a Man: That it was no living Creature, as they at first apprehended; for it lay on the Grass without Motion, and some of them had walked around it several Times: That by mounting upon each others Shoulders, they had got to the Top, which was flat and even; and, stamping upon it, they

found it was hollow within: That they humbly conceived it might be something belonging to the *Man-
Mountain*; and if his Majesty pleased, they would un-
dertake to bring it with only five Horses. I presently
knew what they meant; and was glad at Heart to receive this Intelligence. It seems, upon my first reaching
the Shore, after our Shipwreck, I was in such Confusion, that before I came to the Place where I went to
sleep, my Hat, which I had fastened with a String to
my Head while I was rowing. . . .

(41)

Like so much of *Gulliver's Travels*, this passage is structured as
a sort of riddle.[30] What is so fascinating here is the dramatic
pacing, the gradual revelation of the thing under discussion:
" . . . great black Substance . . . very oddly shaped . . . rising up
in the Middle as high as a Man . . . no living Creature . . . it lay
on the Grass without Motion . . . the Top, which was flat and
even. . . . " Swift toys with us as readers; at first we might guess
something excremental, but hint-by-hint he lets us come to a
recognition of the subject of his riddle. Adding to the dramatic
tension is the fact that the Lilliputians, Gulliver, and Swift's
reader are in a sense locked in a race for understanding. And as
elsewhere, Gulliver's score on this reading comprehension test
is not as high as it should be. One might argue that the lilliputians have an unfair advantage in this particular test, for they
do not have to translate each of Swift's clues, as we do, from the
Lilliputian into the European perspective; for example, the hint
that this object rises up as high as a man could well be confusing—we don't ordinarily think of hats as having such stature.
But then again the Lilliputians have never seen a hat, and when
Gulliver finally guesses what is being described, he has to explain to the Emperor the use of such a thing. Our own reading
of this passage, therefore, is understandably ahead of the Lilliputians' and *should* be ahead of Gulliver's (or else we risk missing the slap-stick humor of the stamping on the hat); that is we
should be able to process the clues faster, more quickly arrive
at the solution to the riddle, than either Gulliver or the Lilliputians.[31] I would guess that most of Swift's readers do indeed pass

his test, but the fact that they or some other readers may not lends a certain element of apprehension, or what I have called danger, to the activity of reading this book.

Perhaps at this point we can refine the distinction we have been working with between the characterized and implied readers of *Gulliver's Travels*, and show in greater detail how this difference functions in the actual reading of the book. To repeat: first there is the characterized reader (addressed by Gulliver) who is often the butt of the joke because he does not understand, or understand fully; second, there is the implied reader, the role of the reader as he is inscribed in Swift's text, and whose wider understanding the actual reader is invited to recognize and emulate. A couple of further complications, however, are necessary if we are to do justice to the sublety of Swift's entrapment: typically, in instances where he springs a trap, he puts his implied reader off guard by encouraging him to separate himself from the slow-footed characterized reader (thus permitting him to feel superior), then leads him into a trap, and finally and most importantly counts on his reader's admitting to himself that he has been fooled and adopting a perspective larger than the one he previously laid claim to. Gulliver is anxious lest he offend his reader. Swift dares offend *his* with the hope that he will learn something from being proved the fool. Of course things could come out otherwise. Swift's implied reader is threatened on every page with the possibility that he may actually *become* Gulliver's characterized reader; he must be perpetually alert to the possibility that he may be drawn in by the seductive rhetoric, or, if he is, he must be broad-minded enough to admit that he has made a mistake. The implied reader is not—unlike the characterized reader—a static figure. There are two necessary steps here. We must be caught napping and then we must rouse ourselves. As Stanley Fish has argued, textual meaning is an *event*.[32]

II

Swift's entrapment of his reader is analogous to the impossible logical situations into which the schizophrenic is put by members of his own family. Gregory Bateson's hypothesis of the double bind—the intense psychological pressure of conflicting injunctions—concerning proper or improper behavior—was first outlined in 1956 in his well known essay titled "Toward a Theory of Schizophrenia." According to Bateson, the necessary ingredients for a double bind are as follows: 1) two or more persons, one of whom is the "victim"; 2) a primary injunction to do or not do such a thing, which is coupled with a threatened punishment for an infraction; 3) a secondary injunction that conflicts with the first on a more abstract level, is often implicit, and is likewise coupled with threatened punishment; and finally, 4) repeated experience, to the point that the victim comes to expect mixed messages.[33] Swift's rhetorical relationship with the implied reader of *Gulliver's Travels* fulfills all four of these criteria for the double bind. The peculiar frustration and confusion that critics have noted in reading the book can be explained by Swift's inconsistent, simultaneous injunctions to accept or not what is being averred.

Over and over the reader's existence as a reader, as an Englishman, or as a human being is challenged, and he is caught with no simple, unambiguously correct reading of the text. He cannot come off well. And his punishment—at least Swift hopes—will be a fresh awareness that he has failed as a reader, has acted in a way unbecoming an Englishman, or has exhibited embarrassingly unkind, inhuman, even animalistic tendencies. It is no wonder we have such difficulty clearly identifying Swift's targets and Swift's own positions. Our frustration is the point. And ultimately we must accept our own reactions as part of the meaning of *Gulliver's Travels*.

The double binds in *Gulliver* are often brief and humorous. A good example is that infamous moment in Brobdingnag:

> The handsomest among these Maids of Honour, a pleasant frolicksome Girl of sixteen, would sometimes set me astride upon one of her Nipples; with many other Tricks, wherein the Reader will excuse me for not being over particular. But, I was so much displeased, that I entreated *Glumdalclitch* to contrive some excuse for not seeing that young Lady any more.

The girl is "pleasant" and "frolicksome" (two essentially positive words), and the stimulating posture in which she places Gulliver on her breast is obviously of interest to the (curious) reader. In fact when I read this passage I crave more of the text's usual reportorial particulars. However, I am to be disappointed, for while my pruriency is inflamed further by Gulliver's vague allusion to "many other Tricks" (did she put Gulliver between her legs?), I am told that of course I will understand, that of course I would not want to have any further particulars.[34] The truth is that I *do* want to hear more, but Gulliver's *assumption* that I would be shocked by further details, and more importantly his final revelation that he himself was so displeased that he asked Glumdalclitch to keep the naughty lady from his presence, makes my male fascination seem like leering. Thus Swift's explicit invitation to be aroused by this tantalizing description is followed immediately by a tacit admission that we of course share a moral revulsion at the very thought of such descriptions. In Bateson's terms, I have been trapped between two contradictory injunctions: sex is stimulating and Brobdingnagian sex is even more so; but sex is obscene and offensive to our higher natures. My choice is between lasciviousness and prudery. Although both of these injunctions to the reader are clearly present in the text, both cannot be true at the same time. I am punished for my indecency by being forced to recognize that my high proprieties do not jibe with my degenerate physical self. Swift has a good laugh—on me.

A more subtle double bind is set up later in Part 2, where Gulliver apologizes to his reader for having permitted the Brobdingnagian King to slander the English in his "little odious vermin" speech:

> Nothing but an extreme Love of Truth could have hindered me from concealing this Part of my Story. It was in vain to discover my Resentments, which were always turned into Ridicule: And I was forced to rest with Patience, while my noble and most beloved Country was so injuriously treated. I am heartily sorry as any of my Readers can possibly be, that such an Occasion was given: But this Prince happened to be so curious and inquisitive upon every Particular, that it could

> not consist either with Gratitude or good Manners to
> refuse giving him what Satisfaction I was able. Yet
> thus much I may be allowed to say in my own Vindica-
> tion; that I artfully eluded many of his Questions; and
> gave to every Point a more favourable turn by many
> Degrees than the strictness of Truth would allow.
>   (133)

Gulliver's frank appeal for an understanding of the double bind
in which *he* was placed by the King makes me for a moment
sympathize with Swift's honest captain. But I pull back from
him when in the next sentence he attempts to vindicate himself
by explaining that on the grounds of partiality to his and his
reader's country he "artfully eluded many of [the King's] Questions; and gave to every Point a more favourable turn by many
Degrees than the strictness of Truth would allow." What has
happened to Gulliver's "extreme Love of Truth"? Is truth not an
absolute but only a matter of "degree"? Having readily accepted
the principle that truth is the highest good, I am then asked to
accept the contradictory principle that untruth in the service of
one's country is sometimes to be condoned. Yet both injunctions
cannot be met. Swift has me again in one of his double binds.
Either I favor truth but am unpatriotic or I am patriotic but
accept untruth. Gulliver's characterized reader—the one ap-
pealed to directly in this passage—reads over the contradiction
without a stutter. Swift's implied reader, on the other hand, is
intended to see the trap set for him and to recognize the difference between abstract principle and pragmatic situation.

But these are relatively simple examples of Swift's technique of entrapment. A comparable but far more complex situation is the paragraph in Part 4, Chapter 8, where Gulliver
speaks of the Yahoos' imitation of his actions. Not far behind
the passage is a struggle between two evolutionary theories: one
that puts man at the summit of the evolutionary scale, and
another that places man at the midpoint between the vicious
Yahoo and the rational horse. Disarmingly, Gulliver whispers
that since he understands human nature so well (does he?), it
was easy for him to apply his Master's criticisms to himself . . . "and my Countrymen," he adds, and suddenly *I* am implicated. Gulliver goes on to admit that with the sorrel nag as
bodyguard he deliberately went among the herds of Yahoos:

For I have already told the Reader how much I was
pestered by those odious Animals upon my first Arrival. I afterwards failed very narrowly three or four
times of falling into their Clutches, when I happened
to stray at any Distance without my Hanger. And I
have Reason to believe, they had some Imagination
that I was of their own Species, which I often assisted
myself, by stripping up my Sleeves, and shewing my
naked Arms and Breast in their Sight, when my Pro-
tector was with me: At which times they would approach as near as they durst, and imitate my Actions
after the Manner of Monkeys, but ever with great Signs
of Hatred; as a tame *Jack Daw* with Cap and Stockings,
is always persecuted by the wild ones, when he happens
to be got among them.

                                                              (265)

Contradictions abound. Gulliver, having admitted that
there are similarities between himself and the Yahoos, goes
among them, tells us how he taunted them into seeing similarities between themselves and himself (flashing his arms and
chest), and then says that they did indeed recognize the similarities and imitated him the way monkeys imitate humans. Incon-
sistently, Gulliver here both willingly surrenders to an identification with the Yahoos and withdraws from them, repelled by
their animal natures. This is typical of the wandering point of
view that characterizes *Gulliver's Travels* from beginning to end;
and such incongruities put the reader repeatedly at a loss to
know where he stands. Gulliver's concluding analogy between
the Yahoos' treatment of him and the tendency of wild jack
daws to "persecute" a tame one who has fallen into their midst,
underscores the reader's problem. Having been encouraged by
Gulliver (most recently, anyway) to see the Yahoos not as human beings but as animals and thus as different from Gulliver,
I am thrown off by these final comparisons between Gulliver and
a monkey and Gulliver and a jack daw. It is Swift's intention, of
course, to trap me between Gulliver's helpful analogies and my
own realization that those analogies contain two insulting comparisons: monkeys conform to mankind's physical shape and use
many of our gestures, and jack daws do not look like us but can

be trained to imitate our manner of speech. Caught again in one of Swift's double binds, I have only two options open to me: I may overlook the comparison with the monkey and the jack daw, and therefore come off as a poor reader but keep my humanity intact; or I may accept the comparisons and come off as a good reader but as an animalistic creature who ranks only a little above the monkey and the bird. Gulliver (misreading the situation) has taken the first option: he seems to miss the significance of his own analogies or else feels oddly secure behind his facile distinction between wild jack daws (= the Yahoos) and a tame one (= Gulliver himself), and he is unaware that this distinction on the basis of *training* is superficial within the context of the larger question of *species*.

For Swift's implied reader things are not so easy. There is a rhetorical contradiction embedded in this passage that I cannot escape without personal compromise. For Swift's reader, as for Bateson's schizophrenic, the conventional logical categories are no longer absolutely defensible. The safe boundaries between Gulliver and the reader on the one side, and monkey, bird, and Yahoo on the other, are discovered to be insufficient to withhold the force of the similarities suggested by Swift.[35]

The inconsistencies of *Gulliver's Travels* have serious consequences for Swift's implied reader. Faced with contradictory messages from what is theoretically a single individual, the reader is put in the position of being unsure how to react to the text he is reading: Swift's meticulous maintenance of Gulliver's single-mindedly literal way of thinking and speaking means that the usual metacommunicative signals that accompany shifts into or out of non-literal statements are strikingly absent. So too the usual markers for indicating a change of a character's mind or a shift in point of view have been deliberately removed from Gulliver's narrative. In spite of Gulliver's insistent intimacy with his reader, the typical lack of connection between one assumption and another, and indeed the lack of any attempt at a bridge between the two, suggest anything but intimacy. Violation of such linguistic rules betrays Gulliver's familiarity with his reader. Of course *Swift* is intentionally flouting the rules in order to make me feel uncomfortable.[36] *Gulliver's Travels* is a disconcerting text that demonstrates the dangers of reading such a text, and the reader's puzzlement—who is talking?

what is his relationship to me? do we really share all the assumptions he thinks we do?—is precisely the reaction Swift has intended to create. "I shall not trouble the reader . . . ," promises Gulliver some ten times. Here lies the difference between him and the real author. Swift has diliberately set out to trouble *his* reader.

III

The deviousness of Swift's entrapment should not be glossed over. For example, in the three passages looked at above, the apostrophe to the reader amidst the several inconsistencies and illogicalities further obfuscate the matter of who is speaking to whom. Implicit in each is the dubious presumption of a mutual understanding: "Wherein the Reader will excuse me for not being over particular," "I am heartily sorry as any of my Readers can possibly be," and "I have already told the Reader how much I was pestered by those odious Animals." In such cases the neat distinction between characterized and implied reader begins to blur. Although we are in effect being addressed, as actual readers of *Gulliver's Travels* we are not altogether pleased with the lack of particulars, we probably distrust Gulliver's sorrow over his untruthfulness, and we wonder how he can separate himself from the Yahoos when a moment earlier he was unabashedly speaking of his similarities with them. We are being spoken to but surely we do not feel totally comfortable in the role of confidant that has been thrust upon us. More generally, such direct addresses to the reader seem always to underscore moments when it would be wise for us to depart from the narrator or his ideas, or at least when we must somehow be on our mettle. Thus at the same moment that we are being invited most explicitly into the text, we are asked to step back from it and take a more objective look. Swift is good at this sort of chicanery. Indeed the difference between these supposed intimacies and the *Tale's* "you will hardly believe, how much it altered her Person for the worse," is one only of degree. That cool grotesquerie is of course more shocking because of the violence of its image, but in *Gulliver's Travels* the quiet insistence on a certain intimacy between

Gulliver and his reader is finally more threatening than anything in *A Tale of a Tub*. The boundary separating the characterized relationship between narrator and reader and that between
Jonathan Swift and his implied reader is in this work not so
clear-cut. And the ambiguity effectively heightens the intensity
of our reactions.

One final point—it should not go unnoticed that Swift's entrapment of his reader suggests on his part a keen awareness of
the process of reading itself. Recent discussions of reading stress
how a reader expects coherence in a text and how a great deal
of his energy is spent in search of varius sorts of consistencies
and in maintaining those consistencies once they have been located. "Consistency-building," says Wolfgang Iser,

> is the indispensible basis for all acts of comprehension,
> and this in turn is dependent upon processes of selec-
> tion. This basic structure is exploited by literary texts
> in such a way that the reader's imagination can be
> manipulated and even reoriented.[37]

The precise way in which the text disrupts the reader's consistency-building is of special interest to Iser, as it was to his spiritual mentor, Roman Ingarden. Ingarden refers to "places of indeterminacy" in a text—called by Iser "gaps" or "blanks"—that
interrupt the flow of reading and that the reader is called upon
to fill. Thus Kenneth S. Goodman can talk about reading as a
"psycholinguistic guessing game."[38] In filling the blanks of a
text "we actually participate in the text," says Iser, "and this
means we are caught up in the very thing we are producing."[39]
Certainly the participatory nature of the reading process—and
there is no reason to expect that it was far different in the eighteenth century—makes available to a satirist like Swift a quite
"natural" tactic for utilizing the reader's own involvement in
the service of his irony. Inside the arena of the text, author and
reader become locked in a dialogue that is, says Paul de Man,
"always a battle for mastery."[40] Surely this is true of reading
Swift.

From the previous discussion it must be clear how cleverly
Swift has used these blanks. In the case of the playful Brobdingnagian maid of honor, Gulliver's authorial prudery has kept him

from giving all the details—there is a gap in his story—and the reader is left to imagine the ungiven details. In leaving this blank in his text, Swift has gotten me to supply what Gulliver tells me he knows I wouldn't want to hear. If anyone is guilty here, it is not Gulliver. Similar things occur in reading the second and third passages (although there the blanks are not brought explicitly to our attention): in both cases the inconsistency of the text suggests that something is missing, that links must exist that would explain how Gulliver could love truth and yet be untruthful, and how he can be like a Yahoo and yet call them "odious," or be unlike them and yet similar to a monkey or a jack daw. As in the first passage, however, any attempt on my part to bridge the gaps in Swift's text—or thinking of Bateson, any attempt to link up the opposing injunctions—will implicate *me* in some way.

A reader can be trapped because he desires coherence and will create it where he finds little or none. A satirist like Swift can thus make him stumble over his own reactions to the text. In such circumstances the only escape open to Swift's implied reader is to admit his entrapment by the slippery prose, to dust off his pride, and to resolve in the future to *try* at least to keep his baser instincts, his English prejudices, or his human egocentricities from dragging down his higher aspirations.[41] Swift hopes that his reader learns something from his experience of reading the text and that he is willing to accept a new and more challenging relationship with the real author.[42] This is asking a lot. Whether the actual reader of *Gulliver's Travels* is capable of such honesty and flexibility is another matter. Nonetheless, it is abundantly clear that Swift, charges of misanthropy aside, had remarkable confidence in his *readers as readers.*

NOTES

1. David M. Vieth, "Entrapment in Restoration and Early Eighteenth-Century English Literature," *Papers on Language and Literature,* 18 (1982), 228–29.
2. I have modified Richard H. Rodino's definition as it appears in "Varieties of Vexatious Experience in Swift and Others," *Papers on Language and Literature,* 18 (1982), 325. Rodino makes some interesting observations on Jonathan Smedley's comments (1728) on Swift's attitude toward his reader.

3. Samuel Johnson, *Lives of the English Poets*, ed. George Birkbeck Hill (Oxford: Clarendon Press, 1905), III, 52.
4. F. R. Leavis, "The Irony of Swift," published first in *Determinations*, ed. F. R. Leavis (London: Chatto and Windus, 1934), 79–108. Reprinted in *Swift: A Collection of Critical Essays*, ed. Ernest Tuveson (Englewood Cliffs, N. J.: Prentice-Hall, 1964), 18; the word "trap" appears on page 26. Leavis, in this respect ahead of his time, likewise refers to Swift's "betrayal" of his reader, to his prose that "continually surprises and disconcerts the reader," and to the Swiftian text as "a fierce and insolent game."
5. Henry W. Sams, "Swift's Satire of the Second Person," published first in *ELH*, 26 (1959), 36–44. Reprinted in *Twentieth-Century Interpretations of "Gulliver's Travels,"* ed. Frank Brady (Englewood Cliffs, N. J.: Prentice-Hall, 1968), 36.
6. Oswald Johnston, "Swift and the Common Reader," in *In Defense of Reading: A Reader's Approach to Literary Criticism*, ed. Reuben A. Brower and Richard Poirier (New York: E. P. Dutton, 1962), 178.
7. C. J. Rawson, "Gulliver and the Gentle Reader," in *Imagined Worlds: Essays on Some English Novels and Novelists in Honour of John Butt*, ed. Maynard Mack and Ian Gregor. Reprinted (in slightly different form) in *Gulliver and the Gentle Reader: Studies in Swift and Our Time* (London: Routledge and Kegan Paul, 1973); see esp. 6. In another chapter of this latter book, Rawson refers to Leavis's essay as "the most acute general discussion of Swift ever written" (59).
8. John Traugott, *"A Tale of a Tub,"* in *Focus: Swift*, ed. C. J. Rawson (London: Sphere Books, 1971), 117; Robert C. Elliott, "Swift's Satire: Rules of the Game," *ELH*, 41.3 (1974), 423; and Wayne Booth, *A Rhetoric of Irony* (Chicago: Univ. of Chicago Press, 1974), 106 and 109.
9. Neil Schaeffer, " 'Them That Speak, and Them That Hear': The Audience as Target in *Tale of a Tub*," *Enlightenment Essays*, 4 (1973), 25–35; Robert Uphaus, *"Gulliver's Travels, A Modest Proposal*, and the Problematical Nature of Meaning," *Papers on Language and Literature*, 10 (1974), 268–78; and Deborah Linderman, "Self-Transforming Ironies in Swift's *Tale of a Tub*," *Comparative Literature Studies*, 16.1 (March, 1979), 69–78, esp. 73.
10. Alain Bony, "Call me Gulliver," *Poétique*, 14 (1973), 197–209. Some aspects of the present study are taken up also in Bony's essay.
11. John Fletcher, "From 'Gentle Reader' to 'Gentle Skimmer'; or Does it Help to Read Swift as if he were Samuel Beckett?" *Hungarian Studies in English*, 12 (1979), 49–59.
12. John N. Morris, "Wishes as Horses: A Word for the Houyhnhnms," *The Yale Review*, 62 (1973), 362.
13. Brian McRea, "Surprised by Swift: Entrapment and Escape in *A Tale of a Tub*," *Papers on Language and Literature*, 18 (1982), 234–44; Donald C. Mell, Jr., "Irony, Poetry, and Swift: Entrapment in 'On Poetry: A Rapsody,' " 310–24; and Richard H. Rodino, "Varieties of Vexations Experience in Swift and Others," 325–47. The essays in the present volume by A. B. England, Louise K. Barnett, and Melinda Rabb appeared previously in somewhat different form in *Studies in the Literary Imagination*, 17.1 (Spring, 1984).
14. Janet Aikins, " 'Reading With Conviction': Trial by Satire"; Louise K. Barnett, "Deconstructing *Gulliver's Travels*,"; Frederik N. Smith, "Style,

Swift's Reader, and the Genres of *Gulliver's Travels*," in *The Genres of 'Gulliver's Travels*,' ed. Frederik N. Smith (Newark: Univ. of Delaware Press, 1990). Note too that several essays in *Approaches to Teaching "Gulliver's Travels*," ed. Edward J. Rielly (New York: The Modern Language Association of America, 1988), demonstrate how the new emphasis on the reader has affected classroom teaching.

15. Clive T. Probyn, "Preface: Swift and the Reader's Role," in *The Art of Jonathan Swift*, ed. Clive T. Probyn (New York: Barnes and Noble, 1978), 9.

16. *A Tale of a Tub*, ed. A. C. Guthkelch and D. Nichol Smith, 2nd ed. (1920; Oxford: Clarendon Press, 1958), 203. Elsewhere the Modern Author refers to "the yawning Readers in our Age" and to "the Fatigue of Reading."

17. Ibid., 185.

18. Daniel W. Nelson, "Readers in Texts," *PMLA*, 96 (1981), 848–63.

19. Ibid., 855.

20. In addition to these direct addresses to the singular reader of *Gulliver's Travels*, there is one reference to a generalized "English Reader," another to the "unwary Reader" of other travel books, and several to "Readers" of books as a group. I have not counted any of these, although obviously they are important to any discussion of readers or reading in Swift's satire.

21. Walter J. Ong, "The Writer's Audience is Always a Fiction," *PMLA*, 90 (1975), 14. But how new was this attitude? Cf. Cathleen M. Bauschatz, "Montaigne's Conception of Reading in the Context of Renaissance Poetics and Modern Criticism," in *The Reader in the Text: Essays on Audience and Interpretation*, ed. Susan R. Suleiman and Inge Crosman (Princeton: Princeton Univ. Press, 1980, 264–91.

22. *A Tale of a Tub*, 181.

23. The adjective "candid" in this context means "free from malice; not desirous to find faults" (Johnson).

24. See Gerald Prince, "Introduction to the Study of the Narratee," in *Reader-Response Criticism: From Formalism to Post-Structuralism*, ed. Jane P. Tomkins (Baltimore: Johns Hopkins Univ. Press, 1980), 7–25.

25. Jonathan Culler, *Structuralist Poetics: Structuralism, Linguistics and the Study of Literature* (Ithaca: Cornell Univ. Press, 1975), 154.

26. Cf. G. Douglas Atkins, *Reading Deconstruction/Deconstructive Reading* (Lexington: Univ. Press of Kentucky, 1983), 108: "The *Tale* thus participates in that important but little-studied Augustan interest in reading and interpretation that Dryden makes the center of attention in *Religio Laici*, which can be read as a layman's approach to reading. The *Tale* may even be 'about' the effort to read and a satire on the perhaps inevitable desire to reduce and make comprehensible."

27. *Gulliver's Travels*, ed. Herbert Davis (Oxford: Basil Blackwell, 1965), 136. Subsequent references will be to this edition and will be included parenthetically within the text.

28. In *A Proposal for Correcting the English Tongue, Polite Conversation, Etc.*, ed. Herbert Davis (Oxford: Basil Blackwell, 1964), p. 252.

29. Gerald Prince, "Notes on the Text as Reader," in *The Reader in the Text: Essays on Audience and Interpretation*, ed. Susan R. Suleiman and Inge Crosman (Princeton: Princeton Univ. Press, 1980), 239.

30. There are numerous other passages that function in this same way; moreover, Part 4 as a whole can be looked at as an incomprehensible riddle:

what has a mane, a tail, hooves, can thread needles, talks, has servants, and is intolerant of any threat to its authority?

31. Cf. Everett Zimmerman, *Swift's Narrative Satires: Author and Authority* (Ithaca: Cornell Univ. Press, 1983), 116: "Gulliver, we assume, will be integrated into a satiric version of the travel book by serving as the neutral observer, a figure characteristic of the travel book, who then absorbs the lessons figured by the scene, although at a somewhat slower rate than the reader."

32. Stanley Fish, "Literature in the Reader: Affective Stylistics," in *Self-Consuming Artifacts: The Experience of Seventeenth-Century Literature* (Berkeley: Univ. of California Press, 1972), 123–62.

33. Gregory Bateson, In *Steps to an Ecology of Mind* (San Francisco: Chandler Publishing Co., 1972), 201–27.

34. There is an additional joke here at the expense of the genre of the travel book, which is of course ordinarily replete with "particulars." Gulliver is thus pretending to be a travel-writer who is more sensitive to his reader than most travel-writers are.

35. Swift's verbal cross-referencing should also heighten our awareness of these similarities. Thus the word "odious" is used here by Gulliver to describe the Yahoos, although the term can hardly be employed neutrally after its appearance in the speech by the Brobdingnagian King. What we have then is an "odious" man deigning to call the Yahoos "odious."

36. For a general discussion of this phenomenon, see Mary Louise Pratt, "Literary Cooperation and Implicature," in *Essays in Modern Stylistics*, ed. Donald C. Freeman (London: Methuen, 1981), 377–412.

37. Wolfgang Iser, *The Act of Reading: A Theory of Aesthetic Response* (Baltimore: Johns Hopkins Univ. Press, 1978), 125.

38. Kenneth S. Goodman, "Reading: A Psycholinguistic Guessing Game," *Journal of the Reading Specialist*, 6 (1967), 126–35.

39. *The Act of Reading*, 127. On the "gaps" or "blanks" in a text, see especially Iser's "Indeterminacy and the Reader's Response in Prose Fiction," in *Aspects of Narrative*, ed. J. Hillis Miller (New York: Columbia Univ. Press, 1971), 1–45. See also Ingarden, *The Cognition of the Literary Work of Art* (1968), trans. Ruth Ann Crowley and Kenneth R. Olson (Evanston: Northwestern Univ. Press, 1973), 241–45.

40. Paul de Man, "Dialogue and Dialogism," *Poetics Today*, 4 (1983), 107.

41. Of course while reading *Gulliver's Travels* we undoubtedly grow increasingly accustomed to Swift's methods of entrapment, and certainly in subsequent readings our experience is of a different kind (not necessarily in any way less); we gradually learn to perceive ourselves being trapped by Swift, or enjoy exercising our wits in attempting to avoid traps we see coming. See Iser, *The Act of Reading*, 134.

42. Cf. John Preston, *The Created Self: The Reader's Role in Eighteenth-Century Fiction* (New York: Barnes and Noble, 1970), 209–10: "The eighteenth-century novelists were pushing forward the possibilities of the novel and were therefore in effect asking for a different kind of reader. Their professed contempt of the 'critic' was not just a conventional joke. It was part of the process of remaking a reader, who would have to be capable of sustaining a much more complex and challenging situation than the mere 'critic.'"

Lures, Limetwigs, and the Swiftian Swindle

John R. Clark

To spot a man who's counterfeit is hard,
But nothing, Kurnos, matters quite so much.
                                    —Theognis[1]

A little reflection will give almost anyone pause when he
or she intends to make any pronouncements about "audience
entrapment." From one perspective, the satiric or the comic author certainly needs to be cautious about assaulting or even
discomforting his audience. The humorist, after all, needs com-
munal consensus; laughter requires some agreed-upon standards, risibility needs must be the permissible discharge of the
vox populi. He must confirm his auditors or win their assent as
concerns the object that triggers public release. He must not
alienate his secular congregation. Consequently, he will *not* violate comic decorum or offend his auditors; he needs *to win friends*

131

in order to influence people. "Entrapment," from this point of view, is a no-no, and out of the question.

On the other hand, the comic artist frequently, as Diogenes the Cynic long ago boistrously demonstrated by unseemly conduct, paradox, and indecency, attracts attention and obtains an assembly and a hearing in the first place. Freud distinguished two kinds of wit and tendency humor, based upon such wit's purport—to destroy or to expose—satire or ribaldry. Yet Eric Bentley rightly notes that

> . . . we may take another step by observing that there
> is destructive force also in the joke that exposes. It is
> hostile either to the thing exposed or to the audience
> watching the exposure or both.[2]

For both rely upon "aggression." In this sense, *both* comedian *and* satirist in some sort startle, ruffle, discompose their audience, and audience manipulation and even entrapment constitute standard operating procedure in their everyday maneuvers.

But normally, I believe, this element of surprise, of the disconcerting and the aggressive, most commonly is encountered *at the outset* of a performance. Initially, "the willing suspension of disbelief" comes into play; once the audience adjusts to or tentatively accepts the strategy, the posture, and the occasion of the jarring humorist, it normally anticipates—and is provided with—smooth sailing thereafter. The audience comes to count upon the *given* boundaries of the saturnalian unseemly excess and release. Like the observers of romance or of tragedy, the witnesses of humor and satire, of Restoration Comedy or of farce, rapidly become familiars; they like to become acquainted, to feel, with tendency humor, that they know where it will venture, how it will run. And here, it is only the daring and the unusual artist who will disturb the pattern and direction of his work in its later—and particularly its climactic—stages.

In this paper, then, I am specifically concerned with the author who reneges his contract at the last, who rattles his audience in the end, who deliberately fails to gratify what his would-be initiates anticipate, who interposes material that he knows his congregation will find intolerable or unacceptable.

Such an author is a wrecker of tacit commitments, a violator of form, a literary disturber of the conventional peace. If such an artist is a dangerous experimentalist in his art, frequently instilling in his work a savage power, he nonetheless earns a bad name for his pains, and he is frequently chastized and maligned—even over the centuries—with tedious consistency. Perhaps this is as it should be: the very sources of his force emanate from his lawlessness and his repulsive bouquet of broken promises. His supposed weakness is literally synonymous with his strength.

Consequently, although I am not at all certain of the precise definition of the term "reader entrapment," I am very much interested here in the artist who inflicts audience discomfiture to the highest degree. *All* satire seeks to some extent to "shock" or discomfort the reader, especially the imagined reader who is implicated as having whatever lax morals or bad taste the satirist at that time is impugning. A central strategy therefore of the more intransigent satirist is relentless parody—a strategy whereby tastes and forms the reader espouses (or at least takes for granted) are deployed *as if* they were acceptable; only later will such forms and ideas be drastically stretched until they become from such distortion grotesque and untenable. The strategy of discomforting parody is archetypal, say, in Aristophanes's *Birds*, as one critic has well observed:

> A treacherous fellow, your satirist. He will beguile the leisure of an Athenian audience, needing some rest, Heaven knows, from the myriad problems of a relentless war with powerful neighbours, by putting on a little play called *The Birds*. Capital; we shall enjoy that. Two citizens of Athens, so the plot runs, take wings to themselves and set out to build a bird city, remote from the daily instance of this subnubilar world. Excellent! That is just what we wanted, a relief for tired brains! And then, the fellow tricked us, it proves, after all! His city in the clouds is, after all, only a parody of an Athenian colony, and the ceremonies which attend its inauguration are a burlesque, in the worst possible taste, of Athenian colonial policy. We

come here for a holiday, and we are being treated to a
sermon instead![3]

Such a "gulling" strategy is a dominant feature in Euripidean
drama: the audience is deliberately invited to "side" with a sympathetic character like Medea or Dionysus—only, in a later reversal, to be repulsed by such characters' overt savagery.[4] Modern theater tactics often deliberately alter characters and scenes
abruptly, to prevent us from what freshmen call "identifying
with" particular people, viewpoints, events. This is the heart of
what Antonin Artaud implies in the devices he calls for in his
proposed "theater of cruelty"; it is the soul of Brechtian alienation or the *Verfremdungseffekt*;[5] and it is the goal of recent
theater's startling utilization of so-called "transformation" strategies.[6]

Moreover, beyond parody and shock, a good many satirists
employ anticlimax: the cliché-ridden plot or idea, the usual practice, is somehow undercut or curtailed, leaving the reader high
and dry.[7] It is a favorite stratagem of Shaw, who, for example,
will at the end of his drama gleefully prevent the marriage of
Eliza and the Professor in *Pygmalion*—and boast about it in a
lengthy and taunting After-word. Dryden similarly "provokes"
his readership at the close of "Absalom & Achitophel" by having
King David—drastically outnumbered by his enemies—against
all probability utterly banish civil strife in an instant by a God-
like *fiat*.

By almost any standards, however, Jonathan Swift regularly goes farther than most satirists in the deployment of such
stratagems at the close of his works. His intellectual preference
for "nettling" by means of "raillery"[8] leads him *repeatedly* to
engineer preposterous inversions, reversals, and contradictions;
indeed, he favors proceeding by a use of logic to overturn logi-
cality itself, so that the reader is continually confounded. Such
playfulness, to be sure, often dismays and exacerbates his readership in a particularly galling manner. One need merely think
of the string of absurdities in the *Tale of a Tub's* Section IX,
whereby the speaker appears to waver back and forth, now accepting Superficiality, now endorsing Depth—only at the last,
in the famous "fools and knaves" climax, to impugn both.[9]

One is similarly immersed in impossibilities when he accepts the very grounds and conditions of "Verses on the Death of Dr. Swift": for the reader "believes" he is reading about a man's demise *described by the deceased;* later, when supposedly "unbiased" third parties (and even "strangers") are introduced for *their* opinions in the case, point of view has been manipulated to run haywire and common sense has been strained to bursting. A similar strategy is operative in the "Argument Against Abolishing Christianity," when the "sides" of the question are neatly drawn and quartered, producing only *two*: abolition (and militant atheism) or vacillating hypocrisy. In every case, the conscientious reader, eager to choose a head or a tail, finds himself becoming the laughable hyena. The commonplaces of *recta ratio* and of a complacent and satisfied readership are themselves brought to naught. The supposed rational "sides" of a question and the reader's own concessive good nature are transmogrified into the horns of a dilemma, and in every case it is the reader who gets gored.

Nowhere is this dismantling of grounds, cases, and occasions for argument better in evidence than in the renowned Fourth Part of *Gulliver's Travels.* The reader is cunningly induced to accept a world consisting of two antithetic entities only: of wise horses and of vicious beasts. Somewhere in between the lines, Gulliver is, as it were, a number of times "converted"; as if by magic, he is forced to recognize with total conviction that the bestial is precisely synonymous with the human; with "horror" Gulliver observes (IV.ii) "in this abominable animal, a perfect human figure" in the Yahoo; and at one fell blow (IV.iii) the designated "masters" or horses similarly perceive that "it was plain I must be a perfect yahoo. . . . " (The oxymoronic use of "perfection" to describe base and abandoned depravity and bestiality is a typical nicety of the Swiftian broadsword.) Though Gulliver denies this identification, he straightway proceeds (IV.iv) *as if he did not*: recounting English history to his "masters" as if it were the proceedings of the vilest of unregenerate yahoos. Hence the identification is in every way complete. The Houyhnhnm "Master" continues in his "conviction" that man is identical with yahoo, arguing that physically Gulliver "agreed in every feature of [his] body with other yahoos" and that intellectually Europeans also reveal "as near a resemblance in the disposition of [their] minds" (IV.vii).

The Master is the exempler, as has been assumed from the outset, of right reason, so who (to pun a little) is to say him neigh—even when he employs the skewered axiom that things similar to the same things are equal to each other! The case has long been settled; IV.viii (with typical Swiftian repetitive overkill) purports to provide irrefutable evidence even for Gulliver—as if he were not long ago "satisfied"; here it is presumed "natural" and "regular" by the Houyhnhnms when the eleven-year-old yahoo brunette sexually assaults Gulliver in the river,

> . . . matter of diversion to my master and his family, as well as of mortification to myself. For now I could no longer deny that I was a real yahoo in every limb and feature, since the females had a natural propensity to me as one of their own species. . . .

We will say nothing of the reader's chagrin to learn that barely pubescent maidens are casually reckoned to be Nabokovian nymphets and sexpots; it is still more disturbing to accept Gulliver's corrosive "chain" of reasoning. In any event, Gulliver has traveled a flightshot from his initially seeing the yahoos as a "herd" of "singular, and deformed" "animals" or "cattle" (IV.i). And the journey to the comically "infallible" conclusion that yahoo = man has been precipitated again and again by repetitious assumptions, faulty comparisons, crippled axioms, and magnificent illogic. Swift intransigently wins the day because of his characters' universal capitulation and docible assent to a wretched hypothesis. If readers have been repeatedly sparked to violent reaction to Book Four—one immediately thinks of Thackeray (or of Huxley, or even of Orwell)—it is doubtless because of the implacable march of a seeming logic toward this finale of militant unreasonableness. Swift doesn't call for the "willing suspension of disbelief"; instead, he seems to proceed naturalistically, only to transform his fiction by invisible stages into the fantastic and thence into the positively repugnant. We cannot put our finger upon a specific place or passage where a *cognitio* or metamorphosis or conversion of Gulliver's conviction transpires, and we are all the more perturbed for being unable to ascertain where this transition takes place. It happens almost everywhere in the early chapters, or it happens nowhere: for the Houyhnhnms have been certain from the start. Hence the reader finds himself tricked into accepting the unacceptable.

But whatever the reader's reservations, objections, and frustrations at this point, he is going to be still more confounded by this Voyage's conclusion. For, however much we might question Gulliver's new-found conviction, we have nevertheless been assuredly led to expect that if this new-made monomaniac has learned one thing in all his life, at least, now that he has obtained that modicum, *he will stick to that*: he will have attained to a kind of stubborn valor, displaying the courage of his misapprehensions. We expect such consistency because of the very conventions of travel literature and of literary romance: the hero undergoes trials and initiation, endures the fires of experience, emerges to maturity and with the illumination of the convert of religious rite and the *Bildungsroman*. In short, the protagonist traditionally confronts, withstands, and then incorporates the wisdom of the Nether World, and progresses, in Jungian terms, "to higher consciousness."

But Gulliver does not. Gulliver does no such thing. For one thing, he closes his mind; he refuses to be adaptable, to assimilate new experience, to accommodate himself to new cases. This is clearly the situation when he refuses to acknowledge the exemplary humaneness of Don Pedro de Mendez, the Portuguese Captain. Moreover, in his withdrawal from so-called English yahoos and his denunciations of their "pride," Gulliver increasingly evinces a prime delusion: that he himself is their superior, that he, somehow, is himself more Houyhnhnm than Yahoo. Hence, in Gulliver's crippled geography, all Gaul is divided into *two* parts—and Gulliver has removed himself to the better camp. Blandly defying the opinion of the Houyhnhnms, he has become in his own eyes an illustrious Houyhnhnm himself. In this honorable posture he remains implacably fixed and firm. Furthermore, Gulliver manifests another delusion: he confounds form and content; for he equates English stone-horses with Houyhnhnms, and takes to feeding with equine beasts and sleeping in stables. For him, a horse, no matter what the circumstances, is a Houyhnhnm. Just as implacably, Gulliver concludes that men are yahoos: form and physiognomy are everything. It does not matter to him that certain men are intellectually wise or sensitively benign, or that European horses are mentally vacant or depraved: a rule is a rule. Hence he confuses substance with accident, crucial traits with superficial manners—and we find him concerned with imitating and admiring a horse's whinny, its odor and its gait, *as if* these were the characteristics worthy of honor and emulation. Five years have passed, he tells us (IV.xi), since his return into England, yet he still maintains for his wife and children his "hatred, disgust, and contempt." It would seem that Gulliver's confusions are at least sustained by a kind of grandly obtuse perseverence and inflexibility. At any rate, we are conned into thinking so.

Yet it is not so: for Gulliver has elected to write a book for the delectation of the hopelessly vicious English yahoos. Although they are elsewhere considered incorrigible and unregenerate, he nonetheless deigns (in the manner and jargon of authors) to address his audience as "gentle" and "courteous" and "judicious" readers, to write to them employing the intimate *thou*–form, and to explain that he wishes to "inform" them and "to improve their minds." In short, he seeks "the PUBLIC GOOD" of those whom he absolutely condemns, despises, and abhors. Indeed, although it took him *two years* under Houyhnhnm tutelage to purge himself, as he tells us, of the vices of "lying, shuffling, deceiving, and equivocating," he complaisantly estimates that his compatriots, upon reading his book, need but *six months* to amend ("Letter . . . to Cousin Sympson").

But if all of this conduct reveals Lemuel Gulliver as constantly inconstant and shakily steady, nothing better serves to undermine his position than Swift's final cut of the knife. For Gulliver *cannot adhere* even to those truths that he takes to be self-evident and eternal. Instead, he wavers and changes. During those selfsame five years that he mentions (IV.xi), he has come to "endure my wife [and] children in my presence." Just "last week" he "began to permit [his] wife to sit at dinner with [him]. . . , and to answer . . . the few questions [he] ask[s] her" (IV.xii). And he "hopes" to "suffer" neighbors in his company before long. Soon the back-sliding is nearly complete. In "The Publisher To the Reader," Richard Sympson speaks of Lemuel Gulliver, a short time later, as an "intimate friend," as one "in good esteem among his neighbours."

With this final sea-change, even the lunatic Gulliver is robbed of the last shred of dignity and consistency: he simply *cannot* even hold to this one scrap of new-found faith and dogma, without insensible regression and apostasy. Swift will not allow him even to bask in the steady light of error and insanity. Among all the changes wrung upon the characters and ideas in the final pages of this master-work, surely the most dazzling is this unkindest cut of them all: Gulliver cannot adhere to any simple doctrine or hold to any steady course! Perhaps that is, in such a whirligig of transformations, the most telling piece of information.

Neither those who condemn Gulliver's initial horse-philosophy nor those who applaud it are permitted self-gratulation or satisfaction. For, laughingly, Jonathan Swift is showing us what a poor, bare forkèd thing is unaccommodated man—a yahoo in all affairs, but most pathetically so in his frivolous indeterminacy. If he be the archetypal representative of the human condition, Swift appears to tell us (laughing and shaking in Rab'lais' easy chair), then Lemuel Gulliver is a wretched captain of our soul, and very much at sea.

—And the reader?—He has been rocked and knocked and turned and overset so repeatedly in the satire's last pages, that I daresay he is willing to concede just about anything. And that, of course, is precisely where Swift wants to have him. Yet one thing is certain: the reader has been conned into making what has to be described as a "bad trip"; he won't want to thank Jonathan Swift for such coarse transportation, although he will never forget the Voyage. That, too, is exactly where Swift aims to have him.

NOTES

1. *Elegies* 117–18 in Hesiod, *Theogony; Works and Days;* Theognis, *Elegies*, trans. Dorothea Wender (Harmondsworth, England: Penguin, 1977), 100.
2. Eric Bentley, *The Life of Drama* (New York: Atheneum, 1964), 237.

3. Ronald A. Knox, *Essays in Satire* (London: Sheed and Ward, 1954), 24–25. See also the Introductory comments by William Arrowsmith in Aristophanes, *The Birds*, trans. Arrowsmith (Ann Arbor: University of Michigan Press, 1961), 1–5. The ire caused by entrapping the reader may be illustrated by the uproar caused by publication in the *New Yorker* of Shirley Jackson's "The Lottery." Among many irate letters, this one sums up readers' general sense of having been victimized: "You have betrayed a trust with your readers by giving them such a bestial selection. Unaware, the reader was led into a casual tale of the village folk, becoming conscious only gradually of the rising tension, till the shock of the unwholesome conclusion, skillful though it was wrought, left him with total disgust for the story and with disillusionment in the magazine publishing it" (in Shirley Jackson, *Come Along With Me*, ed. S. F. Hyman [New York: Viking Press, 1968], 222).

4. The first author clearly to stress Euripides's unsettling strategy of dramatizing the victory of forces of illogic and chaos was E. R. Dodds, "Euripides the Irrationalist," *Classical Review* 43 (1929), 97–104. William Arrowsmith emphasizes the fact that Euripides reflects his troubled era, by forging a "*created* disorder," utilizing "fragmentation" and "juxtaposed incongruities" to reflect his world's "divided culture" ("A Greek Theater of Ideas," in *Ideas in the Drama: Selected Papers from The English Institute*, ed. John Gassner [New York: Columbia University Press, 1964], esp. 9, 13, 14).

5. See Bertolt Brecht, *Brecht on Theatre: The Development of an Aesthetic*, trans. John Willett (London: Methuen, 1964), esp. 91 ff., 94–96, 101–2, 143–45, 191–95.

6. "Transformation" is a Second City Workshop device of initiating in the midst of the action a sudden change of scene, character, pace, continuity with the intent of destroying conventional theatrical realities. See Peter Feldman, "Notes for the Open Theatre Production" (of *Keep Tightly Closed in a Cool Dry Place*), in Megan Terry, *Viet Rock; Comings and Goings; Keep Tightly Closed in a Cool Dry Place; The Gloaming, Oh My Darling: Four Plays*, intro. Richard Schechner (New York: Simon and Schuster, 1967), 200–1.

7. For the prevalent use of the anticlimactic to parody and induce shock, consult my study, "Anticlimax in Satire," *Seventeenth-Century News*, 33 (Spring–Summer 1975), 22–26.

8. "An Epistle to a Lady" (1733), lines 213–22:
   "THUS, I find it by Experiment,
   Scolding moves you less than Merriment.
   I may storm and rage in vain;
   It but stupifies your Brain.
   But, with Raillery to nettle,
   Set your Thoughts upon their Mettle:
   Gives Imagination Scope,
   Never lets your Mind elope:
   Drives out Brangling, and Contention,
   Brings in Reason and Invention."
   Swift always sought any strategy that would obstruct the reader's complaisance and ease, prevent the reader from

bandying the guilt feelings the satire might stir away toward someone else; he wanted every reader to feel a direct hit.

Naturally, most critics have spoken to some extent about Swift's employment of the device of audience entrapment; some of the more pertinent comments on this topic may be found in Henry W. Sams, "Swift's Satire of the Second Person," *ELH* 26 (1959), 36–44; Irvin Ehrenpreis, "Swift and the Comedy of Evil," in *The World of Jonathan Swift*, ed. Brian Vickers (Cambridge: Harvard University Press, 1968), esp. 216–19; and C. J. Rawson, *Gulliver and The Gentle Reader* (London: Routledge and Kegan Paul, 1973), esp. 5–7. As concerns the deliberate use of illogicality and anticlimax: Robert M. Adams provides an interesting survey of the ways in which Swift and Kafka alike jar the reader by use of "disorganization," "dislocation," and what Adams calls "open form" (in *Strains of Discord: Studies in Literary Openness* [Ithaca: Cornell University Press, 1958], 146–79).

The early 1980's witnessed a flurry of interest in audience and reader entrapment by Restoration and early eighteenth-century authors. Swift, as might be expected, virtually leads the pack. Consult issues of journals devoted to such "entrapment": *Papers on Language and Literature*, 18 (1982) and *Studies in the Literary Imagination* vol. 17. 1 (Spring, 1984). See also David M. Vieth's article on Pope and entrapment in *SEL* 23 (1983), 425–34.

9. On the contention of "credulity" and "curiosity" as a dominant motif, see my own study, *Form and Frenzy in Swift's "Tale of a Tub"* (Ithaca: Cornell University Press, 1970), 17 ff., 39ff., 41–48; 48–51; 72–75.

The Smiler with the Knife: Covert Aggression in Some Restoration Epilogues

Anthony Kaufman

> For you must know there is, in nature, but two ways
> of making very good prologues. The one is by civility,
> by insinuation, good language, and all that, to—a—in
> a manner, steal your plaudit from the courtesy of the
> auditors: the other, by making use of some certain per-
> sonal things, which may keep a hank upon such censur-
> ing persons as cannot otherways, a gad, in nature, be
> hindered from being too free with their tongues.
> —Buckingham, *The Rehearsal*

Civility, insinuation, good language—here is the very stuff
of satirical entrapment, that covert method of misleading the

reader or audience under the guise of sincerity and straightfor-
wardness. Surely the Restoration prologue and epilogue are vehicles well suited for such entrapment, for so often civility, insinuation, and good language, seemingly in the service of flattery
or licensed abuse, instead covertly ensnare the reader or viewer
into false expectations and misleading assumptions. Indeed, the
very convention of the prologue and epilogue, the actor or actress
standing before a relatively small audience in an intimate theater, speaking the lines of the playwright, perhaps in the person
of a character of the play, may lend itself perfectly to a deliberately ambiguous meaning. Although not all Restoration playwrights were as purposeful in their making of prologues and
epilogues as was Mr. Bayes, I wish to cite some examples of
deliberate satiric aggression, conveyed by the vehicle of entrapment.

The prologues and epilogues of the Restoration were mark-
edly different from those few of the earlier period of English
drama. Soon after 1660 the theater audiences came to expect
more than a polite plea for the good will of the audience in a
prologue and in the epilogue a genial call for applause. Although
Ben Jonson had in *Every Man Out of his Humour* attacked the
audience with characteristic roughness, the satiric aggression
of the Restoration is not often found in the earlier drama. Soon
after the Restoration, however, the audiences came to expect a
witty, often quite satirical, prologue and epilogue, often delivered in the easy, urbane tone so admired in the period. Although
the hundreds of prologues and epilogues are various in their
subjects and their manner of delivery, even a superficial glance
at a collection of them suggests that satiric attack, either
straightforward or oblique, was particularly relished.

The causes of these new expectations are beyond the scope
of this paper, but I should note that it cannot be firmly linked
to the appearance of a somewhat new audience, upperclass or
court-oriented. Recent scholarship has suggested (although perhaps not proved) that the Restoration audience was more heterogeneous in its makeup than previously thought. Rather than the
coterie audience described by earlier theater historians such as
Nicoll and Beljame, we now suspect the presence of a rather
various audience made up of persons from all or most of the

strata of Restoration society. Apparently there was an important group of middle class persons there, as well as courtiers, soldiers, law students, prostitutes, servants, persons grave and sober as well as persons drunk and disorderly. Pepys was there and so was John Evelyn.[1]

And, indeed, one cannot link the appearance of the new witty satirical prologues and epilogues to the alleged dominance during the period of the so-called comedy of manners. One might think that if the audiences were exclusively attracted to comedies like *The Man of Mode, The Country Wife,* and later, *The Way of the World,* comedies witty, urbane, satiric, they might demand prologues and epilogues that were also witty, urbane, and satiric. But we have been reminded in the last several years of what has been known for some time—that Restoration drama is various; that farce, historical plays, low comedy, high (or high-sounding) tragedy, the heroic play and many more types, were as appealing as the comedy of wit.

Perhaps the emergence of the new witty-satiric prologue and epilogue can be associated to some extent with the love of witty discourse that distinguishes the period. Men and women apparently were serious about fine talk and responded to it on stage or in everyday life. There are jokes on the Restoration stage about certain would-be wits coming to the theater to store up bright sayings and witty cracks, garnered both from the stage and from the wits of the audience. It appears that people also bought prologues and epilogues, which were sometimes published separately from the plays, in order to study their wit. The prologues and epilogues, then, provided a kind of how-to-do-it manual for those who wanted to sound as bright as Dorimant or Horner, Etherege or Wycherley. And it has been noted that, despite the fact that the prologues and epilogues are usually monologues, delivered by the actor or actress to the audience, they often have the sense, even when read today, of being a kind of repartee—a witty, aggressive, dialogue between stage and audience. Granted that the reader/audience, does not directly partake, but it is easy enough to infer the questions, objections, cracks, that the audience could be imagined as making. As James Sutherland pointed out some years ago, "It is true that this was repartee in monologue, but what the speaker of the prologue was, so to speak, replying to could easily be supplied by the imagination."[2]

And perhaps we can also infer that the emergence of the new witty-aggressive prologues and epilogues had something to do with the sense of intimacy at the London theaters of the period. However various the audience may have been, the small theaters, with their extended stages, the actors and actresses playing in close proximity to the audience, encouraged a sense of intimacy—especially since the repertory theaters featured the same stars in a variety of roles day after day. Surely the prologues and epilogues encouraged this sense of rapport between the company and the audience, implying, as they so often do, a bond between them. Often the suggestion in the prologues and epilogues, even when they seem to be satirically abusive of the audience, is that the speaker and his company and the audience are all witty, urbane types, men and women of the world and the *bon ton*—that however various the components of the audience may be, for the moment at least both Royal in the boxes and footman in galleries could feel themselves subtly flattered and seduced.

But whatever the cause, collections of Restoration prologues and epilogues reveal a preponderance of pieces that are witty, urbane, and satirical—either overtly or in hidden, more devious ways. And these were studied by the town for their wit, for their sense of repartee.

What we must understand about these prologues and epilogues is that they are types of fictional discourse. It would be a serious mistake, as recent scholarship has pointed out, to take the prologues and epilogues at face value, as genuine reportage of the behavior of the audiences for example, or as reflecting the real displeasure of the playwright with the low standards of the town when it came to the theater. First, they are artificial attempts to gain the good will of the audience through a variety of means. Even when the playwright berates the audience for its noisy behavior, or its allegedly low literary standards, there is an attempt to gain the favor of the audience. Second, often the prologues and epilogues are integral parts of the play, extending its themes through a variety of ways. Not all of them do this of course, but many do.[3]

So, although James Thompson in the present volume is correct to point out the element of hostility and distrust between playwright and audience during the period, the prologues and epilogues, I believe, are best seen as works of rhetorical discourse, intended to persuade the audience to favor the play, to enter and depart from the fictional world with good will, and the first step is by means characteristic of the time—licensed and acceptable abuse. That the period was attracted to witty verbal aggression is well known; much of the dialogue of the comedies is devoted to highly polished banter, to the repartee that Dryden thought the very essence of comedy: "As for Comedy, repartee is one of its chiefest graces; the greatest pleasure of the audience is a chace of wit, kept up on both sides, and swiftly managed."[4] Thus the clever verbal fencing of Dorimant and Harriet, Mirabell and Millamant, and a hundred other truewits. The would-be wit, of course, relished without understanding. He understood that witty banter was fashionable, but had neither the wit nor judgment to appreciate truly its subtlety. Any sort of verbal aggression was meat to him. Sparkish of *The Country Wife* is a good example; he ignores even the most direct insult, thinking it mere witty banter and an implied compliment to his understanding. Anthony Witwoud of *The Way of the World* is his successor. "He is one whose conversation can never be approved, yet it is now and then to be endured," says Mirabell shortly before the entrance of Witwoud. He has indeed one good quality, he is not exceptious; for he so passionately affects the reputation of understanding raillery, that he will construe an affront into a jest; and call downright rudeness and ill language, satire and fire."[5]

The prologues and epilogues, themselves a species of witty repartee, aimed at persuading the audience to approve, very often offer abuse to a willing and applauding audience. Examples of this abound, but one may suffice. We recall Sir Car Scroope's Prologue to *The Man of Mode:*

... heav'n be thanked, 'tis not so wise an age
But your own follies may supply the stage.
....
'Tis by your follies that we players thrive,

As the physicians by disease live;

....

Since each is fond of his own ugly face,
Why should you, when we hold it, break the glass?[6]

Here is a seeming paradox: why is it that an audience of men and women of at least middling intelligence pays good money to be abused by the playwright and the players? But the paradox is only apparent—as long as the abuse was conveyed through wit, with charm, in the intimate setting of the theater, as a means of introducing the audience to the fictional world of the play or bringing him out of this world, the players were licensed to abuse. No doubt each member of the audience was also willing to think that the attack applied only to his neighbor, and not to himself. And, moreover, even today we respond to popular and not so popular entertainment that takes a satirical look at our own values and way of life. Despite George S. Kaufman's grouchy maxim that "satire is what closes Saturday night," we still pay good money to be laughed at. The fact is that the audience of 1660 and following expected witty abuse and responded to the ritualized attack on "the wits," "the critics," "the beaux," "the ladies," "the pit," "the cit," "the galleries," "the boxes," and so on. Harold Love notes that the audiences relished "the almost ritualized abuse of such groups," and may "have welcomed the targets as a mode of acknowledgment rather than resented as an affront."[7] He quotes Dryden's second prologue to *Secret Love, or The Maiden Queen* (1668) in which the playwright suggests that the best way to gain the favor of the audience is to abuse them:

The most compendious method is to rail:
Which you so like, you think your selves ill us'd
When in smart Prologues you are not abus'd.
A civil Prologue is approv'd by no man;
You hate it as you do a Civil Woman.[8]

And so it appears that there is a tacit agreement between stage and audience; satirical abuse is, as Love suggests, expected and favored—perhaps as a kind of indirect compliment to the various components of the Restoration audience. To see this is to understand the Restoration stage better, and yet perhaps to defang the satire of the prologues and epilogues. For if the satire is almost ritualized, if it is expected and relished, a means of compliment, if it does not describe contemporary realities, then surely we have satire that, to misappropriate Congreve's words, ". . . scarce dares grin, 'tis grown so mild,/Or only shows its teeth, as if it smiled. (Prologue to *Love for Love*)

But what of a satire, seen in prologues and epilogues, which does not sooth and flatter, acknowledge and invite? There are prologues and epilogues where the audience is deliberately misled and baffled, where the response, even when reading them today, must be a certain vexation. Here the satiric aggression takes the form of entrapment. The attack is covert, and our response is uncertain: we may be irritated or confused. What does the playwright (or whoever wrote the prologue or epilogue) mean? Is he having us on?

I want to note three examples of entrapment as a satiric technique. I have chosen three epilogues because in them we see how the sense of entrapment stems from the playing-off of the epilogue against the dramatic action we have just seen or read in the play. The epilogues to *The Country Wife, Amphitryon,* and *The Wives' Excuse* in quite different ways are subtle extensions of the plays' satiric themes.

It is clear that Wycherley's *The Country Wife* goes beyond mere bedroom farce, mere pandering to the taste for sex comedy in the 1670's, and recent critics have shown a variety of ways in which the play is to be enjoyed and valued. Although the play's satire ranges from the direct and obvious to the oblique and subtle, the epilogue is notable as Wycherley's smiling final jab. The audience has just seen Mr. Horner seemingly triumphant, surrounded by his gulls and doxies amidst "A dance of cuckolds," a seeming sign of his victory—or apparent victory. The audience, or at least the men of the audience (some of the women apparently disliked the play and this is significant), have to a greater or lesser extent identified with Horner, the Don Juan figure of the play. They have shared for the moment his energy, wit, poise, and audacity—although they may have been troubled from time to time in the play at the implications of and motivations behind Horner's actions. Now the audience sees Mary Knepp, still dressed as the bawdy lady of the play, Lady Fidget, step forward. (I assume that there is no break between the last quatrain of the play and the epilogue.) Her great scene with Horner, the china scene, is well remembered. There is some fun here for the audience, since Knepp is presumed to be a sensual woman (Pepys' favorite of course) and so the role and the actual person quite fit. Typecasting you might say; just the opposite of Nell Gwyn as "a Princess, acting in S. Cathar'n."

We have just heard Horner end the play with a quatrain:

> Vain fops but court, and dress, and keep a pother,
> To pass for women's men with one another;
> But he who aims by women to be priz'd,
> First by the men, you see, must be despis'd.[9]

Now, as Knepp begins the epilogue, it seems that the question of how men are to be prized by women will continue. And Lady Fidget/Mary Knepp are certainly women who have earned the right to speak on this question. In fact, we have had throughout the play a wonderful demonstration of how men are to be prized: through cleverness, audacity, and of course a high level of sexual energy. Having to some extent identified with Horner, we expect an acknowledgment and an amplification of what we have just seen, a confirmation that we are Horners and that we "the vigorous" can be expected to thrive.

Instead we are startled by an unexpected attack. Knepp's tone is contemptuous and amused: addressing the men of the audience, she charges us with being much like Sparkish. We preen, she says, and invite the vizard mask to come out, and yet

> ... when she says, "Lead on," you are not stout;
> But to your well-dress'd brother straight turn round
> And cry, "Pox on her, Ned, she can't be sound!"
> Then slink away, a fresh one to engage,
> With so much seeming heat and loving rage,
> You'd frighten listening actress on the stage. . . .
>
> (ll.5–10)

We are, she says, only appearance and fraud. And the attack is delivered not only by Knepp/Fidget, but also by the playwright, Wycherley, the "Plain Dealer" as he will soon come to be known. His satirical judgments we have just witnessed and approved. He has exposed the vice and folly of Sir Jasper, Sparkish, and the others, encouraging us to identify with the cunning and energetic Horner. Now we must instead identify, it seems, with the "well-dressed," the "Falstaffs of fifty" (1.14), the "essenc'd boys" (1.18). We may enjoy thinking of ourselves, it is implied, as Horners, but all we are, says the playwright and his knowledgeable agent, Knepp/Fidget, is show and failed deceit. And, near the end of the epilogue, it seems that although the town is corrupt and "the vigorous" experienced at deceit, our victories are only partial. "Men may still believe you vigorous" (1.32), but there is one test that even the most cunning deceiver cannot pass, one moment of truth from which there is no escape, one court from which there is no appeal: "we women—there's no coz'ning us" (1.33).

What is our response to be? How do we deflect the attack? By acknowledging smilingly the truth of the charge? By believing silently that it applies only to our neighbors in "the pit"? Our willingness to identify with the Don Juan is aborted; yet we can hardly permit ourselves to identify with the primary targets of Wycherley's satire. The epilogue calls for applause, but what are we to approve of? The playwright has turned on us, and his is a moral judgment we cannot easily avoid since his play has led us to join the laughter against a vice and folly that we ourselves are, apparently, a part of. There's a twist, though. By our applause and purposeful grinning, we approve the author's judgment, and by doing so, we remove ourselves (as best we can!) from the author's indictment. It is an uncomfortable removal, and perhaps we are conscious of our expediency. Perhaps we find ourselves in the position of Walpole at *The Beggar's Opera*—grinning and applauding furiously and when the time comes we acknowledge that, "That was leveled at me."

In Dryden's *Amphitryon,* produced about 1690 (the exact date is not certain), we again see that the playwright offers an epilogue that plays against the action we have just witnessed, an epilogue with a speaker (in this case Mrs. Mountfort) whose lines leave a certain puzzling ambiguity. Mountfort appears as Phaedra, the conniving maid to Alcmena, whose chief action in the play has been to chisel money from god and man alike. A throwback to Dryden's intelligent and witty gay mistresses of the earlier comedy, she is smart and savvy, and pretty enough to attract Mercury himself, who, as god of thieves, recognizes an affinity with Phaedra, Queen of Gypsies.

Although Phaedra's chief interest in this play is money, not sex, she has constantly used sex as a weapon for her economic advancement. She begins the epilogue by regretting the passage of the Pagan Age:

> I'm thinking, (and it almost makes me mad,)
> How sweet a time, those Heathen Ladies had.
> Idolatry was ev'n their Gods own trade;
> They Worshipt the fine Creatures they had made.[10]
>   (11. 1–4)

She laments the passing of that golden age in which Cupid was all the fashion in the skies, when "The Treasury of Heav'n was ne're so bare, / But still there was a Pension for the Fair" (11. 9–10). John Loftis has suggested that the epilogue embodies Dryden's ironic lament for the Restoration court,[11] and surely it is easy to find an echo of *Absalom and Achitophel* in such lines as: "In all his Reign, Adultry was no Sin; / For *Jove,* the good Example did begin" (11. 11–12). The golden age of Jove was one of bounty for such cunning and lusty ladies as Phaedra. But Phaedra's regret for the passing of the heathenish age of Jove, or Charles, plays off oddly against the treatment of the gods in the play we have just witnessed, where Jupiter and his sons Mercury and Phoebus are seen as degraded and without majesty "Black-brow'd and bluff like Homer's Jupiter; / Broad-back'd and brawny, built for love's delight. . . ." is how Dryden describes Jupiter in *The Hind and the Panther* (pt. 3; 11. 1144–45), written shortly before *Amphitryon,* and here in the play Jupiter is a coarse and equivocal seducer, whose interference in human affairs causes grief to an Amphitryon and Alcmena clearly his superiors in decent feeling and in dignity. Dryden, as Earl Miner points out, is obviously concerned with the invasion of an uncontrollable external power into human life, limiting our capacity for freedom and joy.[12] Phaedra's lament for an age of love and money—for the age of Charles II—charms us. She is, in the person of Mrs. Mountfort, attractive and witty. Yet Jupiter's lies and evasions—the coarseness and arbitrary power he embodies—obviously compromise any sense we may entertain of a lost golden age. Dryden's view, late in his life, of the age of Charles is seen in the famous lines from "The Secular Masque": "Thy lovers were all untrue. / 'Tis well an old age is out; / And time to begin a new" (11. 95–97). Yet in the epilogue to the play the satire turns back on the audience, or at least the men of the audience. Jove was a civil god, says Phaedra, "Civilly he sav'd the Ladies fame. / The secret Joys of Love, he wisely hid" (11. 14–15). His generous actions are contrasted with those of the men of the audience. While Jove gave his cuckolds "New Honours to content 'em," and "in the kind remembrance of the Fair, / On each exalted Son, bestow'd a Star" (11. 18–20)—the London seducer mocks his victims, "to their face torment 'em" (1.17). The god's munificence, though purposeful and dishonest, contrasts with the meanness of the Sparkishes and Witwouds of the pit.

Yet even the gods grow old, and although the age of Jove flourished two thousand years,

At last, when He and all his Priests grew old,
The Ladies grew in their devotion cold;
And, that false Worship wou'd no longer hold.
  Severity of Life did next begin;
(And always does, when we no more can Sin.) (11.
                                        23–27).

Our present age is one of severity, says Phaedra mockingly—the severity of the old and impotent, but severity of life cannot be long practiced. The next age may see another practice: "Then, Pagan Gods may, once again, succeed; / And *Jove,* or *Mars,* be ready, at our need, / To get young Godlings; and, so, mend our breed" (30–32). What is our response to this? Jupiter and his ilk mend our breed by begetting godlings? The play opens with the admission by Phoebus and Mercury that they are bastards:

... for, to confess the Truth, we two are little better
than Sons of Harlots; and if *Jupiter* had not been

> pleas'd to take a little pains with our Mothers, instead
> of being Gods, we might have been a couple of Linck-
> Boys. (I.i. 15–19)

And Jupiter's suave promises that Amphitryon will be well compensated for his horns by the birth of Hercules, "Who shall redress the Wrongs of injur'd Mortals, / Shall conquer Monsters, and reform the World"—are aptly answered by the witty god, Mercury, who says, "Ay, Brother *Phoebus;* and our Father made all those Monsters for *Hercules* to Conquer, and contriv'd all those vices on purpose for him to reform too, there's the Jeast on't" (I.i. 126–30).

In short, Phaedra's pious hope that the pagan gods may once again arise is compromised by the observance that godlings got by Jupiter will be closer to the London street mobs than to majestic Olympians. Yet the suggestion that our breed must be mended, that severity of life has led us to become an enervated breed, incapable of sin, is disturbing. We have found some comfort in the play from having seen that Amphitryon himself and Alcmena, the human beings devastated by the needless intrusion of Jupiter, have real human dignity; but even this comfort is compromised by the appearance of Sosia, the coward and fool—alas, another element of human nature. We might expect after the puzzling and unsettling ambiguity of the play some reassurance. Instead the playwright extends the deliberate ambiguity of the play through a disturbing epilogue.

In Southerne's *The Wives' Excuse,* Mrs. Barry speaks the epilogue and we sense at once that there is an absurd incongruity between the character she plays, the virtuous Mrs. Friendall, and the audience's perception of Elizabeth Barry as a woman of pleasure. Mrs. Friendall, although treated brutally by her foolish husband, refrains from accepting Lovemore's invitation to place the horns on the erring hubby. Her sense of honor and self-respect triumphs over her freely admitted inclination to her energetic pursuer, Lovemore. In the epilogue she wittily asks the audience not to think that she disparages the good old English custom of cuckolding, which first evolved when "the priests first made all Pleasure Sin."[13] We are reminded of her sense in the play itself of the division between her sexual inclination and her belief that she has invested her self-respect in an artificial social convention. Mrs. Friendall is in the epilogue laughingly tolerant of the old English rite of horning, and she concludes that "Whether I've done my Husband right, or no; / Most Women may be in the right, that do" (11. 10–11)—that is, cuckold their husbands.

This suggestion that most women have good reason to revolt against inadequate husbands begins the process in this epilogue of identifying the men in the audience with the odious Mr. Friendall. "Our Author does not set up for reforming," she says, "Or giving hints to Fools who won't take warning" (11. 12–13). She reinforces her identification of the men in the audience with the inadequate Friendall by commanding: "Compare at home the Picture with the Life, / And most of you may find a *Friendall* there. . . ." (11. 20–21). Yet at the end, Mrs. Friendall/Mrs. Barry admits that, ultimately, such virtue as she has portrayed on stage is the stuff of fiction only—the Friendalls of the pit needn't worry that her stage example will spoil their daily round of cuckolding and license by converting the ladies to virtue.

> You only fear such Plays may spoil your Game:
> But Flesh and Frailty always are the same:
> And we shall still proceed in our old way,
> For all that you can do, or Poets say.
>
> (11. 34–37)

We are assured that nothing of fiction can touch the female human nature that Mrs. Barry herself embodies. But the assurance is equivocal: our fair game will always be in season for the satisfaction of our immoral desires. The twist of the knife lies in the last couplet. Men's best efforts to keep their rambling wives content will be of as little use as the well-wrought but finally ineffective morality of Mr. Southerne. All this is guaranteed by Mrs. Friendall, whose moral example we admire as we admire her charm, and Mr. Barry, whose offstage activities suggest that she knows whereof she speaks.

Wycherley, Dryden, and Southerne sensed that they were allies in the theater and in their satirical vision. In the epilogues I have examined each playwright has gone beyond the printed word to a more comprehensive and complex method of genuine satire. He has relied on the total theatrical situation; that is, the fact that he has a living audience in the theater, a charming and accomplished actress to speak his lines, an actress who maintains her identity as a fictional character in the play that we have just seen. All attack the audience, not through the expected licensed abuse, the banter of the cits and fops and so forth, but by an attack the more formidable because unexpected, covert, and false to our expectations. Wycherley has allowed us to identify with a masterful trickster, and then in the epilogue he smilingly suggests that a truer identification would be with the "essenc'd boys"—the empty and impotent false wits of the play. Dryden, writing some fifteen years later, extends the satire of *Amphitryon* by suggesting in the epilogue that neither past nor present, god nor man, is fully satisfactory and that majesty may be compromised by an all too human coarseness and meanness of spirit, and that if human beings can embody dignity, they can also embody a variety of weaknesses. And Southerne suggests in his epilogue that well-intentioned exemplary comedy will probably reform no one. The Friendalls of the pit need not worry, and, says the virtuous wife, played by the notorious actress, women will always incline to the duplicity and sensuality of their sex. These three playwrights exceed the usual boundaries of the epilogue. They used Mr. Bayes' *civility, insinuation,* and *good language* to provoke a response more complex, more disturbing perhaps, but finally more valuable.

NOTES

1. There are useful studies of the Restoration audience by Harold Love, "Who were the Restoration Audience," *YES,* 10 (1980), 21–44, and Arthur H. Scouten and Robert D. Hume, " 'Restoration Comedy' and its Audiences, 1660–1776," *YES,* 10 (1980), 45–69. James Sutherland's "Prologues, Epilogues and Audience in the Restoration Theatre," in *Of Books and Humankind: Essays and Poems Presented to Bonamy Dobrée,* ed. John Butt (London: Routledge and Kegan Paul, 1964), pp. 37–54, is an excellent study. There are additional helpful accounts by Mary E. Knapp, *Prologues and Epilogues of the Eighteenth Century* (New Haven: Yale University Press, 1961), and *Rare Prologues and Epilogues: 1642–1700,* ed. Autrey Nell Wiley (1940; rpt. Port Washington, New York: Kennikat Press, 1970). Also of use are William Bradford Gardner, *The Prologues and Epilogues of John Dryden A Critical Study* (New York: Columbia University Press, 1951), Emmett L. Avery, "Rhetorical Patterns in Restoration Prologues

and Epilogues," in *Essays in American and English Literature Presented to Bruce Robert McElderry, Jr.* (Athens OH: Ohio University Press, 1967), 221–37. David M. Vieth's concise and most useful study, "The Art of the Prologue and Epilogue: A New Approach Based on Dryden's Practice," *Genre* 5 (1972), 271–92, should also be consulted.

2. Sutherland, 42.
3. Love, *passim*. This is very much the point of Love's article.
4. "An Essay of Dramatic Poesy," in *Essays of John Dryden*, ed. W. P. Ker, I (1926; rpt. New York: Russell & Russell, 1961), 72.
5. *The Way of the World*, ed. Kathleen M. Lynch (Lincoln: University of Nebraska Press, 1965), I.ii. 200–207.
6. *The Man of Mode*, ed. W. B. Carnochan (Lincoln: University of Nebraska Press, 1966), 4–5.
7. Love, 25.
8. Love, 25.
9. *The Country Wife*, ed. Thomas H. Fujimura (Lincoln: University of Nebraska Press, 1965), V.iv. 408–11.
10. *Amphitryon*, ed. Earl Miner, George R. Guffey, Franklin B. Zimmerman, vol. 15, of *The Works of John Dryden*, (Berkeley: University of California Press, 1976).
11. "Dryden's Comedies," in *John Dryden*, ed. Earl Miner (London: G. Bell & Sons, 1972), 54.
12. *Amphitryon*, 471.
13. *The Wives' Excuse or Cuckolds Make Themselves*, ed. Ralph R. Thornton (Wynnewood, Penn.: Livingston Publ. Co., 1973), 125.

Ideology and Dramatic Form: The Case of Wycherley

James Thompson

It is my contention that the financial and political structure of the Restoration theatre during the reign of Charles II led to a peculiarly hostile relationship between playwright and audience. Hostility and distrust are manifested in the overly aggressive prologues and epilogues, as well as in confusing, dislocating, and disturbing plays, espousing unpalatable ideas that writers attempted to force upon uncooperative audiences. In turn, the messy, unbalanced, and unpredictable forms of tragi-comedy, split-plot play, and even semi-opera are determined by an aesthetic of indirection, surprise, and trickery. What appear to us as hopelessly disunified and inexplicably contradictory plays, encompassing poetical justice and the interpositions of Providence, along with cynical doctrines of hedonistic appetite, reflect ideological conflict in the years between England's two revolutions. The drama of William Wycherley provides a brief example of these forces, as his plays get demonstrably more aggressive.

To judge from contemporary accounts, it would seem that no play was ensured a smooth production on the Restoration stage. Diaries and stage histories detail the many ways performances were disrupted, leading one to conclude that stage personnel were continually and often unsuccessfully engaged in a struggle to capture and hold the audience's attention. Spectators habitually fell asleep, talked, hissed, damned the players or the play, threw fruit, or rioted.[1] For their performances on and off the stage, the players, on occasion, were beaten, imprisoned, or run through.[2] Playwrights were in less immediate danger, for their plays could absorb most of the audience's hostility. But dependent as they were upon the volatile humor of playgoers, poets were often less than appreciative in their dedications, apologies, and epilogues. Shadwell's scorn of theatregoers is typical:

> They never read, and scorn all those that write.
> They only come the boxes to survey,
> Laugh, roar and bawl, but never hear the play;
> In monkey's tricks they pass the time away.[3]

Contemptuous of the taste as well as the conduct of those he writes for, Dryden complains that his comedies were not vulgar enough to be popular:

> Low comedy especially requires, on the writer's part, much of conversation with the vulgar . . . [which] confirms me in my opinion of slighting popular applause, and of contemning that approbation which these very people give, equally with me, to the zany of a mountebank . . . a true poet often misses of applause because he cannot debase himself to write so ill as to please his audience.[4]

In theory, preface or prologue, like a classical exordium, ought humbly to elicit the good opinion of the audience, yet in this period direct addresses to the audience are more often marked by hostility than by humility.[5] If poets expect their works to be damned, patrons seem to expect to be bored; we are told again and again that the poets envy the wits, while the wits envy the poets. In short, the relationship between poet and theatre patron in this period is not a harmonious one but rather is characrterized on both sides by distrust, hostility, and violence.

The literary mode of production aggravates, if not determines, this uncomfortable situation.[6] As is well known, Charles II took an unprecedented interest in the theatre.[7] His patentees, Sir William Davenant and Thomas Killigrew, were courtiers, and no mere bureaucratic Office of the Revels controlled them: Charles himself mediated in such difficulties as labor disputes. The closeness and affection that Charles felt for the theatre paradoxically led to a certain license, for he was as tolerant as he was interested and powerful. If he intervened directly in political or personal affairs of the stage, he also allowed the monopolies relative economic freedom. Thus, the Restoration theatre contains elements of both the vestigial feudal relationship between aristocratic patron and his artistic producer, as well as the bourgeois independence from patronage that Pope was to point the ways toward. Direct royal intervention in theatrical matters during Charles's reign may indicate a last, exaggerated flourish of an eroding patronage system. The production of plays falls in between the control of patrons and the control of theatre managers. Where in the Elizabethan and Jacobean theatres, playwrights were paid a flat fee per play, Restoration playwrights were paid from within and without the theatre: from third day receipts and/or from patrons and publishers. This indefinitely controlled system, which is at once highly competitive but within a highly controlled market, evolved during the first decade of the Restoration, and can be said to mediate between the plays' representation of ideology and the massive economic changes that took place during the seventeenth century. If in the 1670s and 1680s plays indicated some perceptible shift away from conservative, aristocratic, providentialist values, toward values of individualism and initiative, these plays reflect the changes consolidated in the Glorious Revolution of 1688.

For writers, three independent sources of income can promote confusion of allegiance. At the least, the diversity suggests that playwrights were not entirely dependent upon pleasing the playhouse audience. For courtiers especially, "the Mob of Gentlemen who wrote with Ease,"[8] pleasing the single royal patron could be far more rewarding than satisfying the rest. Perhaps the literary judgment of the two classes was rarely in conflict, but gentlemen authors like Boyle, Buckingham, Etherege, Sedley, and Wycherley could always say that they were content to please their own class, the gentility in the boxes. Writes the Earl of Rochester:

> I loathe the rabble; 'tis enough for me
> If Sedley, Shadwell, Shepard, Wycherley,
> Goldolphin, Butler, Buckhurst, Buckingham,
> And some few more, whom I omit to name,
> Approve my sense: I count their censure fame.[9]

It is impossible to determine how much the desire for recognition, approval, or simple court preferment weighed with aristocratic poets, but they were at least financially, if not socially, better prepared to face public disapprobation than were professional poets like Dryden and D'Urfey. My case in point is Wycherley, who, in fact, spurned one source of income from his plays: two of his plays have no dedication and the other two are dedicated to his mistress and to a notorious bawd, a trick that Dryden never could have afforded. Whatever mixture of needs drew him to the stage, the gentleman author appears to be indeterminately dependent upon audience approval: too much to be indifferent, enough to be resentful.

Writing as sublimated hostility may sound suspiciously Swiftian, but I would argue that here it is not due either to personality or to the genre of satire: in this case, aggression toward the audience is the consequence of the particular historical situation of a class of writers. Where Swift adapts a hostile posture of "savage indignation," that is, the traditional satiric persona of Juvenal, here hostility is a precondition of writing, where author faces an audience whom he cannot respect nor can hope to win respect from and vice versa.[10] In such a rhetorical situation, no writer can proceed by direct audience appeal or obvious modes of persuasion such as compliment, but rather by indirection, confusion, and surprise, for this is an audience that can only be entrapped into approval. The need to cozen the audience is overdetermined, by the economic conditions of the theatre, by class structure and court patronage, by aesthetic ideology of literary fame and worth, and by individual desires for approval, all of which result in attempts to move the audience against its will.

These conditions of rampant distrust help shape the rhetoric of prologues and epilogues and of the plays themselves. The speaker of the epilogue projects a heterogeneous audience, distinguishing those listeners whose true taste will approve of the performance, from those rowdy vulgarians in the pit and the whores' gallery. (Such class polarization will be seen in the form of split-plot plays, as well as in the political allegories of the 1680's.) The dynamics of socially differentiated appeal is illustrated in the stratified response to *The Plain Dealer,* when, as John Dennis reports, the courtier class imposed its judgment upon the others:

> There was Villers Duke of Buckingham, Wilmot Earl of Rochester, the late Earl of Dorsett, the Earl of Mulgrave . . . Mr. Savil, Mr. Buckley, Sir John Denham, Mr. Waller &c. When these or the Majority of them Declard themselves upon any new Dramatick performance, the Town fell Immediately in with them. . . . And when upon the first representation of the *Plain Dealer,* the Town, as the Authour has often told me, appeard Doubtfull what Judgment to Form of it; the foremention'd gentlemen by their loud approbation of it, gave it both a sudden and a lasting reputation.[11]

My point here is not to rephrase old and questionable clichés about class conflict between the court and the citizens, but to look anew at the confusion of response that Dennis describes. Whatever the immediate causes, Restoration playwrights were unaccustomed to docile audiences, from whom they could expect polite cooperation. As Robert Hume has shown, these were not audiences on whom a single formula could be successfully repeated season after season.[12] The theatrical career of Wycherley, for example, rises and falls like a sine wave: his first play, *Love in a Wood,* was extremely popular, his second, *The Gentleman*

Dancing-Master, a disaster. Subsequently, *The Country Wife* succeeded, while *The Plain Dealer* met with confusion. In point of fact, no Restoration playwright met with success after success: not one playwright ever figured out how to please the audience all of the time.

There are many factors involved in the successful run of a play, not the least of which is having friends in high places. The personal and literary quarrels of poets and their patrons cannot all be attributed to politics and economics. Nevertheless, writers never tired of observing that this is a factious age, an age of unprecedented political instability, and in the 1680's of the Popish Plot, the Exclusion Crisis, and Monmouth's Rebellion, the factionalism and violence of the theatre becomes openly political. Ravenscroft draws the explicit parallel in the epilogue to *Dame Dobson* (1683):

> And Criticks here with the same spirit stickle
> For Liberty, as Whiggs in Conventicle.
> 'Gainst Sheriffs and Poets equally you Baul,
> You Riot in a Play-House, they't Guild-Hall.

The prologue and epilogues to Dryden and Lee's *Duke of Guise* (1682) are astonishingly direct and aggressive, attacking Whigs, Trimmers, and all those who seek to "Make *London* independent of the Crown; / A Realm apart; the Kingdom of the Town."[13] This is offered, not to the court, but in a public London theatre. While this audience was considerably more homogeneous than in the Elizabethan theatre, it was by no means a "court coterie."[14] Pepys writes of the audience at Lincoln's Inn Fields on January 1, 1667/8:

> Here a mighty company of citizens, prentices, and others; and it makes me observe that when I begin to be able to bestow a play on myself, I do not remember that I saw so many by half of the ordinary prentices and mean people in the pit, and 2s-6d apiece, as now; I going for several years no higher then the 12d, and then the 18d places, and though I strained hard to go

in then when I did—so much the vanity and prodigality
of the age is to be observed in this perticular.[15]

Pepy's observations of "the age" indicate that this mixture of
classes was not unusual. Even if the admission was high enough
to exclude the lower classes (save those with business to trans-
act, prostitutes and orange sellers), the leisured, property hold-
ers left over do not constitute a homogeneous class with common
interests. The latter group still includes royalists and parlia-
mentarians, aristocrats and commoners, monopolists, courtiers,
landed gentry, and merchants. In effect, the public theatres of
the second and third decades of the Restoration represent the
antithesis of earlier court theatre, exemplified in the masque:

> The masque presents the triumph of an aristocratic
> community; at its center is a belief in the hierarchy
> and a faith in the power of idealization. . . . As a genre,
> it is the opposite of satire; it educates by praising, by
> creating roles for the leaders of society to fill.[16]

Charles II could never recreate the absolute autocracy of his
father, and as a result, Wycherley addresses a far more mixed
audience than Jonson wrote for, an audience without center, and
without unifying interests, political, financial, or aesthetic. It is
impossible to satisfy any one section of this crowd at the expense
of another, which may explain why Wycherley's plays come to
insult the entire social range, from aristocracy to commoners. It
is as if in the decade between the relative peace of the 1660s and
the open violence of the 1680s, each class of theatregoers could
be contented only with seeing its enemies attacked, even if they
themselves were satirized. Contemporary remarks on Wycherley's plays praise them for the breadth of attack; Dryden writes
of *The Plain Dealer* as one of the "most general, and most useful
satires that has ever been presented on the English theatre."[17]
Evelyn too writes as if no one or class is left unmauled: "As long
as men are false and women vain. / While gold continues to be
virtue's bane / In pointed satire Wycherley shall reign."[18]

In the development of Wycherley's dramatic career from
1671 to 1676, the object of his attack grows larger and more

diffuse, while his plays move toward more and more untenable conclusions.[19] Wycherley's first play is a relatively straight-forward and conventional intrigue comedy, where we know whom to approve and whom to disapprove. But as he experiments with more and more flawed characters, moving the most extreme figures from the periphery to the center of his plays, it becomes difficult to identify the protagonist with any certainty. With the exception of his second play, Wycherley employs two male leads, Valentine and Ranger, Harcourt and Horner, and Manly and Freeman, pairs of characters who contrast noble idealism and rakish expediency.[20] *In Love in a Wood,* their rivalry is easily resolved, as the two figures divide attractive and complementary qualities and share the audience's approval. Later they come to work against each other, calling each other's values into question, exposing one another's deficiencies, and ultimately denying one another the possibility of heroism.[21] Harcourt could easily be the protagonist of *The Country Wife* in the absence of Horner, and vice versa, but when they are together, we cannot fully approve of either. Similarly, in *The Plain Dealer,* Freeman undermines Manly, while Manly undermines Freeman, leaving no unqualified values. The play takes every opportunity to demand that we approve of Manly, but his actions give us insufficient reason.[22] Story and plot work against each other here in such a way that the story denies the response that the plot attempts to elicit.[23] (That Wycherley took to calling himself "Manly" only confuses the issue more.) By the time we get to Manly, the basic character types defined originally by Ranger and Valentine have become far less attractive. The more idealistic characters seem more and more out of place and incapable of action, while the pragmatic characters seem more harsh, cruel, and greedy. While Manly has obviously descended from Valentine, Manly also has inherited his jealous temper from the maddened, exaggerated, vengeful, and violent Pinchwife. Both Pinchwife and Manly are types of Malvolio or Jacques, in Northrop Frye's terms, the *agroikos* figure who is driven out of society in order to reassert comic festivity.[24] Adapting this figure from Moliere's *Le Misanthrope,* Wycherley perversely rewards his Alceste, Manly, with Célimène, while leaving Philante, Freeman, dangling, unfulfilled, and forgotten. (To use Frye's generic scheme, these comedies move further away from the romantic mode toward irony and satire.) Wycherley's fools, for example, range from the silly and amusing Daperwit of *Love in a Wood,* through Monsieur and Sparkish, who are noticeably more malicious, to *The Plain Dealer*'s Novel, whom we find characteristically laughing at "a wooden Leg" (II, i, 499).[25] *The Plain Dealer* is altogether darker and more violent, more questionably comic than the other plays, as here with Manly's sadism: "her Lips—but I must not think of 'em more—but yet they are such as I cou'd kiss,—grow to—and then tear off with my teeth, grind 'em into mammocks, and spit 'em into her Cuckolds face" (IV, i, 113–116).

Even before Manly, Wycherley poses problematic protagonists, particularly Horner, who is, in turn, clever, witty, likable, vicious, and despicable. He dominates the stage, manipulating and out-smarting all of the other characters, bending them to his will and exposing their weaknesses. But after Horner triumphs over them all, the last scene of the play is designed to show his inadequacy. As many point out, this is a disturbing scene, with the violence of Pinchwife, who draws his sword on his wife, the lack of poetic justice (Hume observes that Horner could easily be rendered impotent in fact) and the wholly unsatisfactory conclusion in which they all agree to believe what they know to be lies: [26] "For my own sake fain I wou'd all believe. / Cuckolds like Lovers shou'd themselves deceive" (V, iv, 410–1). Horner, whom we have admired for most, if not all of the play, has the last word: "But he who aims by women to be priz'd, / First by the men you see must be despiz'd" (V, iv, 417–8). Such a choice leaves us in an uncomfortable position, for either we must align ourselves with Lady Fidget and Margery or we must find Horner despicable. That we may find him despicable is made possible by the nasty turn of this last scene. Just prior to Horner's unsettling confrontation with Alithea, Horner's ladies, "the virtuous Gang" (V, ii, 90), gather together to drink, gamble, sweat, boast, and talk lecherously. The ugliness of this gathering, which parallels an earlier gathering of Horner's former friends, Harcourt and Dorilant, serves to remind us that Horner has given up everything, including friendship, in his pursuit of these dubiously attractive women. This is the first time that we can see clearly what Horner has argued all along: that sexual pleasure is the only good. Hitherto, Horner has passed himself off as the only alternative to the inadequate husbands of the play, setting up an opposition between their vacuous respectability and his offer of sexual service.[27] Certainly Horner is far more attractive than Pinchwife or Sir Jaspar, but in this last scene he is forced into opposition against Harcourt as well. When Harcourt offers himself as a husband who can provide both sexual service and respectability, we finally see that Horner is no better than Pinchwife, for Horner's insistence that sex is the only good is as equally one-sided, as equally defective, as Pinchwife's insistence that reputation is the only good. Our change in attitude toward Horner is precipitated by his confrontation with Alithea, the play's most naive and idealistic character. Until this last scene, Wycherley has been careful to keep these two extremes of idealism and expediency apart, but in the end they collide and Horner is forced to choose. Wycherley emphasizes the difficulty of the choice, and in so doing, he forces us all to reexamine our allegiances, in effect, forcing us to choose sides too. Nothing emerges from this confrontation unqualified; Alithea appears foolishly and even dangerously naive, while Horner comes out, not chastened, but as rapacious and appetitive as ever. In the end, we are left feeling that we have been duped into admiring and trusting one whom we should have known was untrustworthy.

The dramatic turn with which *The Country Wife* closes is usually ascribed to the mode of satire or the theme of hypocrisy, yet it is the very form of Wycherley's plot that brings about this peripetia. Through Act Four, Harcourt's pursuit of Alithea is presented as nothing more than an extraneous subplot, and Alithea never speaks with Horner before their confrontation. By working a distinct plot and subplot, Wycherley can suspend key issues and then force the audience to address them and choose sides. Wycherley uses the multiplot form to manipulate audience response even more forcefully in *The Plain Dealer*, which can be seen as an especially well-integrated split-plot play.[28] Like *Marriage a-La-Mode*, *The Plain Dealer* consists of two related but distinct plots: one is elevated, full of idealistic characters who display grand passion, noble sacrifice, and sometimes speak in blank verse; the other is an inversion of the noble generosity espoused in the courtship plot, and is filled with low life and crude insult, bordering on farce. Though Manly's plot has humorous elements, it is essentially serious, while Freeman's plot is consistently comical; Manly is so idealistic that he always demands the best from men and so is usually disappointed, while Freeman is much more realistic and so is not surprised but rather amused by frailty. Their continuous conflict of response governs the play, as Manly and Freeman disagree about everything, particularly the pageant displayed before them in Westminster Hall. Act Three contrasts their views of justice, as the play as a whole comes to question the place of justice, perfection, and idealism in an imperfect world. This question is not an idle one, for it reflects all of the real problems of audience and patronage discussed above: indeed, the split-plot should be seen as a form determined by political and class polarization. The heroic plot reflects the hegemonic view of order based on faith and trust in Providence and the divine right of kings. In social relationships, it celebrates the values of devotion, generosity, and sacrifice; in politics and economics, monopolies and hierarchical authority rule. This view is set in violent conflict with Freeman's individualism and free enterprise. The lower plot rewards aggression, independence, self-reliance, initiative, and social mobility.[29] As a younger son, Freeman looks forward to cash, not backwards to familial land. Manly, bereft of his ship and command, is paralyzed until the naval authorities see fit to give him another post. Freeman does not even acknowledge authority, but immediately sets up his own business, selling his services on the open market.

Wycherley's resolution to this conflict is no simple, straightforward validation of one over the other, though just such validation is what we expect of this form. In *Marriage à-La-Mode,* for example, Dryden ever so carefully resolves his polarization with a slight, though gracious, deference to the values of the court. Despite their overwhelming self-interest, Rhodophil and Palamede instantly respond to their king: "no Subject e'r can meet / a nobler fate, than at his Soverign's feet" (V, i, 501–2). In *The Plain Dealer,* however, we do not know what to expect, largely because no character or set of values has been privileged. Manly has done nothing to deserve the reward of Fidelia's love or Freeman's friendship, while Freeman has certainly worked hard enough to win the Widow Blackacre, but she is no reward. If, in the interests of symmetry, we expect Freemen to marry Eliza, they never even speak to one another. On the other hand, because Manly stands higher in the military, social, and literary hierarchy, we would expect his idealism to be validated over Freeman's self-interest. Yet in the end, Manly's values are attacked from within, as he is defeated by internal doubt and inadequacy, without, in turn, validating Freeman's: Freeman's expedience is shown to be corrupt, but Manly's idealism is impossible. The fairy tale ending by which both are rewarded does nothing toward resolving the problems that the plot has posed. It is as if Wycherley has dragged us to the heart of a crux that he has no intention of solving. The split-plot is used to present two equally unsatisfying protagonists, while it refuses compromise. The very character of Manly poses the problem of idealism in an age of pragmatism and trimming; in all but condemning and exiling him, Wycherley suggests that his idealists are vestigial and cannot live in the real world any longer. In Freeman, Wycherley presents an even nastier picture: in his preditory acquisitiveness, we are forced to see the values celebrated by this age. By our lives and our conduct, we deny Manly's principles, making us all Olivias, Novels, or, at best, Freemans. Rammed down the throat of an unwilling audience is the galling message that this is an age that has made idealism, highmindedness, and heroism look stupid, impractical, and ossified. In his last play, Wycherley does not simply polarize the classes with an appeal to the educated and a snub to the vulgar. Rather, he has peopled *The Plain Dealer* with no one whom the audience can approve, a trick that Otway will use with great success in his horrific comedies of the eighties.

In his last two plays then, Wycherley removes the middle ground, the easy compromises, the comfortable places where audiences so like to rest. It would be very nice to see Harcourt and Alithea as representing the Horatian mean, the locus of value in *The Country Wife*, but they are too dull and weak to support this interpretation. Eliza in *The Plain Dealer* is similarly honest and attractive, more so than anyone else in the play, but still she remains minor and forgotten in the end. These uncomplicated characters are atypical, because Wycherley is more interested in his ambiguous characters, paradoxical plots, and labyrinthine scenes that entice the audience into irresolvable contradictions. *The Plain Dealer*'s penultimate scene epitomizes all of these devious maneuvers. Here, the Widow Blackacre and her professional liars, the Knights of the Post, pause in their perjury to complain about breach of promise:

Widow.	Ay, that's all, Gentlemen; and so, here's to you again.
2 Knight.	Nay, 'twou'd do one's heart good to be forsworn for you: you have a conscience in you wayes, and pay us well.
1 Knight.	You are in the right on't, Brother; one wou'd be damn'd for her, with all ones heart.
2 Knight.	But there are Rogues, who make us forsworn for 'em; and when we come to be paid, they'll be forsworn too, and not pay us wages which they promis'd with Oaths sufficient.
1 Knight.	Ay, a great Lawyer, that shall be nameless, bilkt me too.
Widow.	That was hard, methinks, that a Lawyer shou'd use Gentlemen Witnesses no better.
2 Knight.	A Lawyer! d'ye wonder a Lawyer sou'd do't? I was bilk'd of a Reverend Divine, that preaches twice on Sundayes, and prayes half an hour still before dinner.
Widow.	How? a Conscientious Divine, and not pay people for damning themselves! Sure then, for all his talking, he does not believe damnation. But come, to our business: pray be sure to imitate exactly the flourish at the end of this name.

(V, ii, 389–406).

With its wonderful tone of injured innocence, this scene suggests the proverb, "there is honor among thieves," though while they fear being defrauded, they are engaged in fraud themselves. Even so, these petty liars are dwarfed by the grand liars, lawyers and the Swiftian divine, who preaches, prays, corrupts, and cheats all in one afternoon. But, at the same time, should we speculate about relative honesty, we have been seduced into believing liars. We have, in short, been drawn into the famous Cretan liar paradox: says the Cretan, "all Cretans are liars." In this one scene, Wycherley poses radical, unstable irony.[30] The conversation expands, entangling, apparently, all of society in its corruption, asserting, in effect, that only those outside the law are honest. But of course this conclusion is dependent upon our willingness to believe the testimony of proven liars. Once again, we are all Alitheas, fools for believing Horner honorable or liars truthful.

It is in the tremendously disturbing plays of the late 1670s and early 80s that this problematic relationship between play-wright and audience reaches almost hysterical proportions. From *The Plain Dealer* in 1676 to *The Atheist* in 1683 runs a string of plays designed to assault their viewers with unpalatable cynicism. The form as well can be related to the literary mode of production. The messiness of much of Restoration drama reflects the premium paid for novelty, variety, and surprise, which holds for sensational and spectacular semi-operas as well as for the reduplications of split-plot and multi-plot plays. If, as I have argued, these plays are designed to work on a fragmented audience pulling in several directions at once, then the multi-plicity of incidents and plots and characters is not used to cele-brate the formal properties of balance and symmetry, as Laura Brown has argued, but rather are used to keep the audience off center.[31] Balance, symmetry, unity, and resolution are the least desirable formal features in this period; as Dryden snarls in the preface to *Secret Love,* "I would tell the reader that it is regular, according to the strictest of dramatic laws, but that is a commen-dation which many of our poets now despise, and a beauty which our common audiences do not easily discern."[32] The very last drama to succeed on the Restoration stage would be the regular-ity and restraint of Corneille and Racine: what did succeed was Elkannah Settle's untidy *The Empress of Morocco.* If we may glorify these practices with the term, this is essentially an "af-fective" aesthetic, as Eric Rothstein has argued, where drama is defined by the emotions it generates in its audience.[33] And yet Aubrey Williams is certainly correct to point out that a purely affective theory of drama is inconsistent with the hegemonic aesthetic ideology of the period, with its overwhelming emphasis on didacticism and Providence, concepts employed to legitimate and reinforce presently constituted order.[34] Playwrights must answer to these two forces, and if they stoop to affective drama, they are all willing to blame their audience, as does Cibber: It is "to the vitiated and low Taste of the Spectator, that the Corruptions of the Stage . . . (of what kind soever) have been owing." Cibber goes on to bemoan the spectators' refusal to be instructed:

> However gravely we may assert, that profit ought al-
> ways to be inseparable from the Delight of the Theatre;
> nay admitting that the Pleasure would be heightened
> by the uniting them; yet, while Instruction is so little
> the concern of the Auditor, how can we hope that so
> choice a Commodity will come to a Market where there
> is so seldom a Demand for it?[35]

Cibber's marketing metaphor is suggestive; while the monopolistic privileges of theatre patents could, through royal patronage, control competition, they could not force the clientele to buy. And so the economic structure of the theatre causes its drama to mirror the adversary relationship between King and Commons, with the playwright caught betwixt and between.

NOTES

1. For the first decade of the Restoration, Pepys's diary remains the fullest and most vivid picture of life in the pit. For a thorough collection of complaints about audience behavior, see Montague Summers, *The Restoration Theatre* (1934; rpt. New York: Humanities Press, 1964), 67–81.
2. See, for example, the effect of off-stage violence on the career of Mrs. Bracegirdle, in Stoddard Lincoln, "Eccles and Congreve: Music and Drama on the Restoration Stage," *Theatre Notebook* 18, (1963), 7–18. For a much more elaborate study of the relationship between on and off-stage behavior of actors, see Jackson I. Cope, "*The Constant Couple:* Farquhar's Four-Plays-in-One," *ELH,* 41 (1974), 477–93.
3. Epilogue to Lewis Maidwell's *The Loving Enemies* (1680), 11. 9–12.
4. Preface to *An Evening's Love* (1671), in *Of Dramatic Poesy and Other Critical Essays,* 2 vols., ed. George Watson (London: John Dent, 1962), 145, 146.
5. For a brief survey of the form, see David M. Vieth, "The Art of the Prologue and Epilogue," *Genre,* 5 (1972), 271–92.

6. I employ here Terry Eagleton's theory of the literary mode of production from *Criticism and Ideology* (1976; rpt. London: Verso Editions, 1980), 44–63.
7. On these matters of royal control, the best summary is still Emmett L. Avery and Arthur H. Scouten, *The London Stage 1660–1700, A Critical Introduction* (Carbondale: Southern Illinois University Press, 1968), particularly xxi-xxx. More recent work on theater management, finances, and audience is conveniently summarized in the collection of essays, *The London Theatre World 1660–1800,* ed. Robert D. Hume (Carbondale: Southern Illinois University Press, 1980).
8. Alexander Pope, "Epistle to Augustus," 1. 108.
9. "An Allusion to Horace," 11. 120–24. *The Complete Poems of John Wilmont, Earl of Rochester,* ed. David M. Vieth (New Haven: Yale University Press, 1968). Rochester is referring to private poetry and not public theater, but such class-conscious criticism is evident in and of all forms of Restoration literature.
10. Speech act theorists maintain that discourse is based upon cooperation, as in Grice's Cooperative Principle: "Make your contribution such as is required at the stage at which it occurs, by the accepted purpose or direction of the talk-exchange in which you are engaged." (Quoted from Mary Louis Pratt, *Toward a Speech Act Theory of Literary Discourse* [Bloomington: Indiana University Press, 1977], 153.) "Accepted purpose" involves four maxims which say, in brief, 'be as informative, true, relevant, and perspicuous as is required.' Literary works conventionally "flout" or "blatantly fail to fulfill" these maxims and yet leave the Cooperative Principle intact, because, like a court fool, the poet has special license to deviate from the rules (Pratt, 215). Shakespeare's Chorus in *Henry the Fifth* can bend the rules, just as Sterne's Tristram can trick and amuse his readers, but no such happy relationship exists when the audience is liable to hiss, damn, or riot: in this context, speech acts are characterized by distrust, and the only principle at work is uncooperative. Then, the values of information, truth, relevance, and perspicuity are replaced with indirection, confusion, surprise, and entrapment.
11. *The Critical Works of John Dennis,* 2 vols., ed. E. Niles Hooker (Baltimore: Johns Hopkins University Press, 1939), II, 277.
12. Robert D. Hume, *The Development of English Drama in the Late Seventeenth Century,* (Oxford: Clarendon Press, 1976), 10–19.
13. *The Poems and Fables of John Dryden,* ed. James Kinsley, (Oxford: Oxford University Press, 1958), 298.
14. A great deal has been written on Restoration theater audiences, the most recent by Harry William Pedicord, "The Changing Audience," in Hume, *London Theatre World,* 236–52. In *Development of English Drama,* Hume concludes, and I concur, that "there never was a genuinely *dominant* court coterie, even though court patronage was important" 28. In "The Restoration Theatre Audience," *PQ,* 45 (1966), 54–61, Emmett L. Avery examines Pepys's evidence, concluding that "the audience contained persons of all ranks and classes."
15. *The Diary of Samuel Pepys,* ed. Robert Latham and Wililam Matthews (Berkeley: University of California Press, 1976), IX, 2.
16. Stephen Orgel, *The Illusion of Power* (Berkeley: University of California Press, 1975), 40.

17. *Of Dramatic Poesy,* I, 99.
18. Quoted from Bonamy Dobrée, *Restoration Comedy 1660–1720* (Oxford: University Press, 1924), 82.
19. Rose Zimbardo best follows Wycherley's development. *Wycherley's Drama* (New Haven: Yale University Press, 1965).
20. I must admit that I am unable to fit Wycherley's second play, *The Gentleman Dancing-Master,* into this schema; it is anomalous in many ways, an experiment that failed and was not repeated.
21. In a recent study of Dryden, Derek Hughes has suggestively argued that the heroic plays are designed to assert "the disparity between Herculean aspiration and human reality." *Dryden's Heroic Plays* (Lincoln: University of Nebraska Press, 1981), 2.
22. Ian Donaldson clearly demonstrates that Wycherley uses resources such as the dramatis personae description to present Manly favorably. *The World Upside Down* (Oxford: Clarendon Press, 1970), 101–5.
23. This distinction is drawn from Victor Shklovsky, "Sterne's Tristram Shandy: Stylistic Commentary," in *Russian Formalist Criticism, Four Essays,* trans. Lee T. Lemon and Marion J. Reis (Lincoln: University of Nebraska Press, 1965), 27–57.
24. *Anatomy of Criticism* (Princeton: Princeton University Press, 1957), 175–76.
25. All quotations are from *The Plays of William Wycherley,* ed. Arthur Friedman (Oxford: Clarendon Press, 1979).
26. Hume, *The Development of English Drama,* 99.
27. Here, I differ with David Vieth who argues that Horner is intended to represent an attractive alternative to the play's inadequate husbands. "Wycherley's *The Country Wife:* An Anatomy of Masculinity," *PLL,* 2 (1966), 335–50.
28. In "Dryden's Joke on the Courtiers in *Marriage a-La-Mode,*" *SCN,* 34 (1967), 5–7, A. N. Okerlund argues interestingly that in this play Dryden uses the juxtaposition of comic and heroic plots to manipulate the audience into discovering "its own moral alignment: its preference for sexual intrigue over spiritual ideals."
29. These sets of values ought not to be regarded as exclusive. Manly, for example, is "tainted" with individualism and desires to free himself from social hierarchies; his self-reliance, however, is explicitly one of the qualities that he must abandon in the end.
30. "Stable" and "Unstable" are Wayne Booth's terms. *A Rhetoric of Irony* (Chicago: University of Chicago Press, 1974).
31. Laura S. Brown, "The Divided Plot: Tragicomic Form in the Restoration," *ELH,* 47 (1980), 67–79. Again in *English Dramatic Form, 1660–1760* (New Haven: Yale University Press, 1981), 30, Brown sees the primary object of multiplot plays as "an aesthetic effect of a neat and symmetrical resolution." My reading of Wycherley and his contemporaries of the 1670s comes much closer to her description of "transitional drama," 69–142.
32. *Of Dramatic Poesy,* I, 104–5.
33. Eric Rothstein, *Restoration Tragedy* (Madison: University of Wisconsin Press, 1966), 3–23.
34. Aubrey L. Williams, *An Approach to Congreve* (New Haven: Yale University Press, 1979), 19–57.
35. *An Apology for the Life of Colley Cibber,* ed. B. R. S. Fone (Ann Arbor: University of Michigan Press, 1968), 67.

Entrapment in Eighteenth-Century Drama from Congreve to Goldsmith

William J. Burling

Scholarly interest in Restoration and eighteenth-century literary entrapment has produced a number of recent studies that have focused mainly on poets and prose writers, such as Swift and Fielding, but did dramatists of the period likewise engage in entrapment? Were dramatists concerned, as David Vieth expresses the issue, with luring the audience "into a response whose intensity seems out of all proportion to its cause," and with creating "awareness rather than knowledge?"[1] By examining two of the best known and frequently taught plays of the period—*The Way of the World* and *She Stoops to Conquer*—I hope to demonstrate that in eighteenth-century drama, from William Congreve to Oliver Goldsmith, entrapment was a significant artistic strategy.

Numerous comic dramatists of the eighteenth century regularly incorporated entrapping segments in their plays, notably

John Gay, Henry Fielding, and Samuel Foote,[2] but others, such as Colley Cibber, Richard Steele, Charles Johnson, and Arthur Murphy seem not to have written with such tactics in mind. After considering several plays of each type, I hope to demonstrate that entrapment in drama is not merely a matter of idiosyncratic artistic inclination, but is an essential technique for the presentation of moral epistemology in many plays. Entrapment at first may seem to be merely a different word for irony, but such an assumption belies an important distinction. Irony operates with the implicit understanding that some members of the audience understand the "real" meaning while others do not; playwright and select members of the audience share certain assumptions and thus mutually enjoy the jokes at the expense of others. In entrapment, however, the author catches the entire audience off guard. Thus the playwright offers a considerable challenge to the audience's interpretive sensibilities, making clear that routine assumptions about art and life will be of no value to the audience. In other words, they must reassess their sense of art and life as recontextualized by the playwright's vision of both. With this important axiom in mind, let us consider a classic of the early eighteenth-century stage.

I

William Congreve's *The Way of the World* is taught so widely (as a result of being anthologized, particularly in the *Norton Anthology of British Literature*)[3] and has received so much critical attention that my suggestion that we have not appreciated the full meaning of this play may appear heretical. Nevertheless, by examining the suppositions and the dialogue of the famous "proviso" scene, I hope to show how Congreve relied upon the techniques of entrapment and how an awareness of his method alters interpretation of the play.

Critics are fond of remarking how well the famous couple of Mirabell and Millamant behaves in Act IV. Martin Price's comment epitomizes this view of the play: "In the famous proviso scene, they are fighting, humorously and banteringly but still generously, for a vision of marriage free from the cant and hypocrisy that surround them. . . ."[4] Price's view is seconded by

Shirley Strum Kenny's claim that "Millamant is not being head-strong in her proviso scene . . . when she shows concern to make sure of her will and pleasure before the ceremony. . . ."[5] But does the dialogue actually support these interpretations? What exactly do Mirabell and Millamant expect from each other? What are their demands? The language of this brief scene is so dazzling and rapid that we must proceed at dead-slow speed and reduce the dialogue to an actual listing of the demands one-by-one.[6] Such an analysis will reveal Congreve's use of entrapment.

Millamant demands to be made "sure of my will and plea-sure," which for her means that she be allowed "to lie abed in a morning as long as I please," and that she and Mirabell not indulge in "nauseous cant" or ride about together in their car-riage. To all of these demands, Mirabell replies that the requests seem "pretty reasonable." Indeed, just so; she is asking for little that she did not already have. But she continues: 1) "to pay and receive visits to and from whom I please"; 2) "to write and receive letters, without interrogation or wry faces on your part"; 3) to "wear what I please"; 4) "to choose conversation with regard only to my own taste"; 5) "to have no obligation . . . to converse with wits that I don't like because they are your acquain-tance . . . or to be intimate with fools, because they may be your relations"; 6) to "come to dinner when I please"; 7) "dine in my dressing room when I'm out of humour"; 8) "To have my closet inviolate"; 9) "To be sole empress of my tea table"; 10) "And lastly, wherever I am, you shall always knock at the door before you come in." Of these demands, however, how many actually address the matters of hypocrisy and cant? At least two seem to liberate Millamant from bondage, i.e., the right to receive whatever visitors she wishes and to correspond without interro-gation (or wry faces). But what of the others? The right to dine alone (especially when out of humour)? To expect Mirabell to knock before entering? When did ladies of this period not have these rights if they chose to assume them?

Mirabell does not agree to all of these demands without counter-proposals. In point-by-point fashion he skips over and thus tacitly agrees to the minor points (knocking, etc.) but he addresses and amends each of Millamant's more important mat-ters as follows: 1) only general acquaintances to be allowed and absolutely no confidantes or "decoy-ducks"; 2) no vizard masks (to ensure that she never attempts to appear anonymously in public); 3) no bawds selling door-to-door to be admitted;[7] 4) no lacing during pregnancy; 5) extensive qualifications to the matter of "sole empress of the tea table," including no hard liquor, no conversation other than "authorized tea-table talk" (i.e., gossip), and no drinking of healths or toasting of fellows.

What is the final score, then in this contest of wit? Mirabell clearly has the upper hand. Millamant resists ever so slightly by remarking "I hate your horrid provisos," to which Mirabell confidently counters, "Then we're agreed." Millamant then signals her assent by stating "I think I must have him." In short, she has "won" precious little other than what she already had. Mirabell gains control over who shall be her friends (general acquaintance only), forbids all schemes of deception (as implied in the matters of the vizards), demands control over the matter of any would-be pregnancy conditions, and specifies to the smallest detail the content of tea-table company, conversation, and refreshments. I need scarcely mention that he will also become master of her fortune (£12,000). *None* of her demands (except that Mirabell act cooly toward her in public) affects *his* behavior whatsoever. *All* of his demands restrict *her* behavior. How can we imagine that Millamant has won any victory?

By way of comparison we may recall the mock proviso scene in Act V.x of Henry Fielding's *The Modern Husband* (1732). Here Lady Charlotte and Captain Bellamant play a game of hard-to-get in which each affects utter indifference to the other while both are actually in love. Lady Charlotte makes outrageous demands, hoping to shock Captain Bellamant, who in turn enthusiastically (and maddeningly) agrees to Lady Charlotte's terms (though at the moment he is not "officially" courting her):

> *Lady Charlotte.* In the first place, then, whenever . . . I marry, I am resolved positively to be mistress of myself; I must have my house to myself, my coach to myself, my servants to myself, my table, time, and company to myself; nay, and sometimes, when I have a mind to be out of humour, my bed to myself.

Captain Bellamant. Right, madam; for a wife and husband
always together, are, to be sure, the flattest company in the
world.
Lady Charlotte. O detestable! Then I will be sure to have
my own humour in every thing; to go, come, dine, dance,
play, sup at all hours, and in whatever company I have a
mind to; and if ever he pretends to put on a grave face upon
my enjoying any one of those articles, I am to burst out in
his face a laughing. Won't that be prodigious pleasant? Ha!
ha! ha!

Captain Bellamant agrees that all of these actions would be
"charming, charming," and they banter on for several more ex-
changes with their little game of cat and mouse.[8] Lady Charlotte's demands are funny precisely because they are so extreme,
i.e., unrealistic; Captain Bellamant's responses are amusing for
the reason that he is so uncritically compliant. The lady's wishes
to control her own life are the stuff of genuinely serious personal
freedom, but the flippant tone of the scene and the conditions
under which she presents her case undercut any claim to legiti-
macy and differ sharply from the tone established by Congreve's
Millamant. Fielding's couple is not serious; Congreve's is much
in earnest, and yet both playwrights are employing entrapment.
    The way Congreve has arranged the content and delivery
of this scene suggests that he intended upon and was successful
in entrapping the audience. We see the whirling of skirts and
coats, the snapping of fans, and the rapid exchange of machine-
gun dialogue. The scene, audiences have long realized, is a verbal tour de force that provides performers with splendid opportunities to strut and puff. We see the action; we hear the exchange;
we see the lovers come to terms; we imagine that they have
"worked out" their differences. In fact, Millamant is madly in
love with Mirabell (he is forbidden fruit to her by her guardian's
decree) and will agree to any of his demands. And, after all, how
can any audience be expected to keep track of each of Millamant's dozen or more points and then compare each of Mirabell's
provisos with those original demands? This overwhelming (and
distracting) of an audience is precisely the way entrapment operates in drama: sight and sound subvert sense. One need only

compare Congreve's proviso scene to one in a play not employing entrapment, such as John Fletcher's *Rule a Wife and Have a Wife* (1624), to recognize that proviso scenes can be written "straight," that is, just for laughs, or they can be designed for serious purposes.

With Congreve's play in mind as a model, we might do well to consider some other famous examples from the eighteenth century, particularly by Gay and Fielding, and examine some plays by Cibber and Steele that do not rely upon entrapment.

II

The notoriety and popularity of *The Beggar's Opera* is so well known as not to need review here. Critics' responses to Gay's satiric strategies, as summarized by Robert D. Hume, can be summarized as "soft," "hard," "message-monger," and "mixed,"[9] but all of these approaches emphasize the *effect* of the satire rather than the *method*. An understanding of Gay's mode of entrapment helps to clarify *how* he produced whatever themes he wished to develop. Virtually any scene in Gay's ballad opera could be analyzed in light of his entrapment strategies, but the opening scene is so clear as to be particularly exemplary.

For the first several minutes of the scene the audience does not, cannot, know that the prosperous looking gentleman before them auditing his account book is none other than a notorious criminal. Even Peachum's opening air, which in fact sets up the thematic agenda for the entire play, does not immediately contradict his ostensibly honest image. Generalized attacks on the corruption of the clergy, the legal profession, and politicians were routine in drama and literature. Nowhere in Air I does Peachum reveal that *his* trade is blatantly illegal. Not until Filch's entrance and his update on the status of Black Moll's trial is Peachum's character revealed. In response to Moll's request for legal assistance, Peachum remarks, "you may satisfy her that I'll soften the Evidence."[10] To a similar request regarding Tom Gagg, Peachum decides otherwise: "A lazy Dog! . . . This is Death without Reprieve. I may venture to Book him" (II, 5). The audience, to its shock, thus learns that Peachum, not the court, decides the fate of these arrested felons. Peachum's subsequent decision respecting Betty Sly— "I'll save her from Transportation, for I can get more by her staying in *England*"—and Filch's assessment of her character— "Without dispute, she is a fine Woman!" (II, 5)—force the audience into the position of being witness to a display of extreme, unmitigated, debased morality as disturbing as it is humorous.

More than a few audience members on reflection were shocked by the play's content and presentation. James Boswell records the ongoing concern from 1775 in his *Life of Johnson*:

> *The Beggar's Opera,* and the common question, whether it was pernicious in its effects, having been introduced;
> *JOHNSON.* As to this matter, which has been very much contested, I myself am of opinion, that more influence has been ascribed to *The Beggar's Opera,* than it in reality ever had; for I do not believe that any man was ever made a rogue by being present at its representation. At the same time I do not deny that it may have some influence, by making the character of a rogue familiar, and in some degree pleasing.[11]

Johnson's reactions highlight well Gay's success in entrapping the audience. The "common question" of the "pernicious" effects of the play is illuminated by Johnson's acute perception that a rogue is made "familiar, and in some degree pleasing." The various scenes and songs are humorous and pleasing to the degree that an audience *separates* itself from the world of crime being presented; likewise the play unsettles an audience that is caught off-guard by and cannot free itself from the disturbing scenes being presented. In either case, the audience constantly finds itself unbalanced. The play's essential technique is to present as commonplace a world and mindset that most of the audience members have never before witnessed. One viewer may squirm while another laughs, but the play relentlessly proceeds to shock and disorient by forcing the spectator into an alien, uncomfortable acceptance: except as a spectator at a play, under what other conditions would a person willingly consent to be a witness to such goings on?

A similar but even more unsettling example of entrapment occurs in Henry Fielding's *The Modern Husband* (1732). The audience is witness to the shockingly immoral activities of the Moderns, a couple that subsists by the husband pimping for his wife. Her hypocrisy and his callous indifference to any matters of morality are summed up in Mr. Modern's remark that "to me virtue has appeared nothing more than a sound, and reputation its echo. Is there not more charm in the chink of a thousand guineas, than in ten thousand praises?" (17). The first several acts of the play require the audience to witness not only the repulsive activities of the Moderns but also the deceitful and even cruel actions of Lord Richly and his following of lowly sycophants. This is not irony: decadent immorality is presented as commonplace. The net effect of these characters grates on audience sensibilities, relieved and countered only somewhat by the forces of virtue headed by Mrs. Bellamant and Lord Richly's heir, Mr. Gaywit. Gaywit, in a stroke of satisfying irony on Fielding's part, undermines a plot to sully the Bellamants' reputation. Morality is upheld, but none of the play is pleasant.

Contemporary audiences found *The Modern Husband* a curious hybrid that both offended and pleased. As Hume recounts, the press attacked the play, but audiences supported the comedy for fourteen nights, bringing to the author considerable financial success.[12] The play achieves its effect, however, at least partially by the unrelieved intensity of the first act. Fielding seeks no balance of vice and virtue; we see only continual and unsettling vice. First Mrs. Modern appears. Ostensibly she is a typical lady of the *beau monde* at her toilet, very much like Pope's Belinda, but we soon learn that she has no interest in paying bills owed to her tradesmen, whom she terms "duns" (14). We next learn of her extensive social calendar, which consists of engagements for playing at cards—i.e., gambling. If to this point we imagine that Fielding is merely criticizing the misguided and shallow world of the *beau monde,* we are soon convinced otherwise upon her husband's entry. Mrs. Modern remarks, "Husband did I say? Sure, the wretch who sells his wife, deserves another name. But I must be civil to him while I despise him" (15). Thus the audience learns, as in the case of *The Beggar's Opera,* that what at first appeared to be one kind of behavior was something quite different indeed.

After the *tete-a-tete* conversation between husband and wife, the scene changes to the residence of Lord Richly, who has been named as one of Mrs. Modern's most important customers. Captain Merit, an excellent army officer, attends Lord Richly's leveé hoping that the peer may help him to obtain a command position. The ostensible workings of patronage and influence seem realistic (if discomforting) until we meet Lord Richly and his company. The conversation quickly turns to discussions of "fine women," and the point is brought home that his lordship has little else on his mind. The scene and first act conclude with Lord Richly's remark, "But great men, justly, act by wiser rules; / A levee is the paradise of fools" (25).

If we have been willing to suspend judgment concerning Lord Richly's character, imagining that he might simply be the cully of Mrs. Modern, we now learn otherwise. The "juster rules" are soon revealed in II.vii as flagrant disregard for common decency and utter contempt of his fellow human beings. Lord Richly has tired of Mrs. Modern and now demands that she assist him in his plans to seduce Mrs. Bellamant. For reasons that are not clear, the contemporary audience, while rightly acknowledging that Lord Richly and Mrs. Modern were a fine slimy pair, were not *offended* by them, imagining the lewd characters as unfortunate blemishes in an otherwise acceptable aristocratic hierarchy.

A decade later in *The Wedding Day* (1743), Fielding presented another lecherer and his female assistant, Millamour and Mrs. Useful. Despite the best comic efforts of David Garrick in the role of Millamour and the fact of this character's utter and complete moral reform by the finale, the audience hated the play.[13] We are left to conclude that either Fielding had a better sense of craftsmanship in respect to entrapment in *The Modern Husband* or that audience tastes had changed over the eleven years, or both. With the exception of *The Wedding Day,* Fielding rarely dabbled with "realistic" social satire after 1732; he turned increasingly to farce, burlesque, and topical satire (often political). The kinds of entrapment he employed in such plays as *The Author's Farce* (revised 1734 version) and *The Historical*

Register for the Year 1736 (1737) resemble more closely the tone and style of *The Beggar's Opera*.

III

Further insight into the nature of entrapment can be seen by a consideration of plays in which the technique is absent, notably in comedies by Colley Cibber and Richard Steele. The most important comedies by these playwrights present either problems of moral reform within marriage or are concerned with courtship. In the first class we have three exceptional plays by Cibber—*Love's Last Shift* (1696), *The Careless Husband* (1704), and *The Provok'd Husband* (with Sir John Vanbrugh, 1728)—and one by Steele—*The Tender Husband* (1705); in the second group we have (among others) the delightful fluff of Cibber's *Love Makes a Man* (1701) and *She wou'd and she wou'd not* (1702) and Steele's exemplary role models in *The Conscious Lovers* (1722). All of these plays were enduring successes throughout the eighteenth century.[14]

In neither class do Cibber or Steele depict scenes that intentionally deceive or irritate the audience. In Cibber's *The Careless Husband,* for example, Lord Charles Easy may at first be depicted as a bad husband, but we have Lady Easy's word that her husband has an "unforgiving heart" and "good nature," while he recognizes her as "the best of wives."[15] The audience knows from the beginning what the outcome will be in this most predictable of plots. The pleasure comes from the circumstances of the reformation. In straight courtship comedies, Cibber has great fun with the prospect of Charino's daughter choosing between Antonio's two wildly different sons in *Love Makes a Man*. In *The Conscious Lovers* the audience is kept in the dark as far as the details of Indiana's foggy past are concerned, and a few tense moments occur when Bevil, Jr., and his friend Myrtle nearly come to swords, but the play derives its appeal from the absolute certainty of a satisfying moral resolution that is never in question. Entrapment is unnecessary in plays delivering fluff or sermons.

IV

I would like now to turn to a play that seems an unlikely candidate for entrapment, being neither a political nor a social satire, *She Stoops to Conquer* (1773), and in so doing offer a few comments on other later eighteenth-century plays. Critical consensus avers that Goldsmith's play is one of the century's greatest comic achievements, but the few critics who choose to discuss the play's content (rather than, as many have done, the sources) are surprisingly casual, starkly limited, or even silent as to the play's specific merits. John Butt, in the widely read *Oxford History of English Literature* volume, finds the play's main interest in the reversal of who chases whom and remarks generally that the play's reputation rests "on the comic invention and originality shown in developing the farcical situation"; Robert H. Hopkins's detailed study of Goldsmith's career omits the play entirely.[16] These critics exemplify the minimal assessments that abound in the critical literature concerning the play.

Two lines of enquiry take Goldsmith seriously; unfortunately, neither argument is given much force by its proponent. The main advocate of Goldsmith as serious dramatist is Ricardo Quintana, in *Oliver Goldsmith* (1967) and "Oliver Goldsmith, Ironist to the Georgians" (1970). Quintana insists on Goldsmith as ironist but provides little in the way of convincing argument, spending most of his attention on the historical circumstances of the play's original production. The only other line of criticism that sees anything other than broad comic humor in *She Stoops* is best (if very minimally) posited by Bernard Harris: "The play is very much about . . . liberation, and Goldsmith managed this by not directly challenging too violently the acceptance of his audience, but by subversion, and by capturing a mood in his own society that . . . remains renewable and available to subsequent experiences in totally different circumstances."[17] This potentially illuminating assessment—particularly on the points of liberation[18] and subversion—ends an essay that begins with the remark, "It is peculiarly senseless to attempt to analyze comedy" (139); and, indeed, Harris provides no discussion whatsoever to develop his contentions. We are thus left with yet another dead end in the way of discussion of Goldsmith as serious comic dramatist. In sum, no one has satisfactorily made the case that the play has any kind of a message.

So why do audiences love *She Stoops*? The explanation always asserts the "obvious": this is a funny farce. Numerous critics thus maintain that Goldsmith felt that he was creating, at least to some extent, a play that reestablished the authority of the "laughing" school of comedy as opposed to the rising sentimental tide that was supposedly choking the stage. Hume has convincingly demonstrated, however, that we have seriously overestimated and misinterpreted Goldsmith's supposed paranoia in the famous "An Essay on the Theatre" concerning the sentimental comedy: sentimental plays constituted a tiny minority of actually staged performances.[19] Nonetheless, Goldsmith himself provides a hint of his own seriousness in the "Essay"; he comments on a specific component of laughing comedy that characterized, for him, the essence of the genre—"ridiculously exhibiting the Follies of the Lower Part of Mankind."[20] Taking his cue, if we posit this premise as necessary for an understanding of *She Stoops to Conquer,* we come away with some conclusions that fly in the face of standard interpretations of the play. While virtually all critics agree that the zany antics of Tony Lumpkin and Mrs. Hardcastle—i.e., low characters—embody much of the play's comic appeal, no one has considered the possibility that the romantic relationship between young Marlow and Kate—also a low character (she is, after all, Tony's half-sister—may be of equal comic value.

The differences in the aims of comedy as one may infer from Goldsmith's remark are quite profound and signal his intentions to play upon audience expectations and to entrap the audience by the very structure of the play. The play ostensibly portrays the comic courtship of a "typical" couple—Charles and Kate—but if we inquire into the crucial matter of social station, we detect a fundamental discrepancy between the relative ranks of the families: Sir Charles Marlow, an hereditary baronet, and his son, Charles, are distinctly of a higher class; Hardcastle is a country squire—respectable, to a relative degree (at least by rural standards) but *not* an aristocrat. Hardcastle tells Kate that the meeting of the young people has been arranged by

agreement with Sir Charles, "my old friend . . . of whom you
have heard me talk so often" (I.i.139).[21] The audience is slickered
in by this very first explanation for the engagement of the couple. Kate may have heard her father "talk so often" of Sir
Charles, but she has never seen either the knight or his son.
The reason? The Hardcastles and the Marlows, in fact, do not
socialize; they are of different levels of society. The friendship is
one that the audience could conceive of as *theoretically* possible,
but upon close examination, the proposed alliance is simply not
credible. We have here a genuine mismatch that nicely demonstrates Goldsmith's use of entrapment.

This play, unlike virtually every other comedy of the century involving the pairing of lovers, is conspicuously silent on
matters of class and wealth. In this play, as far as these points
are concerned, no problems exist whatsoever. Later in the play
when Sir Charles finally appears on the scene, a telling exchange between the fathers occurs:

> *Hardcastle:* . . . Yes, dear friend, this union of our families
> will make our personal friendship hereditary; and tho' my
> daughter's fortune is but small—
> *Sir Charles:* Why, Dick, will you talk of fortune to *me?* My
> son is possessed of more than a competence already, and
> can want nothing but a good and virtuous girl to share his
> happiness and increase it. . . .
>
> (V.i.23–30; 197).

And so the audience is lead to believe that Sir Charles speaks
the truth, that his son needs not money but a virtuous wife. To
what extent is Sir Charles's remark to be accepted as a believ-
able and sufficient response? Essential to my argument here is
our understanding that a *modern* audience would think nothing
of Kate's freedom of choice or the differences in social position,
while an *eighteenth-century* audience would be susceptible to
entrapment. Therefore we must attempt to recover some sense
of courtship and marriage conventions during Goldsmith's day,
a task requiring a brief but necessary digression.

Recent socio-historic studies have shown that marriage options in England were quite flexible within certain general limits and allowed for a fair degree of social mobility. Compared to

other European countries, as Lawrence Stone states the matter, "the English enjoyed greater freedom of choice of a marriage partner . . . than was the case on the Continent."[22] To understand the full dimensions of the marriage issue, however, we need to separate theoretical freedom of choice from practical precedents of propriety and tradition.

In the matter of choice of partners, the play sets up the first laughable violation of custom: the woman has complete freedom while the man has little to say about matters. When Hardcastle assures his daughter, "Depend upon it, child, I'll never control your choice" (I.i.137; 112), he was indeed echoing mainstream attitudes of the time, as convincingly documented by Alan Macfarlane in *Marriage and Love in England 1300–1840* (1986) and aptly expressed in the following passage from the diary of an early eighteenth-century father: "I long since told her I would not compel her to marry, much less to marry one she could not love and so to make her miserable as long as she lives, so leave her entirely to please herself." Such a liberal remark from a half-century *before* Goldsmith's play would seem to indicate that no humour was intended in the plausibility of Kate being personally responsible for her choice of a husband; but our early diarist has a bit more to say on this matter of choice: "all I require is that he be a Gentleman of a competent Estate, one of a good character, and a Catholic."[23] In other words, his daughter may marry whomever she wants from a specified subset of the available population, i.e., men of rank and affluence (and Catholic to boot)—but no mere laborers or tradesmen (or non-Catholics). Young people in eighteenth-century England may have had quite a bit to say about their choice of marriage partners but always *within limits*. Stone sums up the prevailing notion as follows: "freedom of choice can be most easily conceded by parents . . . when there is little chance that the children will come into contact with members of a lower social class" (316). But what were the possibilities of marriage *between* classes? Here we must consider matters of class, wealth, and tradition.

Scholarly opinion on the subject of inter-class marriage is split. Macfarlane asserts, "intermarriage between different ranks was very common" (257) and provides some striking examples, yet J. A. Sharpe contends, "marriage between peers and commoners was very unusual" during the years 1550–1760,[24] a view seconded by Stone's comment that "cross-class marriages were universally condemned in theory and very rare in practice" (394).[25] A somewhat flexible social system offering *opportunities* for intermarriage between classes seems very likely to have existed. Opportunity is not the same, however, as widespread general involvement in such activity, and whatever the actual eighteenth-century statistical norm, each family, of course, worked out its own affairs. The existing data is ambiguous, but the evidence suggests that mixed marriages consisted largely of three situations: 1) younger sons of the upper class (without prospects of inheriting family titles or estates) marrying downward for economic security; 2) younger daughters of the affluent merchant (but non-titled) class marrying downard to a respectable yeoman; 3) daughters of the wealthiest branches of the merchant class marrying upward in a trade-off of money for rank of the kind portrayed by William Hogarth in "Marriage *a-la-mode*" (1745). In addition, studies show that social movement most often took place at the lower edge of the upper crust, at the rank of baronet. This materialistic attitude was widely accepted and even actively promoted. As Macfarlane rightly points out, "there was a mass of literature encouraging people to trade off birth against wealth" (256).

The Charles-Kate affair meets almost none of the requirements for a "plausible" cross-class marriage. He has all of the social advantages, and while his social position does meet one of the criterion for mobility (i.e., the rank of baronet, thus *not* of the rarified upper crust), she brings essentially nothing to their marriage other than her goodness and virtue, and the goodness soon evaporates (of which more later). If we hold Goldsmith to his own logic in his "Essay," then the basis of his play must be "the follies of the *lower* part of mankind" (my italics). Charles cannot be so considered; Tony *and* Kate (and the other Hardcastles) therefore must be the intended comic characters. What could be more of a folly than to attempt to marry a country girl lacking the requisite wealth (and other marriageable amenities) to the son of a wealthy urban baronet?

The key point for our attention, however, remains the *literary* presentation of the situation between Marlow and Kate.

Stone observes that "the literary evidence shows that there was a prolonged public argument during the late seventeenth and eighteenth centuries about a child's freedom of choice in a marriage partner" (280–81). In light of this scholarly assessment concerning marriage for love versus the quest for economic opportunities, a *positive* interpretation of Sir Charles's indifference to Kate's lower social rank and lack of an attractive dowry could be offered as proof of Goldsmith's forward-looking social vision, but such an intepretation deserves close inspection. In the popular literature of the eighteenth century, this "public argument" offers but few precedents for marriage between a poor but virtuous woman and a socially and financially superior man. *Pamela* (1740) springs to mind, but the "Cinderella" aspect of Richardson's story alone, to say nothing of the negative reaction by Henry Fielding,[26] discounts Pamela's marriage to Squire B—— as an impossibility and not one to be seriously advocated as a precedent for other women of Pamela's low station.[27] The public's fascination with story, which sent the novel into five editions the first year, is notable proof of the *novelty* of the idea.

In the drama we find *no* examples of the lopsided social inequity represented in Kate and Charles; in fact, a brief survey of a few of the most popular comedies of the period demonstrates the hegemony of the traditional class status quo. George Farquhar's *The Beaux Stratagem* (1707) portrays the schemes of a "younger brother," the financially strapped Aimwell (and his friend Archer—"two gentlemen of broken fortune"), to marry a wealthy country beauty under false pretense of financial independence and social prestige. When Dorinda learns that Aimwell has neither title nor estate, she remarks, "Matchless Honesty!— Once I was proud, Sir, of your Wealth and Title, but now am prouder that you want it: Now I can shew my Love was justly levell'd, and had no Aim but Love. Doctor, come in."[28] Only a moment later, of course, Aimwell learns that he has inherited his family's extensive fortune and the title of Viscount Aimwell,[29] redeeming him as a suitable husband for the virtuous Dorinda. Perhaps more to the point, *deux ex machina* plot resolution aside, he was *already* a member of an aristocratic family. Dorinda's family would have been disappointed that she married a *poor* member of the upper class, but no one would have faulted her *social* choice.

The case of Charles Johnson's popular *The Wife's Relief* (1713) provides considerable insight about the possibilities for genuinely lasting social improvement through marriage. Sir Tristram, a baronet risen from the cit class, has chosen his nephew Bob Cash as the heir to his fortune ("half a Plumb at least," i.e., £50,000)[30] and his title. His friend Volatil raises a pertinent question, and Sir Tristram's answer reveals much about marriage as represented in drama:

> *Volatil.* Why did you not train him up a Cit, in the Road of your Family—
> *Sir Tristram.* My Nephew's Great-Grandson will be a Citizen again.
> *Volatil.* Again—how so?
> *Sir Tristram.* Why, we Cits, as you call us, tho' we hate Gentlemen, are proud to breed our Children so—but in three Generations they always come back into their Shops—as thus, —We purchase Land, our Gentlemen Children live high and Mortgage, the Grand-Children sell, and the Great-Grand-Children are always Prentices again—
> (16–17)

Sir Tristram's remarks highlight the mobility—upward *and* downward—but the key is, as always, money. Likewise Steele's *The Conscious Lovers* presents an aberrant social mismatch between Bevil, Jr. (a baronet apparent) and the virtuous but apparently social inferior and impoverished Indiana. By play's end, to no audience member's surprise, Indiana's true blood (and wealth) emerge.

While numerous later plays emphasize the value of love in the forming of marriage partnerships, they likewise affirm the general barriers *against* social mobility between classes, confirm the harsh realities of the importance of money, and only rarely question the status quo. Gaywit in Fielding's *The Modern Husband* (1732, discussed at length above) must plot at length to break his arranged marriage to his cousin without losing the extensive inheritance contingent on their nuptials. What at first appears to be an important exception appears in Benjamin Hoadly's *The Suspicious Husband* (1747), but the incongruity between the economic fortunes of Bellamy and Jacintha (he controlling £300 a year, she with an estate worth £30,000)[31] is resolved when we realize that no fundamental *social* barrier exists. Bellamy is a gentleman of genteel social status and excellent character; the lovers are *equals* despite the differences in their fortunes. In George Colman's *The Jealous Wife* (1761), Charles Oakly in his pursuit of Harriot may not have £5000 a year and the baronetcy enjoyed by his rival, Sir Harry Beagle, but Charles enjoys the full benefits of genteel rank, and we always understand that Harriot is his *equal*.[32] Five years later in the Colman-Garrick *The Clandestine Marriage* (1766), the authors state in the play's prologue (also mentioned in the advertisement) their intention to mock the kind of cross-class marriage depicted by Hogarth in "Marriage *a-la-mode*":

> Their one great object, marriage-*a-la-mode!*
> Where titles deign with cits to have and hold,
> And change rich blood for more substantial gold!
> And honored trade from interest turns aside,
> To hazard happiness for titled pride.[33]

Lord Ogleby's pressing need for the £80,000 dowry to unencumber his estate (actually to be delivered to his family via the would-be groom, his nephew, Sir John) and the blatant social climbing of Mr. Sterling, the cit wishing to marry his eldest daughter in exchange for social gain, are exaggerations created for comic effect but well mirror current concerns. The one apparently contradictory moment in the play occurs when Lord Ogleby becomes infatuated with Fanny's beauty and charm, but we cannot take seriously his comment that he would marry the charming but socially inferior Fanny "With any fortune, or no fortune at all" (312). The lord remarks in the finale, "I indulge my own passions too much" (330), an indication that his "love" for Fanny, while not without cause or merit, was impulsive and unrealistic. Of course, there is no chance of this match actually taking place; the audience knows full well that Fanny is already secretly married to Lovewell, who is, by no coincidence, her social equal (and, to boot, a socially inferior relative of Lord Ogleby's). Indeed, it is well worth noting that the play finally does *not* present a cross-class marriage.

Likewise much of the humor in R. B. Sheridan's *The Rivals* (1775) ensues precisely because of Lydia's foolish attempts to overturn traditional economic "rules" for courtship and marriage. Young Absolute ultimately succeeds precisely *because* he is of the right class and financial worth; Lydia rebels at first against the status quo but willingly accepts her fate by the play's end. As even this brief survey indicates (and many other examples could be presented), we see that Charles Marlow and Kate Hardcastle in Goldsmith's play are literally one of a kind on the eighteenth-century stage. They are an odd couple, a study in social and economic contradiction that invites laughter.

If the social/economic "marriage trap" created by Goldsmith was the only feature of his method, the play could still pass for a genuine portrayal of the phenomenon of social leveling or as a sign of the century's growing liberal willingness to allow young people to marry for love. But numerous other traps, which are actually inversions of the conventions of comedy, may be found in Goldsmith's play. Consider, for example, that the parents provide only the most minimal obstacles to the union of the couple; the young people themselves actually stand in each other's way. Goldsmith here overturns the longstanding tradition where the parents (or guardian) refuse permission, a dramatic device taken to the furthest extreme in Susanna Centlivre's *Bold Stroke for a Wife* (1718) where Colonel Fainwell must gain the consent of *four* guardians (none of whom cares for or respects the others) in order to gain Mrs. Lovel's hand (and her fortune of £30,000). Also, as mentioned above, for Charles and Kate money is not an issue; in fact, money is only passingly mentioned (in the main plot) in *She Stoops to Conquer,* a quirky deviation from comic tradition.[34] Also turned topsy-turvy is the matter of gender roles. Charles is courted by Kate (*she* stoops to conquer), while Hastings, the other male lover, wishes to elope but is thwarted by the conventional and money-bound Miss Neville. In short, females dominate the main lines of action in ways most atypical. Women may scheme and be successful in this and other eighteenth-century plays (such as *The Careless Husband*

and *The Wife's Relief*) in reforming their *husbands,* but the men virtually always decide on the ultimate marriageability of *lovers.*

And last, but not least, is the fact of Kate's altered personality by the conclusion. Precisely the mirror opposite of her namesake Kate in *The Taming of the Shrew,*[35] Kate Hardcastle, we are led to believe, *becomes* a shrew: one stage direction indicates that Kate and Charles "retire, she tormenting him"; Marlow a bit later calls Kate "my little tyrant," and we have the unmistakable irony of the epilogue that traces the transition in Kate's character after she and Charles marry: she becomes a loud, impudent coquette who indulges in every vanity of London high-life.[36] If Sir Charles Marlow hoped to find in the lower gentry a kind of goodness not available in his own rank of society, he was dreadfully mistaken.

Those critics seeking to find signs of social progress in *She Stoops to Conquer* will have to go very far, indeed, to establish anything like a consistent, liberal thematic message in this play. From the entire basis of the play's action itself to every detail of the relationship between Charles and Kate, the play is mocking and satirizing dramatic (and probably social) conventions of courtship and cross-class marriage, thus pushing probability to extreme limits and even beyond. While none of the contemporary reviewers specifically remarks on the matter of the improbability of the central marriage match, some criticized the play's general incredibility.[37] And the main characters are hardly the only ones stretching belief. When Hastings and Miss Neville ask for forgiveness (for their aborted elopement), Mrs. Hardcastle (Miss Neville's guardian) remarks on their plea in terms that well characterize Goldsmith's attitude about the whole business of love and marriage in this play: "Pshaw, pshaw, this is all but the whining end of a modern novel" (V.iii.153–54; 215). In other words, Goldsmith was so much as openly stating to the audience that he was toying with their judgment. We might go so far as to say that this is "double" entrapment, that is, employing entrapment in the play, and then telling the audience in tongue and cheek fashion that they have been tricked!

From this brief survey we have seen that entrapment is an important strategy of several important eighteenth-century dramatists. In the cases of Congreve, Gay, and Fielding, their purposes involved sharp satiric comment on society. For Goldsmith, the satire has a softer edge but his *technique* is identical: to create a situation that *forces* the audience to confront a moral or social problem it might otherwise wish to ignore. In all of the cases, the audience finds itself in situations where it is forced to view full face situations that may be most unsettling or oddly curious, and where the audience must reflect on the details of plot and dialogue to understand the full dimensions of the author's intentions. We may conclude that entrapment is one of the most important techniques a playwright can employ when pursuing serious themes, especially in comedy, and that modern interpretations that do not take this technique into account may well be prone to faulty conclusions.

NOTES

1. Vieth's remarks are quoted by Carl Kropf in the Editor's Comment to the issue of *Studies in the Literary Imagination,* 17.1 (Spring, 1984), 1.
2. For a recent discussion that argues that Foote's plays are much more than simple farces that scholars have long believed, see Terrence M. Freeman, "Best Foote Forward," *SEL,* 29 (1989), 563–78.
3. *The Way of the World* appears in all editions except the fourth, where Congreve's *Love for Love* (a much funnier and easier to teach play) was included.
4. I quote here from Martin Price's essay as reprinted in the popular classroom critical edition edited by Scott McMillin, *Restoration and Eighteenth-Century Comedy* (New York: Norton, 1973), 546.
5. Shirley Strum Kenny, " 'Elopements, Divorce, and the Devil Knows What': Love and Marriage in English Comedy," *SAQ* 78 (1979), 89–90.
6. All quotations from the proviso scene are from McMillin's edition (196–98) rather than from Herbert Davis' *The Complete Plays of William Congreve* (Chicago: University of Chicago Press, 1967).
7. Mirabell here is not concerned with Millamant spending money, but rather with the reputation that these bawds had as gossip mongers and confidantes in surreptitious schemings. See, for example, the negative characterization of the orange-woman in George Etherege's *The Man of Mode* (1676).
8. Henry Fielding, *The Complete Works of Henry Fielding, Esq.,* ed. W. E. Henley (1902–1903; rpt. New York: Barnes and Noble, 1967), X, 86–87.
9. For a helpful survey of Gay's various strategies and of the criticism, see Robert D. Hume, " 'The World is all Alike': Satire in *The Beggar's Opera,*" Chap. 8 in *The Rakish Stage* (Carbondale: Southern Illinois University Press, 1983), 260.
10. John Gay, *Dramatic Works,* ed. John Fuller (Oxford: Clarendon Press, 1983), II, 4. All further quotations are from this edition.

11. James Bowell, *Life of Johnson,* ed. R. W. Chapman (1904; rev. ed. New York: Oxford University Press, 1970), 628–29.
12. Robert D. Hume, *Henry Fielding and the London Theatre 1728–1737* (Oxford: Clarendon Press, 1988), 121–29.
13. For a convenient analysis of the play and its reception, see Hume, *Henry Fielding and the London Theatre 1728–1737,* 46–49.
14. See Shirley Strum Kenny, "Perennial Favorites: Congreve, Vanbrugh, Cibber, Farquhar, and Steele," *Modern Philology* 73, no. 4, Part 2 (1976): S4–S11.
15. Colley Cibber, *The Careless Husband,* ed. William W. Appleton (Lincoln: University of Nebraska Press, 1966). Quotations from 102, 105, and 116.
16. John Butt, *The Mid-Eighteenth Century* (Oxford: Clarendon Press, 1979), 188–90; Hopkins, *The True Genius of Oliver Goldsmith* (Baltimore: Johns Hopkins University Press, 1969).
17. Bernard Harris, "She Stoops to Conquer," in *Modern Critical Views: Oliver Goldsmith,* ed. Harold Bloom (New York: Chelsea House, 1987), 139–44; quote from 143–44. Bloom excerpts Harris's essay from a longer piece in *The Art of Oliver Goldsmith,* ed. Andrew Swarbrick (New York: Vision Press; Barnes and Noble, 1984).
18. Harris revives with proper credit this point suggested over a decade earlier by B. Eugene McCarthy in "The Theme of Liberty in *She Stoops to Conquer,*" *University of Windsor Review* 7 (1971), 1–8.
19. Hume, "Goldsmith and Sheridan and the Supposed Revolution of 'Laughing' against 'Sentimental' Comedy," in Hume's *The Rakish Stage* (Carbondale: Southern Illinois University Press, 1983), Chap. 10.
20. Oliver Goldsmith, "An Essay on the Theatre," in *Collected Works of Oliver Goldsmith,* ed. Arthur Friedman, 5 vols. (Oxford: Clarendon Press, 1966), III: 210. All further quotations from Goldsmith's works are from this edition.
21. Goldsmith, V, 112. Friedman does not employ continuous line numbers, so I have provided act, scene, and line numbers for users of other editions.
22. Lawrence Stone, *The Family, Sex and Marriage in England 1500–1800* (New York: Harper and Row, 1977), 318.
23. Blundell, *Diary 1702–1728.* Quoted in Alan Macfarlane, *Marriage and Love in England 1300–1840* (London: Blackwell, 1986), 138–39.
24. J. A. Sharpe, *Early Modern England: A Social History 1550–1760* (London: Arnold, 1987), 174.
25. Stone argues this contention at even greater length in his and Jeanne C. Fawtier Stone's *An Open Elite? England 1540–1880* (Oxford: Clarendon Press; New York: Oxford University Press, 1984).
26. Fielding's *Shamela* (1741), Martin Battestin remarks, attacks Richardson's *Pamela* as a "morally contemptible and technically incompetent novel, a position Fielding would continue in *Joseph Andrews* (1742). See Battestin, Introduction, *Joseph Andrews* and *Shamela* (Boston: Houghton Mifflin, 1961), x.
27. Both Stone and Macfarlane discuss Richardson's *Clarissa* but do not analyze the sociological and financial aspects of *Pamela.*
28. George Farquhar, *The Works of George Farquhar,* ed. Shirley Strum Kenny (Oxford: Clarendon Press, 1988), II, 234. All further quotations are from this edition.

29. Upon hearing the news of his brother's death (by which the title came to him), Aimwell remarks, "Thanks to the pregnant Stars that form'd this Accident" (II, 236).

30. Charles Johnson, *The Wife's Relief* (London, 1713), 16. All further quotations are from this edition.

31. Benjamin Hoadly, *The Suspicious Husband,* 2nd edn. (London: 1747), 8.

32. Among other themes in *The Jealous Wife,* Colman explores the foolish audacity of unpolished, rural squires, long a favorite target for satirists. Sir Harry Beagle, as is well known, is a direct literary descendant of Henry Fielding's Squire Western. But to imagine that Colman is openly attacking the aristocracy would be contrary to the spirit and sense of the play's conclusion.

33. Colman and Garrick, *The Plays of David Garrick,* eds. Harry William Pedicord and Frederick Louis Bergmann (Carbondale: Southern Illinois University Press, 1980), I, 256.

34. Of great interest, however, is the crucial dimension of money to the happiness of Hasting and Miss Neville, the *other* set of lovers.

35. *She Stoops* has often been compared to Shakespearean plays, such as *A Midsummer Night's Dream* and *As You Like It,* but these plays correspond in only superficial ways with Goldsmith's comedy.

36. We cannot discount Goldsmith's own negative opinion of the epilogue, that it was "a very mawkish thing" (*The Collected Letters of Oliver Goldsmith,* ed. Katharine C. Balderstone [Cambridge: Cambridge University Press, 1928], 119), but the epilogue is quite consistent with the development of Kate's character in the last act.

37. For examples of reviewers troubled by Goldsmith's improbabilities, see the anonymous review in the *London Magazine,* 42 (March, 1773), 144–46; and William Woodfall's insightful critique in the *Monthly Review,* 48 (March, 1773), 309–14.

"Inordinate Sallies of Desire" Restrained and "Unutterable Rapture Possessed": The Emplotment of the Reader in *Roderick Random*

John P. Zomchick

Before the narrative of *Roderick Random* begins, its author boasts that he has vanquished romance and relegated it to the "dark ages of the world." In its place the reader will find "an interesting story, which brings every incident home to life," and that "represent[s] modest merit struggling with every difficulty to which a friendless orphan is exposed, from his own want of experience, as well as from the selfishness, envy, malice, and base indifference of mankind."[1] This "friendless orphan," distinguished by the "advantages of birth and education" (xxxv), is

the means by which the "reader gratifies his curiosity, in pursuing the adventures of a person in whose favour he is prepossessed" (xxxiii). In order to make his story "universally improv-
ing," furthermore, the author tells us that he has introduced
occasional satire. Taken together, these authorial directions
mark Smollett's text as a narrative that will offer what Michael
McKeon has called the "conservative critique" of progressive
ideology, in part by incorporating acceptable aspects of the progressive ideology (e.g., merit as the standard of virtue) and in
part by negating the full significance of those elements through
the recuperation of aristocratic traits (e.g., gentle birth).[2] In
what follows I will attempt to construct the "prepossessed"
reader that this conservative critique creates. I wish to argue
that through a complex process of identification, effected
through the text's appeal to its reader's need for mastery over
"the vicissitudes of life . . . in their peculiar circumstances" and
his primary psychical processes, the reader is emplotted as a
bourgeois, gendered subject.[3] This reader is ultimately surprised
by sense and sentiment—sexual fantasies and a yearning for
decency—into accepting the novel's representation of a Hobbesian public society and—as its counterpart—its defensive, eroti-
cized private subject.

The manner in which the reader is surprised into sub-
jecthood and trapped into accepting the novel's representation
of everyday life owes its power to formal "problems" as much as
it does to the thematic material of the text. Many commentators
have noticed a certain indecisiveness in the text as it moves
between the low-life realism of the picaresque and the high-life
fantasy of romance.[4] On the one hand it is possible to read this
formal heterogeneity as the novel's incomplete absorption of its
generic predecessors or as a mark of its author's artistic immatu-
rity. And yet such an explanation is really no explanation at
all, but rather a judgment of Smollett's text against some ideal
narrative type. On the other hand, it is possible to read this
condition as a structure entailed on the narrative by ideological
imperatives.[5] One such imperative is to provide the reader with
a coherent version of the human subject. Looked at in this way,
Roderick Random's generic oscillations can be understood as the

very means by which it satisfies one of its ideological imperatives; for only through the representation of the picaresque
world with its naked brutality and its systemic relations of non-
reciprocity and exploitation can the novel produce its antithesis
in the domestic private sphere with its unadorned affection and
its systemic relations of mutuality and cooperation. Or perhaps
better said, the latter sphere's acceptability is predicated on its
appearance as a refuge from the dangers in the former. Just as
H. F., the "writer" of Daniel Defoe's *A Journal of the Plague
Year,* concluded that because it was impossible to determine who
carried the plague and who did not, one must quarantine oneself
from all social contact; so too for Random and his reader the
domestic sphere becomes the only safe space because it is ultimately impossible to determine the honesty of individuals and
the reliability of their "public" promises. Thus, the picaresque
part of this narrative provides both the moral and ideological
motivation for the domestic romance even as it gives the reader
a coherent logic for interpreting the text: because things are
rarely as they seem and because life in the public sphere is often
nasty and brutish without necessarily being mercifully short,
then to enjoy life's pleasures one must retire to a well-stocked
private sphere.

In addition to this narrative logic, the structural peculiari-
ties of *Roderick Random* also reproduce a split within the bourgeois self between the subject of accumulation and the subject
of affection. This split, however, is partially healed by the narrative as successful accumulation is subsumed by ensuing pleasures of affection. This particular narrative teleology—negating
the destructive effects of accumulation with affection—constitutes the text's objectivity, which Roland Barthes defines in the
following manner: "Objectivity is . . . an imaginary system . . . ,
an image which serves to name me advantageously, to make
myself known, 'misknown,' even to myself."[6] The text's "objective" logic is carried by its syntagmatic structure, which demonstrates how specific actions produce predictable results, elabo-
rated through repetition into paradigmatic moments, where
certain conditions always result in certain consequences. This
logic also produces a reading subject who ultimately (mis)knows

himself as one who masters hostile social relations through interpretation and then moves on to purely "personal" pleasures. In producing the pleasures of interpretation and mastery, the imaginary system creates the (reading) subject in ideology, "where a specific meaning is realised in signification."[7] That is, it creates the subject who will value experience in the public sphere only in so far as it prepares him to enjoy the pleasures of the private sphere, and even then the public sphere's value will be appreciated only in its retrospective negation. The process of mastery actually results in the devaluation of public activity and its consequent replacement by fantasies of self-sufficient pleasures. It bears repeating, however, that the production of this split bourgeois subject is based on a drama of knowing and misknowing the self, social relations, and the function of the self within those social relations: because the text represents social relations as naturally and immutably hostile, the reading subject also feels compelled to defend himself by working to attain "an imaginary position of transcendence to [the representational] system" and—by extension—to the world anterior to the sign.[8] In other words, the reader's pleasure comes from feelings of mastery and superiority over the world in the text. This is a specific kind of pleasure, different from the pleasures that could arise from cooperation. In order to maintain the pleasure of mastery mandated by the natural law of self-defense, the reader must accept the terms of the textual system, must view social relations as defined by those that pertain between adversaries.

In her now classic article "Visual Pleasure and Narrative Cinema" Laura Mulvey offers a model of the psychosexual dynamic of this process of identification and mastery in her summary of Lacan's mirror phase:

> The mirror phase occurs at a time when children's physical ambitions outstrip their motor capacity, with the result that their recognition of themselves is joyous in that they imagine their mirror image to be more complete, more perfect than they experience in their own body. Recognition is thus overlaid with misrecognition: the image recognised is conceived as the reflected body of the self, but its misrecognition as superior projects this body outside itself as an ideal ego, the

alienated subject which, reintrojected as an ego ideal,
prepares the way for identification with others in the
future.[9]

The relation between the reader and Roderick Random is not as
simple as that between the child and his image in the mirror,
for the reader sees the young Random through the eyes of the
older writer, who himself treats his youthful foibles with "playful irony."[10] Nonetheless, from the hero's first victory—the chas-
tisement of the schoolmaster—the reader takes pleasure in the
hero's ability to overcome obstacles to his comfort. Random's
early accomplishments, though often outside the law and visited
with unfortunate consequences, proclaim his superiority over
most of the individual adversaries he faces. At the same time
that the reader admires Random's resourcefulness, he pities his
gullibility. But that pity fails to become the condescension of a
superior ego because the reader also identifies with the narrat-
ing voice that is at once the same and different from the object
of narration. In this way the reader is engaged—one might even
say entrapped—into identifying with the early resourcefulness
that has produced the later authority. And in the process of this
pleasurable identification the ideal ego is transformed into an
ego ideal as the early gullible young fortune hunter becomes the
established man of property. This transformation emplots the
reader in a system of collective or social values that "validate"
his fantasies of power and autonomy.[11] Driven by a desire for
positive identification with narrative authority that orders the
chaotic world by ultimately subjugating social relations to the
desire of the individual, the reader is constrained to accept the
narrative's construction of social conditions and possible forms
of social being in order to insure his own continued pleasure and
the plot's legibility.

Underlying my argument so far is the premise that the
reader of *Roderick Random* is willing to identify with its protagonist and enter into its representations of society. There is, of
course, an alternative "position": in the classic novel, Roland
Barthes notes, one can "either . . . accept or reject the text: reading is nothing more than a *referendum*."[12] One actual reader
who cast a negative vote was Samuel Johnson. Yet even in his

rejection of the new kind of narrative, Johnson implicitly accepts the power of the representational system while rejecting its effects. Johnson is concerned that those "minds . . . easily susceptible of impressions" will be corrupted by the "universal drama" of the new comedy of romance. "[Y]oung spectators," Johnson writes, "fix their eyes upon [the hero] with closer attention, and hope by observing his behaviour and success to regulate their own practices. . . ." Exacerbating this attraction to identification is the "power of example . . . so great as to take possession of the memory by a kind of violence, and produce effects almost without the intervention of the will."[13] In other words, the pleasures of identification override the mind's will to resist. Only the few like Samuel Johnson—who was blessed with a "too great tension of fibres" for his delight in excessive tea-drinking to produce the expected debilitating effects[14]—could be expected to encounter the pleasures offered by the text and remain unaffected by its violently seductive powers. It is an indication of this power that Johnson must reject the entire representational system upon which it is based in favor of a system that "distinguish[es] those parts of nature which are most proper for imitation."[15] In his condemnation of the moral promiscuity of novels like *Roderick Random*, Johnson affirms their power to entrap readers.

The history of the novel proves that Johnson's call for "the highest and purest [virtue] that humanity can reach, which, exercised in such trials as the various revolutions of things shall bring upon it, may, by conquering some calamities, and enduring others, teach us what we may hope, and what we can perform," was antithetical to the pleasures promised by the new writing and the new social formation that gave rise to it.[16] In *Roderick Random* the subject of acquisition momentarily pleases and fascinates the reader as the hero goes about making and recovering a fortune. The subject of affection provides a purer pleasure as romance becomes unconditional love. And finally, both the subject of acquisition and the subject of affection are merged into the ethical subject—the subject in and of modified patriarchal ideology—who takes pleasure as his just and merited due. In the course of the hero's development the reader is urged to judge and condemn the various human excesses and institutional failings that have stood between the hero and happiness. The satirical element in *Roderick Random* strengthens the reader's identification with the hero as the narrative moves forward in time, for the satire involves him in an active process of judgment, a process that enables him to attain transcendence over the objects of satire without necessarily sacrificing a growing identification with the hero. In the rest of my discussion, I want to demonstrate how the text constructs the defensive bourgeois subject, who accepts the text's objectivity in order to find in himself alone the pleasure that the text promises.

Violence is the means by which the text constructs the defensive subject. The reader of *Roderick Random* enters a world made violent by scarcity.[17] Through repetition of violent scenes, *Roderick Random* represents competitive social relations in a state of nature marked by the war of all against all (with certain exceptions in "helper" figures such as Strap and Bowling). The repetition of violent acts creates a condition of expectation and revulsion in the reader. This combination is important, for it is part of the dynamic process of moving the reader to identify with the maturing and ever more defensive hero even as it alienates him from the revolting social world that demands such violent responses.

Random's initiation into the violent world begins at birth (his mother's dream of his birth is a violent one) and continues while he struggles for social status. As the supposedly-orphaned son of a paternally-disapproved marriage, he is subjected to physical and emotional abuse. True to his actual gentle birth, however, he does not suffer torment passively. When his fox-hunting cousin—who is the "old gentleman" grandfather's favorite and heir—sets his dogs upon the young orphan, Random takes action against his cousin's

> preceptor, who, no doubt, took such opportunities to ingratiate himself with the rising sun, observing that the old gentleman, according to course of nature, had not long to live, being already on the verge of fourscore. The behaviour of this rascally sycophant incensed me so much, that one day, when I was beleagued by him and his hounds into a farmer's house, where I had

found protection, I took aim at him (being an excellent
marksman) with a large pebble, which struck out four
of his foreteeth, and effectually incapacitated him for
doing the office of a clerk ever after.

(2: 7–8)

On the surface, the function of this passage seems clear enough:
in the picaresque world, one must defend oneself against the
attacks of the enemy in whatever way one can. And yet there is
more here. Random's reaction carries a childlike satisfaction, a
primitive if feral justice, and a visceral jolt that comes from the
kind of bodily injury that Random inflicts on his enemy. This
sycophant deserves to be disabled from performing his "office,"
because he uses it as a means to advance himself at others'
(notably the hero's) expense. Random's aim fits the punishment
to the crime because the clerk's ambition is wrong. Such ambition will result in either slavish dependency on the will of another or in resentment of those who suffer from the secondary
effects of such dependency. The novel begins its ideological work
by tainting certain means in the quest for status. The graphic
image of the toothless, bleeding clerk reinforces this sense of
taint even when it begins the complex process of identification
with the abused hero, who resorts to violent measures to defend
himself. Given the choice between throwing the stone and losing
four teeth, the reader will not hesitate to choose the former.

In order to construct the proper bourgeois subject, however,
the text must eliminate violence and substitute more effective
means of defense and advancement. The action that Random
takes against the preceptor establishes a pattern whereby violence is shown to produce short-lived gratifications that have
harmful consequences. Sometime after he has knocked the
clerk's teeth out, Random's Uncle Tom Bowling arrives to argue
with the grandfather for the boy's better treatment. The grandfather replies that "he was informed . . . [that Random] was ad-
dicted to all manner of vice, which he the rather believed, because he himself was witness to a barbarous piece of mischief he
had committed on the jaws of his chaplain" (3: 11). The difference
between justice and mischief in this instance is the distance

between the young hero's authority and that against which he struggles. The reader learns from this narrative sequence that defensive aggression works against the powerless because they have no control over the meaning imputed to their actions. The only sure protection from the cycle of violence and retribution is to remove oneself from the cycle. One is either hounded by dogs or one owns dogs. There is no in-between.

In the opening pages of the novel, then, violence is encoded as an inevitable element of an oppressive world, a partially justifiable and fully understandable reaction to that world, and an event that social authority can turn against the powerless. The conditions surrounding Random's violent action against the clerk present the reader with his first bit of useful knowledge, a knowledge that is rearticulated shortly thereafter by Mrs. Potion's reaction to the news that Random's Uncle Tom Bowling has been " 'obliged to sheer off, for killing [his] captain' ": "People should be more cautious of their conduct—she was always afraid his brutal behaviour would bring him into some misfortune or other" (6: 22). And because Mrs. Potion is one of the text's typical minor figures representing an ensemble of social attitudes— "The world would do nothing for her if she should come to want—charity begins at home" (6: 22)—her reflection on Bowling's (and his nephew's) troubles indicates both the danger of violence and the ubiquity of fierce self-interest. That her "discourse" is reported by the narrator rather than dramatized through direct speech adds to the proverbial weight of her statement: that charity begins at home is no idiosyncratic belief; it is worldly wisdom that the reader absorbs even if he suspects the motive of the person who utters it. The "world" waits to capitalize on the folly of the indignant, feeling secure that it can ultimately justify its self-interest by condemning the moral weakness of those who act without caution.

The knowledge that "brutal behaviour" puts one at risk in this world leads the reader to a question: how did the hero, implicated in this risky violence, escape its consequences without succumbing to the violent world that he inhabits? This "enigma" drives the narrative from this early moment, for its answer alone can explain how Random is able to narrate the event of his birth—indeed of the events prior to his birth. Furthermore, if the narrator is to make good upon his first suspended promise ("How I understood the particulars of my birth, will appear in the course of these memoirs" [1: 4])—then the truth of Random's life must negate the narrative of violence that has been opened to the reader in his and his uncle's early misfortunes. To draw on Roland Barthes once more, the "enigma" is an instance of the "hermeneutic" code, which "structure[s] the enigma according to the expectation and desire for its solution." Barthes elaborates on the code's productive function for the reader:

> Expectation thus becomes the basic condition for truth: truth, these narratives tell us, is what is *at the end* of expectation. This design brings narrative very close to the rite of initiation (a long path marked with pitfalls, obscurities, stops, suddenly comes out into the light); it implies a return to order, for expectation is a disorder: disorder is supplementary, it is what is forever added on without solving anything, without finishing anything; order is complementary, it completes, fills up, saturates, and dismisses everything that risks adding on: truth is what completes, what closes.[18]

All that appears before the end of Roderick Random's adventures is mere deferral of the "truth" of his proper and ordered place. Throughout this deferral reigns disorder; moreover, the disorder seems to be "probably infinite in its expansions" as long as the hero seeks his fortune in the violent world.[19] Because violence is the primary means of deferring the solution to the enigma of how Random has come to narrate his own text, and because violence is linked to the disorder in social relations, that which "completes" and provides the reader with the truth of existence must be represented as an antithesis of this violence. On another level, expectation is itself a form of violence; satisfaction brings repose. Truth and satisfaction will drive out violence and expectation.[20]

If violence is both infinitely expansive and counterproductive, then in order to make the reader renounce the satisfactions attendant upon it (as Roderick ultimately does) it must be associated with those forces that stand between the hero and his happiness. The text follows this imperative in inscribing violence with the mark of arbitrary power ignorant of the rule of law that characterizes the liberal politics of bourgeois society. There are countless examples of this association, none as important or as graphic as that in the scenes between the midshipman Crampley and Random. Crampley is especially important for delegitimizing violence and moving the hero and reader toward full-fledged bourgeois subjectivity because the midshipman's authority is not supported by rank or status in the same way that the schoolmaster's, or magistrate's, or Captain Oakhum's is. Through Crampley the text condemns unmerited and arbitrary dominion as well as the aid that corrupt social relations give to an ambitious and unscrupulous man. In this way the text also reinforces its foreclosure of this means of social advancement as the answer to the enigma of the narrator's authoritative discourse.

A recently impressed and bleeding Random's first encounter with Crampley defines his character: "compassion was a weakness of which no man could justly accuse this person, who squirting a mouthful of dissolved tobacco upon me, through the gratings, told me, 'I was a mutinous dog, and that I might die and be damned' " (24: 140). After Random is rescued from this sentence by his uncle's friend and after Crampley takes his place in confinement, the two become inveterate enemies. Random bests Crampley in a fight aboard ship shortly thereafter (27: 155–56), but as might be expected that is not the end of him. Still later, when Random becomes a surgeon's mate (an advancement that he earns), he learns that Crampley "by the dint of some friends about the admiral, had procured a commission constituting him lieutenant on board the Lizard" (35: 200). The rivalry continues with Crampley's slandering the hero, who reacts in the following manner: "This infernal behaviour of Crampley, with regard to me, added such fuel to my former resentment, that at certain times, I was quite beside myself with the desire of revenge, and was even tempted to pistol him on the quarterdeck, though an infamous death must inevitably have been my reward" (36: 205). Although the hero's desire for vengeance almost overwhelms his caution—another instance of the "disorder" that prolongs the enigma of his success—his consciousness

of "an infamous death" signals his movement toward a modified
or emergent bourgeois subjectivity. Whether infamy or death
deters Random in this instance is not entirely clear. But that he
is deterred at all shows that he has begun to internalize the
codes that govern successful or respectable behavior in both aristocratic and bourgeois ideology.[21] Ensuing events prove, however, that the internalization is incomplete.

Crampley's power momentarily increases when he succeeds
to command the ship at the Captain's death. Although Random's
enemy is neither better nor worse than Oakhum or any of the
other figures of authority that Random has met, his humble
beginnings and his securing preferment through patronage reveal that such arbitrary authority as his can only be maintained
by violent means. The least suggestion of opposition evokes repression, and repression evokes resistance and more violence.
The reader learns that such overt destructive forces can only
impede the progress toward happiness and self-sufficiency. The
outcome of this sequence in Random's history is the most brutal
and the most consequential of all his violent encounters. Having
abandoned ship, Random and Crampley "duel" on the shore.
Random offers Crampley a pistol, the narrator writes,

> and before I could cock the other [Crampley] fired in my
> face throwing the pistol after the shot. —I felt myself
> stunned, and imagining the bullet had entered my
> brain, discharged mine as quick as possible, that I
> might not die unrevenged; then flying upon my antago-
> nist, knocked out several of his foreteeth with the but-
> end of the piece; and would certainly have made an end
> of him with that instrument, had he not disengaged
> himself, and seized his cutlass, which he had given to
> his servant when he received the pistol. Seeing him
> armed in this manner, I drew my hanger, and having
> flung my pistol at his head, closed with him in a trans-
> port of fury, and thrust my weapon into his mouth,
> which it enlarged on one side to his ear. . . . I know not
> with what cruelty my rage might have inspired me, if
> I had not at that instant, been felled to the ground by
> a blow on the back part of my head. . . .
>   (37: 210)

Whatever pleasure the reader may derive from participating in the protagonist's revenge is immediately curtailed by the misfortune that befalls his "cruel" actions. Just as negative consequences had followed his striking out the teeth of the clerk, so too negative consequences follow this action. When Random recovers he finds that he has lost everything he has accumulated over the course of his voyage. His violent means of resistance cannot provide the reader with the truth that he seeks. All that it can do is indicate the brutality in social relations by presenting as a paradigm of those relations a cruel fight that ends when an unknown assailant strikes one from behind in order to make off with the property acquired through effort and good fortune.

That Random rises from this fall and from his momentary "resolve[. . .] to lie still where [he] was and perish" functions on one level of the text as an indication of the strength of the human will and its endless desires. The will is cognate with the desire to narrate, and only when the story is told can the will and its desires be at rest. The subject of accumulation (and violence) knows no limit to its desires: like Moll Flanders, he always yearns for more even when he appears to possess a sufficiency. Thus, the subject of accumulation can know no narrative closure, no ultimate truth. As a corollary of this condition the reader begins to suspect that the defensive ego must be supplemented by something else, a something else that will take the form of a complement. This something else is the subject of affection. For the subject of affection absolute satisfaction of the will is projected onto the Other, whose complementary qualities not only provide formal closure to the ceaselessly desiring will, but whose person also transforms violence into a temporarily creative force by providing an "objective" justification for it. In this way, the object of affection provides a bridge between the public sphere (where accumulation occurs) and private sphere (where affection is enjoyed by playing the role of a victim who must be rescued from the latter and installed in the former). She offers the hero the opportunity to exercise his powers in behalf of another who is actually the projection of his own needs. For the reader who has been repulsed by the random violence, this new purposiveness with its promise of static contentment engages assent.

Random and the reader are introduced to the social relations that will produce the private sphere by Mrs. Sagely, who married for love without consulting her parents. As a result of this clandestine marriage, her father (with her mother's concurrence) had "renounced [her] to the miserable fate [she] had entailed upon [her]self" (38: 214). Mrs. Sagely's family history is nearly identical to that of Roderick's mother, and the old "witch" clearly serves as a surrogate for the mother that the hero lost to his grandfather's cruelty.[22] The repetition of the tale of the disobedient daughter and the offended father provides the opportunity for the institution of new affective relations free from the taint of power and greed. Because Mrs. Sagely has felt both the value of love and the powers of the forces that would subordinate it to economic considerations, her experience adumbrates the solution to the enigma: love and power must be joined without being subordinated to economic considerations.

Mrs. Sagely prepares Random's future by recommending him to the service of a lady "who lived in the neighbourhood with her nephew, who was a young fox-hunter of great fortune" (38: 216). The incidental detail of the nephew is important, for Random, it should be remembered, was deprived of his patrimony by a fox-hunting cousin. This additional repetition establishes the conditions for the recuperation of the power that has been hitherto directed against the protagonist. In short, Random has been given a new mother and a new rival or obstacle to his fortunes, and thus a chance to validate his claim to the reader's prepossession. Through a dream-like repetition of events, the narrative initiates a final drive for wish-fulfillment, a drive that is characterized by the desire to rewrite the hero's genealogy in order to erase the forces that formed him. Difficult and heterogeneous social conditions are displaced by the fantasy of a unitary self that owes nothing to the violence associated with primitive accumulation.[23] Such a strong appeal to the reader's fantasies of omnipotence is difficult if not impossible to resist. Not only does it remove the self from the circuit of commerce in the public sphere, but it also makes him beholden to no one for this position of immunity.

The wish-fulfillment is completed with the introduction of the hero's ultimate reward: Narcissa. Her name indicates that she is the reflection of the hero's better self, that self that has survived the deforming influence of social intercourse. As such a reflection, she also becomes a part of the complex process of the reader's identification, an object that the reader needs in order to feel superior to those same conditions of social life that are satirized and made revolting throughout the narrative. At this point Smollett's text begins what Teresa de Lauretis calls the "production of Oedipus": "each reader — male or female—is constrained and defined within the two positions of a sexual difference thus conceived: male-hero-human, on the side of the subject; and female-obstacle-boundary-space, on the other."[24] Narcissa becomes the object of the reader's desire, the only element that can bring meaning to the chaotic succession of adventures. Like the Sphinx, she holds the solution to the enigma of Random's authoritative discourse. At the same time, however, she has no existence apart from the desires of the reader or the hero. This absence of autonomy makes her a willing subject to the mastery that awaits the revelation of truth in the solution of the enigma.

The first hint that Narcissa will complete the process of wish-fulfillment for protagonist and reader comes at her introduction. The conventional nature of the description signals the reader that he is about to view an ideal.

> So much sweetness appeared in the countenance and carriage of this amiable apparition, that my heart was captivated at first sight, and while dinner lasted I gazed upon her without intermission. —Her age seemed to be seventeen, her stature tall, her shape unexceptionable, her hair, that fell down upon her ivory neck in ringlets, black as jet; her arched eyebrows of the same colour; her eyes piercing, yet tender; her lips of the consistence and hue of cherries; her complexion clear, delicate and healthy; her aspect noble, ingen'ous and humane; and the whole so ravishingly delightful, that it was impossible for any creature, endued with sensibility, to see without admiring, and admire without loving her to excess!
>
> (39: 219)

As Random gazes upon this "idol of [his] adoration," he becomes painfully aware of the social distance separating him from it even as he is moved to find ways to diminish that distance. His gaze, however, also signals a power within him: the power of sensibility that will finally move him out of the public sphere where sensibility has no currency. Laura Mulvey has described the pleasure that the reader/spectator gets from a moment like this one in the following way: "As the spectator identifies with the main male protagonist, he projects his look onto that of his like . . . so that the power of the male protagonist as he controls events coincides with the active power of the erotic look, both giving a satisfying sense of omnipotence."[25] Although Random does not yet control events, his gaze fixes the woman as an object worthy of admiration and capable of giving satisfaction. Her idealized characteristics promise that she will be free from all that is ignoble and inhumane: in short, free from all the shortcomings of the social world. The reader who has experienced that world as it has been represented cannot but accept the portrait. And once that reader is trapped into admiring and loving this ideal beauty, he is necessarily trapped into feeling the tortures of the protagonist, whose "servile station . . . placed [him] infinitely beneath the regard of this idol." The unpleasurable social configuration extends the enigma and further incites the wish for the power to possess. In short, it entraps the reader into accepting and approving of Random's aspirations and nurtures his expectation of omnipotence.

The text has already prepared us to accept Random as the suitable consort for this object of perfection by making her the mirror image of the man who was responsible for "ruining" Miss Williams. This man Lothario first rescues Miss Williams from a would-be rapist and then uses the advantage of their friendship to seduce her. Miss Williams tells Random the story:

> If the obligation he had conferred upon me justly in-
> spired me with sentiments of gratitude, his appearance
> and conversation seemed to intitle him to somewhat
> more. —He was about the age of two and twenty,
> among the tallest of the middle-size; had chestnut col-
> oured hair which he wore tied up in a ribbon; a high

polished fore-head, a nose inclining to the aqualine,
lively blue eyes, red pouting lips, teeth as white as
snow, and a certain openness of countenance, . . . he
was the exact resemblance of you.

(22: 119)

This likeness is actually double, and it accomplishes two things.
First, it makes the hero into a romance idol just as Narcissa had
been without subjecting him to the same kind of objectifying
gaze. He himself is never described; rather, a man without morals who turns out to be anything but open is subject to the "active
power of the erotic look." And in this instance, the reader breaks
an identification with this kind of masculine beauty in order to
effect an identification with Random, who saves Miss Williams
from the ultimate consequences of her transgression of sexual
codes. These parallel conventional descriptions mark Random
and Narcissa as complementary, and their union will close the
circuit of the desire to narrate once and for all. Second, by way
of repetition of the scene of rape, the narrative creates a difference that will finally break the cycle of violence that has made
the defensive subject predominant.

This scene occurs when Narcissa's country-admirer Sir Tim-
othy Thicket offers "violence to this pattern of innocence and
beauty." Random tells the reader that he "flew like lightening
to her rescue" and cudgeled Thicket into senselessness. He continues the narration:

Then I turned to Narcissa, who had swooned, and sitting down by her, gently raised her head, and supported it on my bosom, while with my hand around her
waist, I kept her in that position. My soul was thrilled
with tumultuous joy, at feeling the object of my dearest
wishes within my arms; and while she lay insensible,
I could not refrain from applying my cheek to her's,
and ravishing a kiss.

(51: 229)

Instead of fully ravishing the woman he has rescued, Random
shows his true love first by denying a monetary reward that

Narcissa offers, and then by simultaneously revealing his feelings for her, his status as an "unfortunate gentleman," and his resolution to " 'fly from [her] bewitching presence, and bury his presumptuous passion in eternal silence' " (51: 230). This conventional gesture on Random's part further prepares the reader for the romance solution to the enigma even as it demonstrates Random's willingness to sacrifice the immediate pleasures of being in the presence of his ideal to the good and comfort of that ideal. His sacrifice makes him worthy and distinguishes the true lover from the false Lothario. This repetition of the rape scene with a difference, then, prepares the reader for narrative's ideological closure.

All obstacles to ideological closure cannot be removed by the power of romantically-induced self-abnegation alone. The hero's appetites must be chastened by erotic encounters that disgust him, and they must be reeducated through industry. The chastening of the protagonist's appetites begins when Random, while traveling in France with a capuchin, takes the "amiable Nanette" for his "bedfellow." The event shocks him, Random tells us, because his traveling companion had previously bedded both Nanette and her sister; this is close to "downright incest" for the protagonist. Random's disgust "at [the friar's] want of delicacy" marks the action as both "common" and as dangerous to the fantasy of self-contained, unique pleasure that Random imagines with the chaste Narcissa, thoughts of whom had increased his passion for Nanette (42: 240–41). This moment is as close as Narcissa comes to being contaminated by sexual commerce in her identification with Nanette in Random's mind. The event also reveals the text's incestuous drives as well as the need to distance both hero and reader from them. Disgust with promiscuous violence is succeeded by disgust with promiscuous copulation and the special dangers it presents.

More important than this "youthful indiscretion" to Random's and the reader's sentimental education, however, is his pursuit of Miss Sparkle. Believing himself beloved by this young woman—a gentleman's "only daughter, very handsome, who would inherit his whole estate" (50: 301)—because he has received love-letters from her, Random "looked upon [him]self as perfectly secure of that happiness [he] had been in quest of so long" (50: 302). This certainty arises without his ever meeting the woman who is writing him the passionate letters. That he is so transported, even to the extent of his losing "all remembrance of Narcissa" shows the extent to which his vision of happiness remains too much indebted to the promise of accumulating wealth without simultaneously acquiring affection.

In fact, Random is enticed by the promise in Miss Sparkle's letter because he is still intent on getting even with the society that has injured him. As he tells the reader, his "thoughts were wholly employed in planning triumphs over the malice and contempt of the world" (50: 303). Such a triumph would only make Random all the more dependent on the world he has scorned because without it he has no measure of his success. The woman who appears about to make his fortune counts for nothing in the scheme. She is a mere commodity, a possession that will gratify his aggressive impulses, a facilitator of his immature fantasies. When the supposed writer of the letters turns out to be not a young and beautiful Miss Sparkle but an old and hideous Miss Withers, the hero's temporary elation—and the phallic predominance that has enabled him to sparkle in his own imagination—withers to nothing. Or rather worse than nothing, for Miss Withers causes Random a great deal of disgust. Still hoping to turn the misunderstanding to his advantage by using Withers to get at Sparkle, Random submits to the old woman's attentions. As he kisses her "shriveled hand" to take his leave, he describes the climax of the episode in the following way:

> She was so much transported with her good fortune, that she could not contain her exstasy, but flew upon me like a tygeress, and pressed her skinny lips to mine; when . . . a dose of garlick she had swallowed that morning, to dispel wind I suppose, began to operate with such a sudden explosion, that human nature, circumstanced as I was, could not endure the shock with any degree of temper. —I lost all patience and reflection, flung away from her in an instant, . . . and could scarce restrain the convulsion of my bowels, which were grievously offended by the perfume that assaulted me.
>
> (50: 305)

The grotesque nature of this event, emphasized by the hero's physical reaction, signals the reader that Random has picked up a false scent in his search for the trail to happiness. The happiness provided by a Sparkle partakes of the general social corruption instigated by the single-minded and self-interested pursuit of material goods. The gross and decaying carnality of Miss Withers (which also serves an ideological function within the sexist economy of Smollett's text) and her inappropriate erotic desires present a mirror image of the hero's mistaken quest. In order to make that quest acceptable, the text must provide Random with an object of desire free from all taint of gross carnality. Such a provision is necessary on two accounts. First, the reader must be detached from the material world in order to enjoy the feeling of omnipotence that awaits him at closure because the very world's materiality declares its resistance to mastery. In fact, the material-social world makes the reader aware of his own heteronomy, his own susceptibility to the powers that threaten to dominate him by extorting violent reactions that will justify the destruction of his prospects. At closure the reader and the hero must feel active (generative of a new order) rather than reactive (subject to the old regime); in short, they must feel free from necessity. Second, Random's transparently individualist happiness must be repudiated in order that happiness can be constructed in and through the nuclear family. This compromise keeps the individual from becoming monadic and the text from becoming solipsistic even while preserving the illusion of the hero's and reader's detachment from society. Bourgeois ideology thus constructs sociability within the family circle.

Narcissa provides the text with the means for making hero and reader independent of the material world for satisfaction and at the same time with the "material" necessary for the construction of the nuclear family. She motivates the "sublimation" of the primary appetites that have extended the enigma of Random's authority. Having reencountered her in Bath, Random describes his feelings while he sits to dinner with Narcissa: "As I had the happiness of sitting opposite to her, I feasted my eyes much more than my palate, which she tempted in vain with the most delicious bits carved by her fair hand, and recommended by her persuasive tongue;—but all my other appetites were swallowed up in the immensity of my love, which I fed by gazing incessantly on the delightful object" (56: 343–44). As the novelist imports courtly, metaphysical language into his text, he effects the purging of the gross appetites, thereby enabling hero and reader to feast without fear of satiety. At the same time, the chastening of the appetites is accomplished without loss of sensual pleasure, for Narcissa is associated with eyes and palate, hand and tongue. Having been presented with the proper object of desire, one that can be consumed incessantly without fear of depletion, the reader is prepared for the feast of pleasures and the revelation of truth. Never has truth been so enticing, and never has a chastening been so fully rewarded.

Before Random can enjoy his inexhaustible pleasures, however, he must be initiated into industriousness. Rescued from debtor's prison by his uncle, Random sails with him "in quality of his Surgeon" (64: 400), trades to "great advantage" chiefly in slaves (65: 410), and is restored to his patrimony when Random encounters his long-lost and presumed dead father in Paraguay. The mixture of bourgeois *Bildungsroman* and romance convention in the discovery of a lost parent is interesting only insofar that it indicates that merit and industry alone are not enough to secure individual happiness. That, however, has been the burden of this narrative as the reader has witnessed the incompetent promoted over the meritorious or the rich ascend to a position of undeserved influence. The text preserves the value attached to individual effort even while it qualifies it with an innate nobility that will allow that effort to bear fruit in the private sphere. This is the thrust of the text's conservative countercritique of the elements of progressive ideology that it deploys.

More important, however, than the reeducation of the hero is the way that the text attains closure. Shocked at being reunited with his father, Random falls into a fever (thereby effectively purging himself of the remnants of his old life in a "critical sweat"), recovers, and ponders what remains to complete his happiness now that he is possessed of a father and significant wealth: "as the idea of my lovely Narcissa always joined itself to every scene of happiness I could imagine, I entertained myself now, with the prospect of possessing her in that distinguished sphere, to which she was intitled by her birth and qualifications" (66: 414). First, the narrative institutes a new patriarchal order in the figure of Don Rodriguez, Random's once abused and now kind father. Unlike Random's grandfather, whose "resolves were invariable like the laws of the Medes and the Persians" (1: 2), this new-world father approves of his son's "passion," eliciting the following response from him: "though I never doubted his generosity, I was transported on this occasion, and throwing myself at his feet, told him, he had now compleated my happiness; for without the possession of Narcissa, I should be miserable among all the pleasures of life" (66: 415). Random's gesture of submission—like the chastening of his appetites—is a painless one, for the father has "compleated" his happiness. The hero is now enabled to articulate the principle that at once devalues material goods and makes them the means for attaining the consummate happiness that the subject can experience: possession of the "object" that gives meaning to all other sorts of possession.

The enigma that has been suspended can now be solved. On the manifest level of the text—the level of the plot—Random's authority appears as the result of his own efforts in the slave trade and the fortunate coincidence of meeting his father, who has become a wealthy planter. The manifest level, however, engages the reader in the text without entrapping him. It is the latent or ideological register of the text that entraps the reader into a pleasurable acceptance of the terms of closure. That latent content can be described best as the repression of the originary violence that inaugurates the bourgeois subject, the dispersion of the scene of that violence (society), and its replacement by the fantasy of the self-generating subject, dependent for Random's pleasures only upon the narrowly circumscribed world that his new-found powers enable him to control. In Teresa de Lauretis' terms, the text produces the Oedipus by giving Random the power of the father and the pleasure of the mother. This production guarantees generational continuity on one level by providing the hero with a father even while on another, fantastic level it erases all Oedipal conflict by making the will of the father coincident with that of the son, effecting an identity between

Roderick and Rodriguez. This is wish-fulfillment of the highest sort.

The strength of *Roderick Random's* appeal to the reader lies not only in this appeal to Oedipal longings but also in the way that it obliterates the violence that commodity fetishism and the objectification of social relations inflict upon the subject in the capitalist mode of production. John Brenkman's description of such effects within capitalist society are relevant to *Roderick Random:*

> the subject experiences a permanent rift and conflict between the practices of self-preservation and the demands of the erotogenic body. . . . The concept of the "ego" . . . names . . . the disciplining of the body required to make it an instrument of production at the expense of its erotogeneity. This ego now lets itself be invested with the demands of the erotogenic body (the drives) primarily within a space or site of experience separated from the practical domain of labor and value: the intimate sphere of heterosexual love.[26]

Even as *Roderick Random* creates a space "separated from the practical domain of labor and value," it makes that space a consequence of the "progress" of the hero, whose body has been disciplined to no apparent end other than that of making it ready to take up residence in the private sphere. At the same time, the narrative enhances the pleasure by negating the commerce of the public sphere entirely. In this regard, it creates a powerful fantasy, for the subject inside the private sphere has the pleasures of endless "erotogeneity" without the pains of labor.

And yet the text would be untrue to its bourgeois tendencies if it devoted its subject to pleasure alone. To do so would be to reproduce the inverse of the subject of pain that had occupied the first part of the narrative. That pain, it is well to recall, was in part due to the subject's lack of defenses, especially internalized defenses that would prevent him from entering upon self-destructive actions. And so the narrative constructs a self-restrained subject of pleasure. This final drama is played out when Random is reunited with his Narcissa, never to be parted again:

As my first transport abated, my passion grew turbulent and unruly. I was giddy with standing on the brink
of bliss, and all my virtue and philosophy were scarce
sufficient to restrain the inordinate sallies of desire.
—Narcissa perceived the conflict within me, and with
her usual dignity of prudence, called off my imagination from the object in view, and with eager expressions
of interested curiosity, desired to know the particulars
of my voyage.

(67: 425)

Random has one last faculty to master, and he accomplishes this
task with the help of the object that works against mastery of
the turbulent and unruly passions. Thus, Narcissa fills the role
of woman in the bourgeois sphere, she whose function it is to
both incite desire and contain it within acceptable or appropriate
limits. In fulfilling this function, she reflects to the hero not the
negative feelings of repression but the positive accomplishment
of restraint or deferral, a mastery of the self that allows the hero
and the reader to accept the demands of the ego-ideal. In other
words, she gives him a reason for controlling his "sallies of desire" and a sense of satisfaction for doing so; for to indulge those
desires without license would be to taint the idol and sully the
mysteries of heterosexual love.

Narcissa works with Don Rodriguez, Random's father, to
complete the construction of the subject and to keep the narrative from reaching a premature, unsanctioned climax. After satisfying her desire to hear about his travels, Random makes the
following comment: "Having entertained ourselves some hours
with the genuine effusions of our souls, I obtained her consent
to compleat my happiness as soon as my father should judge it
proper" (67: 425). Force is replaced by consent, the mythical
originary moment of bourgeois political structure; and the prolonged Oedipal struggle is resolved by the hero's internalization
of the law of the father. At the same time, the Oedipal structure
is reduplicated in the marriage that is about to take place. Don
Rodriguez identifies Narcissa as the long-lost mother. In this
moment of identification, sexuality is sentimentalized and do-
mesticated: "My father sighing, pronounced 'Such once was my
Charlotte!' while the tear rushed into his eye, and the tender

heart of Narcissa manifested itself in two precious drops of sympathy, which, but for his presence, I would have kissed away" (67: 426). The man's ejaculation is replaced by the woman's tears. The long awaited climax will occur in the privacy of the marital chamber and will generate "the interesting situation, which . . . will produce something to crown [Random's] felicity" (68: 435).

At the end of the text nothing is lacking. The reader finds himself chastened of random sentiments and emplotted by the solution of the enigma. His deepest wishes are engaged in a direct appeal to his sensibilities:

> You whose souls are susceptible of the most delicate impressions, whose tender bosoms have felt the affecting vicissitudes of love, who have suffered an absence of eighteen long months from the dear object of your hope, and found at your return the melting fair, as kind and constant as your heart could wish; do me justice on this occasion, and conceive what unutterable rapture possessed us both, while we flew into one anothers arms!
>
> (67: 424)

The combination of justice and pleasure in this appeal is difficult to resist. Given the dangerous conditions of a random world, who would not wish to find himself in the presence of a "melting fair, as kind and constant as [the] heart could wish"? Who would not wish for the security of acceptance modeled on an unconditional maternal love that negates the harsh conditions of competition reigning in the public sphere, which the text now requires the reader to exchange for the "endearing fondness and tranquillity of love . . . which nought but virtuous wedlock can produce"? In this conclusion with its strong appeal to be loved unconditionally, the reader finds his own truth, and wishing to be free from the fears that the defensive ego feeds on accepts the terms of that truth even as he forgets the oppression and violence that has engendered it. If such oppression and violence continue in the wide world beyond the family redoubt, it is no business of the readers.

NOTES

1. Tobias Smollett, *The Adventures of Roderick Random,* ed. Paul-Gabriel Boucé (Oxford: Oxford University Press, 1979), xxxiii, xxxv. All further references to the novel are included in the text. Both chapter and page numbers are provided in order to facilitate finding passages in other editions.

2. See Michael McKeon, *The Origins of the English Novel, 1600–1740* (Baltimore and London: Johns Hopkins University Press, 1987), 20–21, 169–71. For Smollett's personal politics, see Michael Rosenblum, "Smollett as Conservative Satirist," *ELH* 42 (1975): 556–79.

3. Freud defines *primary psychical process* as the "type of process found in the unconscious," "*freely mobile* processes which press towards discharge. . . . In the unconscious, cathexes can easily be completely transferred, displaced and condensed." From *Beyond the Pleasure Principle,* in *The Freud Reader,* ed. Peter Gay (New York: Norton, 1989), 611, 610. The reader's cathexes (investments) and fantasies are marshaled by the text, as I shall argue below. When speaking of the reader in *Roderick Random,* I shall use the male pronoun because the implied or ideal reader is gendered male. John Barrell has noted that the narrator of *Roderick Random* writes from the position of a gentleman. He gives us "an image of society as a labyrinth, as uncharted country, and also the understanding to find our way through it and so to grasp how it is constructed." In other words, the narrator provides us with mastery over "the vicissitudes of life." *English Literature in History, 1730–80: An Equal, Wide Survey* (New York: St. Martin's Press, 1983), 187. Barrell is referring in this instance to *Ferdinand Count Fathom,* but his remark is pertinent to *Roderick Random* also.

4. For a survey of the literature to 1971 see G. S. Rousseau, "Smollett and the Picaresque: Some Questions about a Label," *Studies in Burke and his Time* 12 (1971): 1886–1904; rpt., with a reply to Rousseau by Paul Gabriel Boucé in G. S. Rousseau, *Tobias Smollett: Essays of Two Decades* (Edinburgh: T. T. Clark, 1982), 53–73. See also Alice Fredman, note 17 below.

5. Reading narrative in order to understand the cultural work it performs is a commonplace among marxist literary critics. See, for example, Fredric Jameson, who describes the novel "as a symbolic act that must reunite or harmonize heterogeneous narrative paradigms which have their own specific and contradictory ideological meaning." *The Political Unconscious: Narrative as a Socially Symbolic Act* (Ithaca and London: Cornell University Press, 1981), 144.

6. Roland Barthes, *S/Z,* trans. Richard Miller, pref. Richard Howard (New York: Hill and Wang, 1974), 10.

7. Rosalind Coward and John Ellis, *Language and Materialism: Developments in Semiology and the Theory of the Subject* (London and New York: Routledge & Kegan Paul, 1977), 68.

8. Ibid., 50.

9. Laura Mulvey, "Visual Pleasure and Narrative Cinema," 1975; rpt. in her *Visual and Other Pleasures* (Bloomington and Indianapolis: Indiana University Press, 1989), 17.

10. Barrell, 192.

11. I am indebted here to John Brenkman's discussion of the ideal ego and the ego ideal. See *Culture and Domination* (Ithaca and London: Cornell University Press, 1987), 196.
12. Barthes, 4.
13. Samuel Johnson, *Rambler* 4, 31 March 1750, in *Samuel Johnson*, ed. Donald Greene (Oxford: Oxford University Press, 1984), 176.
14. James Boswell, *The Life of Johnson*, ed. R. W. Chapman, corr. by J. D. Fleeman (London: Oxford University Press, 1970), 222.
15. Johnson, 177.
16. Ibid., 178.
17. Angus Ross considers the violence as an accurate representation of social conditions. "The 'Show of Violence' in Smollett's Novels," *Yearbook of English Studies* 2 (1972): 118–29. See also Alice Fredman, "The Picaresque in Decline: Smollett's First Novel," in *English Writers of the Eighteenth Century*, ed. John H. Middendorf (New York and London: Columbia University Press, 1971), 199.
18. Barthes, 76.
19. Ibid., 76.
20. For the function of narrativity in satisfying desire, see Peter Brooks, *Reading for the Plot: Design and Intention in Narrative* (New York: A. A. Knopf, 1984), 61.
21. For the ideological significance of dueling, see Donna T. Andrew, "The Code of Honour and its Critics: The Opposition to Duelling in England, 1700–1850," *Social History* 5 (1980): 409–34; and J. C. D. Clark, *English Society, 1688–1832: Ideology, Social Structure and Political Practice During the Ancien Regime* (Cambridge: Cambridge University Press, 1985), 109–16.
22. After listening to her story, Random "contracted a filial respect for her" (38: 215). Later he calls her " 'Dear mother,' " and she greets him with a "truly maternal affection" (65: 404).
23. Random's Uncle Tom Bowling can be viewed in the light of an allegorical figure for such primitive accumulation. He is given to violence, makes his fortune through the slave trade, and has no place within the private sphere. At the end of the novel he returns "to try his fortune once more at sea" (69: 432).
24. Teresa de Lauretis, *Alice Doesn't: Feminism, Semiotics, Cinema* (Bloomington: Indiana University Press, 1984), 121.
25. Mulvey, 20.
26. Brenkman, 197–98.

Confinement and Entrapment in Fielding's *Journal of a Voyage to Lisbon*

Melinda Alliker Rabb

I solemnly declare that unless in revising my former Works, I have at present no intention to hold any further correspondence with the gayer Muses.
> *Covent Garden Journal* 72 (Nov. 25, 1752)

At times we are as different from ourselves as from others.
> La Rochefoucauld, *Maxim* 113

The *Journal of a Voyage to Lisbon* brings Henry Fielding's career to an uneasy (for some, an anticlimactic) close.[1] "A lamp almost burnt out, does not give so steady and uniform a light," some have felt.[2] Questions about the nature and the purpose of the posthumous journal remain unanswered, despite Fielding's avowals that it is an unironic "true history" of his travels, written with a particular concern for maritime reform. In his final narrative, however, the effects of irony, self-representation, and fictionalization complicate the professed simplicity of the text. Travel-literature almost inevitably suggests the conventional idea of life as a journey. In Fielding's *Journal,* this idea is crucially altered. The central metaphor provided by the work is the impeded journey or the journey without progress. Expressed foremost by Fielding's self-portrayal as discontented passenger aboard a slow and claustrophobic ship, the idea also has significance as historical fact, as metaphor, as source of action, as rhetorical strategy, as structural principle, and as theme. By impeding (L. *impedire,* to hold the feet, to ensnare, to entangle the progress of) the subject, Fielding's narrative enacts the entrapment of both author and reader. On this trip, it is difficult to get from one place to another: from England to Lisbon; from the conceptualization of an ideal to the achievement of it; from one consciousness to another; from linguistic signs to meaning. Between these and other "points" lie many snares.

A certain poignancy informs some of the *Journal's* pages: they constitute the last document of a dying man. Moments of great beauty are possible, such the breathtaking sunset and moonrise Fielding watches on deck:

> We were seated on the deck, women and all, in the serenest evening that can be imagined. Not a single cloud presented itself to our view, and the sun himself was the only object which engrossed our whole attention. He did indeed set with a majesty which is incapable of description, with which, while the horizon was yet blazing with glory, our eyes were called off to the opposite part to survey the moon, which was then at full, and which in rising presented us with the second object that this world hath offered our vision. Compared to these the pageantry of theatres, of splendor of courts, are sights almost below the regard of children.

Yet pathos and beauty always contend with a more aggressive Fielding who is in no mood to write another novel or humanitarian social tract. He solicits an audience in a less friendly tone, warning, "I will take my pitch a key lower." Some of the entries display surprising cheerfulness, considering the circumstances of their composition, and this quality has been justly admired. But the pleasures of the *Journal* sometimes are wrested from difficulties both by Fielding and by his reader. The "most amusing pages" are the product of the "most disagreeable hours which ever haunted the author."

The events encompassed by Fielding's "honest" chronicle begin with his departure from England and continue in an apparently methodical chronology. Yet he admits near the end that the "journal" was not written daily; rather, its affect of spontaneity was contrived in retrospect. Fielding also emphasizes the factual accuracy of his account; he claims to epitomize truthfulness among travel writers. Yet his narrative frame seems subjectively contrived. The first page begins under "the most melancholy sun . . . ever beheld," and the last ends in "the nastiest city in the world." Little progress occurs within such a gloomy frame, and this is apt because the *Journal* is not precisely about voyaging.[3] Most pages describe the *absence* of travel, that is, they describe *waiting* in various English ports. Smooth sailing usually receives dismissive treatment, perhaps because brisk progress renders Fielding too seasick to notice much. He condenses "fair weather" and "fresh gale" into a single sentence (67), while he lingers over days when they go nowhere. Least of all, the text is about Lisbon, which Fielding ignores as long as possible and then derides as "the nastiest city in the world."

The inadequacy of each major term in the title (journal, voyage, Lisbon) suggests problems of writing and reading that form a subtext throughout. In explicit and implicit ways, the *Journal* is about striving for uncertain destinations on the journey of life and of writing: to reach nasty Portugal by means of a ship; to reach unreliable readers by means of a text; to reach the inevitability of death. All vehicles prove fraught with difficulties: unpredictable weather and sea impede the ship, while the liabilities of language, of human perception and emotion impede author and audience.

Repeatedly in the *Journal,* Fielding states his intentions and outlines his procedures. Readers may be accustomed to Fielding's intrusive habits as a narrator and yet feel a change in his guidance. Often his overt directions are misleading, while he indirectly reveals better guidelines for responding to the text. The action of the journey procedes against strong undercurrents of psychic/emotional action to which the reader responds. Restricted for the most part to a cabin-sickroom, Fielding speaks candidly about his frustrated isolation. There had been no "season when [he] wanted more food for [his] social disposition, or could converse less wholsomly and happily with [his] own thoughts."

> This . . . being shut up within the circumference of a
> few yards, with scarce a score of human creatures, with
> not one of whom it was possible to converse, was . . . so
> rare, as scarce ever to have happened before, nor could
> it ever happen to one who disliked it more than myself.
> (122)

Alternatives seem relentlessly unsatisfactory. Fielding cannot stay under "the most melancholy sun" of England, whose winters now guarantee his death, nor can he happily stay in Lisbon, where "all idea of beauty vanishes at once," nor can he be content to travel when he is "shut up" and cannot "converse." A work of equally undesirable alternatives may well create confusion about its purpose. Similarly, a work of contending genres (the *Journal* conflates travelogue, diary, novel, autobiography, and essay) may subvert its own well-rationalized purposes. As Robert Uphaus argues, generic confusion frequently signals an emphasis on the affective intentions of the work.[4] Bound within an unwholesome self, Fielding projects a useful, instructive book about maritime affairs. Yet, as his efforts are deflected and checked repeatedly, the idea of entrapment becomes a narrative preoccupation. Fielding shapes his experience into a text, but intractable realities seem to undo his authorial control. Persistently refractory events and an almost freedomless environment contend with the desire that life make sense. These competing impulses engage the reader in the process of questioning more than in earlier works in which Fielding reliably points out the moral.

The history of the *Journal*'s problems precedes its publication. John Fielding read his brother's manuscript with embarrassment and disapproval, judging from the extensive changes upon which he insisted before he would allow Millar to print it.[5] Most of his alterations are designed to make the work more ingratiating to its readers or to alleviate John's discomfort at passages he took as personal slights. Other eighteenth-century readers and reviewers seem incapable of agreement as to the *Journal*'s central issues.

Each finds the text to be about something different: about family demands ("[I]t seems to have been published for the Benefit of his Children" *London Magazine,* Feb. 1755, xxiv. 544); about legal reform ("[M]any intolerable inconveniences which arise either from the defect of our laws, or the ignorance of those by whom they should be executed deserve the attention . . . of the public" *The Gentleman's Magazine* Mar. 1755, xxv. 129); about entertaining episodes, warranting comparison to the novels ("[T]his narrative [is] not greatly abounding with incidents" *The Monthly Review* Mar. 1755, xii. 235). Horace Walpole specifies the grotesque details of Fielding's disease: "Fielding's Travels [is] . . . an account of how his dropsy was treated and teased by an innkeeper's wife."[6] Another reader finds the text ephemeral: "that Fielding should trifle in that manner when immediate death was before his eyes . . . is amazing."[7] Lady Mary Wortley Montagu, perhaps comparing Fielding's earlier and healthier fictive "Bill[s] of Fare," remarks that Fielding could "forget everything when he was before a venison pasty, or over a flask of champagne."[8] The publisher Millar promises readers that the *Journal* will "open every heart" and "call forth a melting tear to . . . blot out whatever failings many be found"; others, like Richardson's friend Thomas Edwards conclude that "the fellow hath no heart."[9]

Reactions to the text are laden with directions or advice on how to read it, yet without much consensus. Ironically, publication of the original unedited manuscript is owing to public interest in the Lisbon earthquake. Millar apparently thought that a work "about Lisbon" would sell. Current critical assessments continue the disagreement. C. J. Rawson, for example, gives it first place in his study of Fielding because Fielding's ultimate rejection of Homer makes a striking contrast to his earlier career; yet Patricia Spacks, who treats Fielding's other self-representations at length, excludes the final narrative completely.[10]

Pat Rogers finds it "one of [Fielding's] most appealing works
. . . as rich in humanity as the best of his novels," while Richard
J. Dircks says that it "is not a happy book."[11]

Contradictory ways of understanding the *Journal* seem all
the more interesting in light of the problematic self-commentary
and self-explanation contained within the text itself. Fielding
persistently urges us toward "what I must be understood to
mean." His remarks sound direct, but in context prove not very
helpful. He lays down "one general rule . . . between relator and
hearer (that he will tell only about things that they could not
know) but (as we shall see) does not adhere to it. He seems
aware that his readers may face difficulties: "[The] particular
knowledge I here mean is entirely necessary to the well understanding and well enjoying of this journal" or "here I cannot be
understood strictly" or "when I said . . . I meant more than I
expressed." He repeatedly claims "this is history," as if wooing
a trust not available to novelist, poet, or playwright: "The following narrative doth . . . deviate less from truth than any voyage
extant"; "every fact" on "the ensuing pages" has its "foundation
in truth." But do these manipulative assertions help the reader?

The claims of honesty and reliability about what the reader
should "perceive" are made dubious by the other surviving docu-
ments associated with the trip to Lisbon. Letters by Fielding
and his companions question both the "true history . . . in humble prose" and the narrator's self-portrayal. Long-suffering,
witty, and wise in the *Journal,* he writes angrily and peevishly
in his letters. His wife, for example, changes from the seasick
heroine in need of protection to a source of "bitchery."[12] An un-
signed letter, probably by Mrs. Fielding's companion, Margaret
(Peggy) Collier, offers a startlingly divergent account of Mr. and
Mrs. Francis and their inn; she calls many of Fielding's "facts"
(including the famous dinner in the barn) "fiction."[13] She characterizes the author as one who "was certainly under great obliga-
tions to anybody that would admit him into their house, whom
disease had render'd offensive to more senses than one." He "had
a napkin put over [the mirror] that he might not be struck with
his own figure, while he was exaggerating that of others." The
Journal's honest traveler becomes in this account one who
"pass'd the last days he saw in his native land, in abusing the

people to whom he was under some obligation, and yet not confining his invective to them only." Can the courageously sick man who still loves life enough to enjoy a glass of good cider also finish his life in "ransacking every place for the means to gratify his depraved appetite, in tormenting himself, and all about him"? While he wrote the grotesque characterization of Mrs. Francis, was he also "afraid to see his own figure, unwilling to correct himself" so that "he exposed that of others, and railed at their Faults"?

Fielding admits some unwholesome things about himself, but as an undeserving victim. The physical grotesque often merges with metaphor: there had been no "season when I wanted more food for my social disposition, or could converse less wholsomly and happily with my own thoughts." Contradictions between historical accounts of Fielding and his own version of the voyage elude reconciliation, but do suggest ways of reading contradictory impulses within the text of the *Journal*. Repeated configurations of opposites characterize its structure, concepts, tropes, and rhetoric.

To read the *Journal* is to experience a sense of oscillation between different subjects and kinds of language. The movement of a typical sentence may be compared with that of an earlier work, *Joseph Andrews*. In the novel, the narrative voice proceeds by increments of increasing irony. A sentence paves the way for the reader's perception: step by step, each phrase advances a little more information, leading ever closer to the author's "meaning." To read such a sentence is to move confidently and steadily toward fuller understanding. A diagram (Fig. 1) illustrates this process. The passage moves the reader deftly from death to seduction; each phrase extends the preceding one. Crucial words ("None," "a good reason," "disconsolate," etc.) emerge, and ironies become progressively clearer ("None but Mrs. Slipslop *and three female friends*"). Transitions and conjunctions are rapid, yet they function as obvious markers of additional related material. A coherent view of Lady Booby evolves: she grieves not for her husband, but for the constraints mourning places on her freedom. She will find ways to enjoy various liberties, gossip, gaming, and sex, even while "confined to her House."

Figure 1

At this time an Accident happened which put an end to the agreeable Walks, which probably would have soon puffed up the Cheeks of Fame and caused her to blow her brazen Trumpet through the Town,

and this was no other than the death of Sir Thomas Booby,

who departed this life, left his disconsolate Lady confined to her House

as closely as if she herself had been attacked by some violent Disease.

During the first six Days the poor Lady admitted none

but Mrs. Slipslop

and three Female Friends

who made a Party at Cards:

but on the seventh she ordered Joey,

whom for a good Reason we shall hereafter call Joseph,

to bring up her Tea-Kettle.

The Lady being in bed,

called Joseph to her,

bad him sit down,

and having accidentally laid her hand

on his,

she asked him, *if he had never been*

in Love?

(Joseph Andrews 1.5.28–29)

The *Journal,* in contrast, enacts in its expressive syntax the configuration of frustration and entrapment. Progress in one direction is impeded or erased by a constraining counter-movement. Series of phrases do not proceed cumulatively toward fuller perception. Rather, they alternate opposing kinds of information and attitude, as the diagram (Fig. 2) illustrates. The passage oscillates between phrases that inform us of a normal, tolerable world ("I received a message from his Grace the Duke," "to attend his Grace . . . upon some business of importance," "ease and lightness," "Gaity of the morning," "many agreeable objects with which I was entertained") and those invoking murder, disease, and pain ("fatigued to death," "gangs of street robbers," "being lame . . . very ill . . . my distemper," "suppressed and overcome by . . . pain, which continued increasingly to torment her"). Transitions are absent or insufficient for the sudden shifts from sunshine to gloom. It becomes difficult to locate the central point of such passages, or to hear a consistently appropriate tone of voice.

Similar examples of impeded movement occur on a larger scale. Fielding begins a paragraph (among many possible examples) by distinguishing "two general ways" of conveyance, and he continues by enumerating "much variety" within each. But he unexpectedly dismisses all of his careful categories at the end: "it is fully sufficient to comprehend them all in the general view, without . . . such minute particulars as would distinguish one method from another." Or, he begins to describe the shipyards of Woolrich and Deptford as "noble sights" that exhibit "the perfection to which we are arrived in building those floating castles." But later in the paragraph, the "floating castles" become "useless, vast and unwieldly burthen[s]": "[T]here is more of ostention . . . in ships of this vast and unwieldly burthen, which are rarely capable of acting against an enemy" (52–53).

These counteractive phrases and sentences set snares for the reader, whose expectations are irregularly satisfied and undercut. Fielding seems to advance an idea and then to place obstacles before it that drive it back again. He asks, "For what, indeed, is the best idea which the prospect of a number of hats can furnish to the mind but of men forming themselves into a society. . . ?" But he begins to challenge his own ideal by listing

Figure 2

Within a few days after this, whilst I was preparing for my journey and when I was almost fatigued to death with several long examinations, relating to five different murders all committed within the space of a week, by different gangs of street robbers,

I received a message from his Grace the Duke of his Newcastle by Mr. Carrington, the King's messenger to attend his Grace the next morning in Lincolns-Inn Fields upon some business of importance but I excused myself from complying with the message as besides being lame I was very ill with the great fatigues I had lately undergone, added to my distemper.

[T]he ease and lightness which I felt from my tapping; the gaiety of the morning, the pleasant sailing with wind and tide, and the many agreeable objects with which I was entertained during the whole way were all suppressed and overcome by the single consideration of my wife's pain, which continued increasingly to torment her till we came to an anchor.

a series of opposing ideas that "step in before it" and overwhelm it: "But in truth there is another idea ready to step in before it, and that is of a body of cutthroats, the supports of tyranny, the invaders of the just liberties and properties of mankind, the plunderers of the industrious, the ravishers of the chaste, the murderers of the innocent, and, in a word, the destroyers of the plenty, the peace, and the safety of their fellow-creatures" (91).

This movement of advance and regress expresses Fielding's disillusion and encourages the reader to share it. Thus, the most beautiful ship the travelers see ("so delightful an object to our eyes") is also the most evil ("carrying . . . desolation and ruin"). The sensation of hope ("In neither of these had we any reason to apprehend a disappointment") eventually is canceled out ("Unluckily, however, we were disappointed in both"). He encourages us to feel that progress forward (in this case, literally progressing toward their destination) brings loss instead of gain. Lisbon looks "very beautiful at a distance," but up close, "all idea of beauty vanishes at once" (130). Perhaps if every sentence, paragraph, or episode exactly repeated this movement, the reader could catch on and have appropriate expectations. But varieties of counter-movement are too great.

For example, Fielding elicits the reader's admiration when he forgives a suppliant Captain Veal ("I did not suffer a brave man and an old man, to remain a moment in this posture"), but then reveals that admiration is an inappropriate response ("I forgave him . . . because it was convenient for me to do so") (115). Consecutive statements may be difficult to reconcile. Fielding writes: "I suffered more than I had done in our whole voyage; my bowels being almost twisted out of my belly. However, the day was very serene and bright, and the captain, who was in high spirits, affirmed he had never passed a pleasanter sea." Extremes of pain and pleasure are brought together by the term "however." Although we might read the sequence as offering a brighter alternative to the contemplation of Fielding's misery, Captain Veal's "high spirits" seem unpleasantly insensitive to his passenger's suffering. Neither man's sensation—twisted bowels or high spirits—is appealing.

The most sardonic instances of striving and being driven back occur in the Introduction. Fielding labors hard at "curing the evil" of London's robbers. He "actually suppressed the evil for a time," but only after sacrifice, effort, and expense. Then, at the season of his apparent "success," the winter, a more potent and uncontrollable adversary, swiftly and cheaply "murders" more innocent "wretches" than the street gangs had victimized. Fielding is helpless to suppress this "evil." In this example and the others, the narrative voice does not articulate ironies, as it might have done in the novels. Statements remain in a state of irresolution. The critical Preface typically obscures the focus of potential ironies. Fielding makes extensive claims and defenses about inventing yet another new kind of writing. Yet the Preface concludes with a comparison of the *Journal* to a farcical scene in a play.[14]

The larger actions—or more precisely, inactions—of the *Journal* follow this pattern. Fielding plans "to go immediately to Bath" and writes "that very night" to engage rooms, but he never leaves London. Later, the travelers rush to board the ship, but it does not sail. They send ahead fresh provisions for a hot dinner at the inn, but nothing gets cooked. They arrive in Lisbon, but cannot disembark. They dare to anticipate; they are surprised, and usually disappointed. Over and over, the *Journal* forces its readers to re-experience the frustrated progress of the journey.

II

Fielding's "true history" of "facts" in "humble prose" owes many of its strongest effects to its figurative language. He claims to "relate facts plainly and simply as they are," and avoids the flamboyantly self-conscious simile and metaphor familiar to readers of the novels. Yet the prose subtly weaves together image and metaphor in order to "relate facts plainly." The *Journal's* important tropes contribute to the experience of frustration and entrapment. The central image of the windbound ship begins as a physical reality but becomes a metaphor for unwilling restraint of many kinds. The ship first offers escape from London's dangerous winter. But the ship imprisons Fielding, so that he describes himself as "shut up within the circumference of a few yards." The ship, in turn, is "shut up" by a wind that refuses to blow. Images of ships that go nowhere are kept before us by Fielding's daily entries about their lack of progress and by descriptions of other ships docked and waiting in various ports.

Soon, he himself becomes a metaphorical ship, described as having "lain so long windbound in the ports of this kingdom" (105). Eventually the metaphor's connotations broaden to include the frustration of all worthy human endeavor as boats confined to shore or driven back by dangerous natural forces:

> I could not help reflecting how often the greatest abilities lie wind-bound, as it were in life; or, if they venture out and attempt to beat the seas, they struggle in vain against the wind and tide, and, if they have not sufficient prudence to put back, are most probably cast away upon the rocks and quicksands which are every day ready to devour them.
>
> (120)

The windbound ship serves as a metonymy for the general concept of impeded journeys and for the contrary movement of release and constraint. Tom Jones had "not sufficient prudence," but has any reader thought that Tom, who has the "greatest abilities" would "most probably [be] cast away upon the rocks"?

Perhaps even more convincing of the pessimism of the *Journal* is its contrast to Fielding's late but optimistic project, the Universal Register-Office (established in 1750). He has very different things to say about human ability and human progress in promoting this enterprise. Unlike the alienation and isolation of traveling to Lisbon, the Register Office would "bring the world as it were together into one place." Unlike the idle ships and wind-bound talents of the voyage, he claims in the "Plan of the Universal Register-Office," "no talent in any of [Society's] members, which is capable of contributing to the general Good, should lie idle and unemployed, nor any of the wants of its members which are capable of relief, should remain unrelieved" (*Plan*, 3). Rather than being cast away and destroyed by a world in which malevolent forces daily "devour" the good, "it is most probable that every human talent is dispersed somewhere or other among the members and consequently every person who stands in need of that talent, might supply his need if he knew where to find it" (*Plan*, 5).[15]

The external world in the *Journal* consists of realities that can be as unhealthy as Fielding's "unwholesome" thoughts, offering few satisfactory alternatives to the collapse of his personal affairs. In addition to the windbound ship, important images come from nature and natural processes, problematic forces with which human life must contend. Conventional gender constructions of nature as feminine are asserted with a difference. Nature is not admired uncritically as a bountiful source for human activity or for artistic inspiration (compare Pope's "Nature to advantage dres't"). "Nature is not, any more than a great genius, always admirable in her productions," Fielding observes. Nature makes mistakes, and she also may be stingy, "truly a parsimonious distributor of her richest gifts." Or she may be unpleasantly lavish, generous only with her most disgusting products, so that "[you] have your taste affronted with every sort of trash that can be picked up at the green-stall or the wheel-barrow." She becomes a duplicitous seductress, cruelly toying with Fielding's emotions: "[S]he made as great a fool of [him]" and "drew [him] in to suffer" the good-byes to his children. "I doubt not," he writes of Nature's trick, "whether, in that time, I did not undergo more than in all my distemper."

His representation of the actual women on his journey reinforces a generally negative construction of femininity. Good Mrs. Fielding, immobilized at crucial points by seasickness and toothache, is absent and silent. Bad Mrs. Francis, ugly, shrewish, and dishonest, is all too present. Maternal, life-giving qualities are transferred, by means of figurative language, elsewhere. Trade becomes "that *alma mater,* at whose plentiful breast all mankind are nourished." Captain Veal, who feels toward his former ship "as a widower of a deceased wife," assumes motherly affection for his new ship: "we have . . . set down a pregnant example in his demonstration of love and tenderness towards his boats and ship."

Fielding's imagery frustrates other conventional connotations of the feminine. Disease has rendered his own body impotent and disfigured. After explaining that pregnant women were afraid to look at him for fear of miscarrying, he refers to his own "burthen," that is, to the water in his grossly extended belly, "under which [he] laboured" until he was "delivered." Male writers have appropriated metaphors of female biological creativity to describe the production of works of art, but Fielding's childbirth metaphors describe his own physical decay. Other characters described with natural imagery fare little better: Mrs. Francis becomes "brisk wind to a standing-pool." Fielding asserts that "nature is seldom curious in her works within; without employing some little pains on the outside" and cites the example of "venomous insects" like the wasp that openly displays its"sting or saw," or the rattle-snake who sounds its tail. These external warnings are nature's way of protecting "man . . . that innocent lambkin." "Bestial" is here distinct from "human," a boundary that is transgressed when Mrs. Francis becomes "the most venomous of human insects."

Recent feminist attempts to revise critical assumptions about Fielding as "this man among men" are persuasive. His views on "the woman question" in The Champion, Tom Jones, and Amelia may be understood more sympathetically by feminists.[16] Sophia who defies convention and Amelia who transcends it, convey Fielding's increasing esteem for the value of genuine tenderness and friendship as enabled by women. Yet these revisionist insights serve to highlight another contrast in the Journal. Tenderness is rare or misplaced (Captain Veal's toward his cat or ship) during the voyage, and friendship succumbs to convenience and ill-humor. Women seem without the creative sexuality that strengthens them in the novels.

In earlier works, Fielding often gives food metaphoric significance. In the "Bill of Fare to the Feast" in Tom Jones, for example, Fielding promises to nurture and satisfy his readers' appetites. The meal shared by Tom and Jenny Waters suggests hearty sexual desire (just as the image of Blifil dining on an ortolan suggests his frigidity). References to food and eating run through the Journal as well, along with their counterparts, deprivation and hunger. Comments about the amount, quality, or scarcity of meat, fish, tea, or other refreshment figure in almost every entry, and focus on the traveler's persistent physical malaise. The gnawing hungers of appetite and desire take on other figurative significance. In addition to vanity, Fielding writes, hunger is the "inducement to writing." He craves actual food, yet also "never needed more food for [his] social disposition."

At times, the contradictory actions (constantly consuming food while constantly being consumed by disease, eating without satisfying) are captured metaphorically. He describes the cool summer as rotting and "mould'ring away," and the summer fruits as having "some appearance of ripeness without . . . any real maturity." Yet he describes his swollen belly as "ripe for the trochar" (39). Narratives become something to be "gulped down," (95) and the gifts of fresh vegetables from a kind gentlewoman are "offals which fall from a table moderately plentiful" (86). Mrs. Francis's complexion "turn[s] milk to curds." Fielding may feel "gloriously regaled" by a dinner or angered by a poorly cooked roast venison. The reader cannot easily respond to the recitation of each menu. Distasteful images of dropping offal or of searching "in the dirtiest kennel" contribute to the *Journal*'s sensory ambivalence. They contribute the narrative's obsessive, unprogressive movement.

Ordinary physical realities and actions during the voyage are transformed into greater importance by the language with which Fielding records them and by his tendency to turn exposition into metaphor. In contrast, imaginative sources for travel literature, like the *Odyssey,* reverse the process. Fielding deflates the figurative power of these sources into "humble prose." Odysseus and his crew of hero-sailors become "the gang of Captain Ulysses" and Circe is demoted to "some good alewife who made his crew drunk." Otherwise, the "fable," writes Fielding, "seems very strange and absurd" (100). "Facts" about what was served at the inn acquire figurative power, while classical "fictions" are demythologized and literalized. I have dwelt so long on figurative language because it most obviously resists Fielding's overt claims of writing factual history in unadorned prose. Other sources of resistance are also important.

Comic characters enacting comic incidents accompanied the novel-journeys; on the way to Lisbon, too, some comic incidents occur, but they seem peripheral, not central, to the narrative. Urgency and disillusionment surround them: "[S]ome of the most amusing pages, if indeed, there be any which deserve that name, were possibly the production of the most disagreeable hours which ever haunted the author" (122). Despite partial resemblances and occasional reminders of the novels (such as the Francis/Tow-wouse parallels), in which characters and adventures punctuate a journey, the exact course of Fielding's travels is imposed upon him. His typical narrative—"the continuous conversion of act into reflection and experience into spectacle"—becomes partial conversion. It is neither fiction nor objective "truth."[17]

Restrictions of many kinds affect the work: Fielding narrows his aims and his subject matter; he restricts his affection to his small family circle; he senses the approaching endpoint of his life; the limitations of his income threaten privation to his heirs. Above all, he is now a cripple and is literally confined to his chair. The forces from which he cannot escape widen around him, even as they press in on him with increasing strength. They are represented by his chair, his cabin-sickroom, the ship that he cannot leave and that is itself confined by the caprices of the wind, and, more abstractly, the social ideals to which he devoted his professional life.

The travelers, especially Fielding, cope with a world pinched by monetary want and physical pain. These conditions change his former comic attitude toward laughter. In 1742, he claimed that "laughter in a good and delicate mind will begin to change itself into compassion"; it is "wholsome physic for the mind" and can "purge away spleen, melancholy, and ill-affections." It draws people together:

> Surely he hath a very ill-framed mind who can look on
> ugliness, infirmity, or poverty, as ridiculous in them-
> selves; nor do I believe any man living, who meets a
> dirty fellow riding through the streets in a cart, is
> struck with the idea of the Ridiculous from it.[18]

By the time Fielding sailed to Lisbon, people with ill-framed minds had disillusioned him. He had become an example of poverty, infirmity, and disfigurement of such proportions that "timorous women with child had abstained from looking at [him]." He is strapped to his chair and lowered awkwardly into the boat

while a crowd hoots and jeers. Their derision epitomizes laughter
in a world in which "that cruelty and inhumanity in the nature
of men . . . leads the mind into a train of very uncomfortable and
melancholy thoughts." While he may attempt comic laughter in
his earlier manner (for example, in the incident of the captain's
nephew) to laugh now also means to join the crowd at the dock
in deriding the solitary sufferer. We are far from the roasting of
Parson Adams whose innocence, save for his pride in his sermons, resiliently survives.

The insistence on writing "true history" raises further problems for the *Journal*'s characterization. Mrs. Francis and Captain Veal seem most closely to approximate comic characters.
Fielding uses familiar descriptive techniques in order to ridicule
vanity and hypocrisy. But the characters on his travels are people who really annoy him. They are partially transformed into
textual constructs, yet ridicule of them cannot be completely
benign. Formerly, the people who inspired his comic portrayals
were cloaked in anonymity and authorial magnanimity. These
buffers allowed laughter without cruelty. Now Fielding exposes
those he most dislikes. Mrs. Francis, a lurid composite of Mrs.
Tow-wouse and Richardson's Mrs. Jewkes, is also a real woman
to whom Fielding deals a direct insult.[19] He subverts the restric-
tion set forth in the Preface to report true facts without exagger-
ation. No human creature precisely mirrors the character of
Mrs. Francis. He breaks his own rule to achieve peevish revenge
on her inhospitality. He once wrote that "the party himself may
laugh as well as any other." But it is impossible to imagine Mrs.
Francis's being amused by the description of her body (51) or by
such remarks as "She exerted, therefore, all the ill-humor of
which she was mistress, and did all she could to thwart and
perplex everything during the whole evening."

The characters of the voyage offer few possibilities for relationship, for Fielding is on a ship of fools. The liveliest moments
involve the grotesque, without the affection felt for a grotesque
like Mrs. Slipslop. Admirable characters (Fielding's family, the
generous gentlewoman) remain in the background with neither
vivid description nor dialogue. At times, they begin "to creep
out of their holes" but soon retreat. The gentlewoman requests
anonymity, and a seasick Mrs. Fielding takes to her bed. Other

examples of human nature—the jeering sailors, the boatmen who overcharge passengers, the self-seeking men who refuse to build the causeway, the inconsiderate Duke, the insolent nephew, the insulting customs' official, the Swiss captain, Captain Veal and Mrs. Francis—surround and press in on Fielding.

Restrictions on the *Journal*'s content and aims call to mind by contrast the bold declarations of the novels. Formerly, his subject matter was vast and inclusive, like the limitless potential of *Joseph Andrews* in which "life everywhere furnishes . . . the ridiculous," like *Amelia*'s "models of life," or like the "prodigious variety" of *Tom Jones*'s "Bill of Fare": "[A] cook will have sooner gone through all the several species of animal and vegetable food in the world than an author will be able to exhaust so extensive a subject." But grandiose schemes are set aside in the *Journal*. It replaces the endless feast of *Tom Jones* with the sparser provisions of the travelers. Its subject matter is narrowly defined: "[T]here are few things which a traveller is to record, there *are fewer* which he is to offer his observations" (24). He now delimits a topic that is "surely more feasible than that of reforming a whole people." And this diminished scope focuses on restrictive "laws" rather than on ungovernable "people."

Like his earlier fictive narrators, Fielding himself provides the dominant "character"; however, the narrative voice is more bleakly autobiographical, is more unheroic than mock-heroic. Traces of the burlesque appear; the authorial voice recalls (if it does not achieve) intimacy with the reader ("where the author, to use George Eliot's metaphor, draws his armchair to the proscenium to address his audience in person"[20]). This new unheroic mode results partly from his loneliness. Heroes (like those epic heroes evoked comically in Parson Adams and Tom Jones) also experience a kind of isolation, but only in order to explore special freedoms and distinctions, to exercise boundless energy and will. Fielding, to the contrary, is bound literally (when strapped to his chair) and metaphorically. Even when he is able to strike a deft blow at some "enemy," he is at pains to undercut himself. When Captain Veal is brought to his knees, Fielding's forgiveness is made to seem small and self-serving:

> And here, that I may not be thought the sly trumpeter
> of my own praises, I do utterly disclaim all praise on
> the occasion. Neither did the greatness of my mind
> dictate, nor the force of my Christianity exact, this
> forgiveness. To speak truth, I forgave him from a mo-
> tive which would make men more forgiving if they
> were wiser than they are, because it was convenient
> for me to do so.
>
> (115)

Such defensive writing subverts the possibility that the reader
will enjoy the triumph over Captain Veal or even know the point
of the episode.

Fielding's unheroic self-portrayal begins in the Introduction, an autobiographical background to his eventual departure
from England. He describes the progress of his diseases, a long
series of physical sieges and mental trials. But he seems uneasy
about asking for admiration. For example, he writes of his efforts
against street gangs: "Though the visit cost me a severe cold, I
notwithstanding, set myself to work. . . . Though my health was
now reduced to the last extremity, I continued to act with utmost
vigor against these villains." But he also represents himself as
the antithesis of strength and grace: "I was almost fatigued to
death, . . . had I strength remaining to go thither," he reports
"in the utmost distress." His body is "so entirely emaciated that
it had lost all its muscular flesh," while his stomach is so dis-
tended that "[he] was tapped and fourteen quarts of water drawn
from [his] belly." Enumerated afflictions form a refrain: "a distemper," "a severe cold," "deep jaundice," "being lame," "a
dropsy," "an asthma," "the agonies of death."

If the Introduction is a matter-of-fact background to the
voyage of a public servant (as Fielding claims it is), the detailed
account of his sickness is too prolonged (see especially 31–39),
too liable to set his own vulnerability and mortality against the
immortal achievements of a hero and a martyr: "Having thus
fully accomplished my undertaking, I went into the country in
a very weak and deplorable condition, ... The sudden relaxation . . . so weakened me that within two days I was thought to
be falling into the agonies of death . . . I began in earnest to look
on my case as desparate."

Less intense yet constant mundane problems beset his "odyssey": money (the cost of the ship's passage, of supplies, of the inn), provisions (cider, tea, the quality of various meats, wines, cheeses), and physical discomforts (deafness, toothache, sea-sickness, hunger, dropsy, gout). A perpetual need for replenishment, an attention to common trivia, make the traveler/hero seem both durable and vulnerable. His trials lack glamour and even border on the morose. Caught in such snares as gout and poverty, death ignobly becomes

> indeed, no other than the giving up of what I saw little likelihood of being able to hold much longer, and which, upon the terms I held it, nothing but the weakness of human nature could represent to me as worth holding at all.
>
> (35)

III

The Preface announces an opposition between history and romance, in which the author chooses fact (what he calls "real and valuable knowledge of man and things") over fiction. He defines both sides of the antithesis. Romantic "lies" are condemned out of hand. The rejection of fiction for fact has overt and subtle consequences. The narrative sometimes moves from a description that activates the imagination to a harsh reminder of what is "real." For example, Fielding comments with comic irony on the bustling port between Redriffe and Wapping, encouraging the reader to imagine its sights and sounds and to compare it to another work of imagination, a Hogarth print. He captures the

> sounds of seamen, watermen, fish-women, oyster-women, and . . . all the vociferous inhabitants of both shores, composing altogether a greater harmony than Hogarth's imagination hath brought together in that print of his, which is enough to make a man deaf to look at. . . .
>
> (46)

But he immediately directs attention to grim facts about himself: "I had more urgent cause to press our departure, which was, that the dropsy, for which I had undergone three tappings, seemed to threaten me with a fourth discharge, before I should reach Lisbon." This pattern of alternating moods curbs all fanciful flights from present distress.

The narrative's patterns of impediment have multiple consequences. Contrasts between control and helplessness, preparations and delay, hate and inertia project Fielding's vulnerabilities onto the world at large. This process is suggested by the parallel between his life and the ship's course. He is constantly at the mercy of his illness, of the Duke, of watermen, innkeepers, and the captain; the ship is subject to forces of wind and weather. The wind, especially, comes to represent the flimsiness of all their plans; even Captain Veal calls it "bewitched." All the voyagers become involved in incidents that begin with hurried preparation but end in disappointment or inaction. False starts become the rule. Vacant lodgings at Bath, raw venison on a cold hearth, empty sails, sums of money paid for items that never materialize—these details give concrete shape to disappointed expectation.

The pattern of hurry and delay manipulates the sense of time in the *Journal,* so that even time becomes a means of entrapment. Fielding had long been interested in the relationship between time and textuality. In *Tom Jones,* for example, a chapter may be titled "Containing three hours," and another, "Containing about five pages." During the voyage, textuality does not presume to control time, although readers feel a continuing awareness of its representation. Days, weeks, and months may race by, or a few moments may drag on interminably, depending on Fielding's perceptions. For example, the progress of his illness is speedy: "The sudden relaxation which [the tapping] caused, added to my enervate, emaciated habit of body, so weakened me, that within days I was thought to be falling into the agonies of death. (37)" If it takes only two days to arrive at death's door, the progress of recovery is painfully slow, requiring two months for "some little degree of strength": "I began slowly, as it were, to draw my feet out of the grave; till in two months time I had again acquired some little degree of strength, but was again full of water." Similarly, he watches the summer "Mouldering away" and wonders if the year has postponed the warm season indefinitely: "[T]he early fruits came to the fulness of their growth . . . without acquiring any real maturity" (40). His belly, however, is "ripe for the trochar"; his diseases develop with breakneck speed:

> I saw the dropsy gaining rather than losing ground; the distance growing still shorter between the tappings, I saw the asthma likewise beginning again to become more troublesome. I saw the Midsummer quarter drawing to a close. So that I conceived . . . I should be delivered up to the attacks of winter.
>
> (40)

The momentum of his decline gathers force while his efforts at recovery, even at stasis, are overwhelmed. The unripe fruit and the ripe belly, both unnatural images, reinforce the sense that time is out of joint. Similarly, the ship's retarded progress suggests that human endeavor falters against the relentless march of time. Occasionally a gale quickens the voyage, but often they attempt to sail "in direct opposition to the tide" and manage only "three miles in as many hours" (119).

Fielding's sense of the passage of time may indicate the emotional intensity of an event. Minutes may seem longer than a year, as they do during the arduous, embarrassing business of hoisting him by pulleys onto the deck. He experiences "a fatigue" that is "more intolerable" than he had "undergone in a land journey of twelve miles which [he] travelled with the utmost expedition" (40). Time rapidly runs out for Fielding. He can no longer, as he could in *Tom Jones,* make his history "move backwards." Discoveries come tardily, bringing regret for "what I had thought of too late."

"Too late" come thoughts of family and health: again, an unresolved conflict ensues. The *Journal* constantly weighs public and private responsibility; in a way, it is a result of their antagonism. Fielding writes to support his family, but also to continue social reform. He "cures" the body politic of its affliction (crime) while his own body succumbs to disease. During his last months in England and during the trip, legal proceedings and proposals alternate with attacks of dropsy, tappings, and colds. Ironically, as crime lessens, Fielding himself wastes away. The public good proves a parasite, and Fielding a kind of host.

The unresolved struggle between public and private worlds finds further expression in the *Journal*'s attention to the systems of value by which an individual functions in society. Moral values are least discussed. Money and food, which are measured, recorded, and evaluated, figure in almost every entry. Cost becomes a minor theme. Four entries in a row, for example, dwell on accounts (74–90), with little relevance to maritime reform. Typically, his only comment about the first night in Lisbon, for which he had risked the perils of the sea, is about the expense of dinner: "Here we regaled ourselves with a good supper, for which we were as well charged, as if the bill had been made on the Bath road, between Newbury and London" (131). Transactions of money belong to a world in which one either cheats or is cheated. These unpleasant choices irritate Fielding. He complains, for example, of the Captain's exorbitant provisions:

> I am firmly persuaded the whole pitiful £30 came pure and neat into the captain's pocket, and not only so, but attended with the value of £10 more in sundries, into the bargain. I must confess myself therefore at a loss how the epithet *pitiful* came to be annexed to the above sum . . . nor do I believe it is so thought by the greatest men in the kingdom; none of whom would scruple to search for it in the dirtiest kennel, where they had only a reasonable hope of success.
>
> (119)

Money draws people to the "dirtiest kennel," yet it is also the commonest measure of the "worth" of a life. Fielding even calculates his own value in the Introduction by tallying up the sums he cost or saved the government. Parliament dispenses £600 "to demolish the then reigning gangs" of London robbers, although only £200 reaches Fielding. In return for this investment, he manages a huge profit: "not only no such thing as a murder, but not even a street-robbery [was] commited." There is no satisfactory system with which to evaluate such an achievement; there is only £200 of "the dirtiest money upon earth."

To the account of his finances, Fielding adds the history of his physical decay, expressed in a mixture of monetary and medical details. After explaining the exact disposal of government funds, he writes, "I was tapped, and fourteen quarts of water drawn from my belly" (37). The quarts of water in his belly become a kind of currency with which he measures the cost of reform; his salary and expenses weigh against the number of tappings.

Within the harsh world that entraps him, hope survives. His hope of recovery motivates the voyage; his hope of reform and of a pension motivate the writing of the journal. Most events prove that anticipation leads to disappointment, and the concluding entries are no exception. Safe arrival at their destination immediately turns into frustration: "I never yet saw or heard of a place where a traveller had so much trouble given him at his landing as here" (129). Just as he had hoped *en route* for a dish of "beans smoking on the table" or for some good conversation, he expects comfort, if not escape, in Portugal. But his perspective changes as he nears the city:

> As the houses, convents, churches, &c. are large, and
> all built with white stone, they look very beautiful at
> a distance, but as you approach nearer, and find them
> to want every kind of ornament, all idea of beauty van-
> ishes at once.
>
> (130)

Promises of relief are broken. Fielding may be glad to sup on dry land, but nothing bears close inspection: "as you approach nearer, . . . all idea of beauty vanishes."

IV

Fielding implies that writing is therapeutic, that it can be an effective means of relief from personal distress. Most readers would support such writing: keeping a journal is better than dwelling on unwholesome thoughts. If Fielding solicits sympathy, he also harbors anger at his plight and toward the public

he holds responsible for it. This anger takes the form of estrange-
ment between narrator and implied reader. He no longer claims
"the liberty to make what laws I please. . . . And these laws my
readers, whom I consider as my subjects, are bound to believe
in and to obey." Under such permissive and open-ended laws,
everything is possible. But the *Journal* lacks freedom: it narrows
everything down to "one general rule" based on selectivity and
restraint:

> I shall lay down only one general rule; which I believe
> to be of universal truth between relator and hearer; as
> it is between author and reader; that is, that the latter
> never forgive any observations of the former which
> doth not convey some knowledge that they are sensible
> they could not possibly have attained of themselves.

No confident assumptions (like *Tom Jones*'s "we doubt not but our
reader may be rendered desirious to read on forever") justify this
defensive maneuver. The rule anticipates readers who "never for-
give" an artistic lapse. Self-absorption (however understandable)
makes him disregard the audience's pleasure. He displays an
emaciated body and bloated belly. He addresses his work not to
love, wisdom, or friendship, but to "the public utility which will
arise from it" and to his "slenderly provided for" family.

Accusation and apology can place the reader in the enemy
camp. The Duke of Newcastle, exemplary of a social system that
feeds off of loyalty and hard work by (civil) servants, abuses
Fielding's delicate health. With palpable anger, the Introduction
groups the reader and "men" in general with the Duke. Fielding
is particularly touchy about suspicions of his personal honor and
ethics:

> But, lest the reader should be too eager to catch at the
> word vanity, and should be unwilling to indulge me
> with so sublime a gratification, for I think he is not too
> willing to gratify me, I will take my pitch a key lower,
> and will frankly own that I had a stronger motive than
> love of the public to push me on: I will therefore confess
> to him that my private affairs at the beginning of the
> winter had but a gloomy aspect; for I had not plundered

the public or the poor of those sums which men, who
are always ready to plunder both as much as they can,
have been pleased too suspect me of taking.

(34)

Almost no one is welcome unconditionally in this narrative. Fielding esteems his family but suspects the public. He would no longer "become a voluntary sacrifice to the public good" but would do so out of "love for [his] family" (35). "Were I desirous of playing the advocate," he writes, "I have occasion fair enough; but I disdain such an attempt." The presumed friends of *Tom Jones*'s "Farewell to the Reader" are now presumed to be begrudging and distant acquaintances. "Public praise is the last gift they care to bestow," so "let the world draw from [the journal's facts] what conclusions they please." At one point Fielding abruptly apologizes for speaking urgently of his private affairs:

> But, not to trouble the reader with anecdotes, contrary
> to my own rule laid down in my Preface. I assure
> him . . . that my health begun to decline so fast that I
> had very little more of life left to accomplish what I
> had thought of too late.

As he contrasts the "anecdotes" with the reader's supposed indifference, we see how the "one general rule" has become a strategy of entrapment.

Even when Fielding indulges an occasional impulse to joke with the reader, the appropriate response is unclear. One such "joke" contrasts with the hyperbolic apostrophe to Vanity in *Joseph Andrews:*

> I know that thou will think that, whilst I abuse thee,
> I court thee, and that the love of thee hath inspired me
> to write the sarcastical panegyric on thee; but thou art
> deceived; I value thee not a farthing; nor will it give
> me any pain if thou shouldst prevail on the reader to
> censure this digression as arrant nonsense; for know,
> to thy confusion, that I have introduced thee for no
> other purpose than to lengthen out a short chapter.
> (*Joseph Andrews*, 57)

> Can I say I had no fear? Indeed, I cannot. Reader, I was
> afraid for thee, lest thou shouldst have been deprived
> of that pleasure thou art now enjoying; and that I
> should not live to draw out on paper that military char-
> acter which thou didst peruse in the journal of yes-
> terday.
>
> (97)

The second passage cuttingly suggests that the reader will be angered, not by Fielding's death, but by missing a few moments of pleasant reading.

The reader is left to negotiate the significance of ironies or of such phrases as "infants just born" in a list of "wretches": "women in labor, people in sickness, infants just born, prisoners, and captives." His shrill rejection of romance's "stupid, sense-less, incredible lies" and his rigid insistence on historical fact differs greatly from the latitude granted historians to distort fact in, for example, *Covent Garden Journal* #12.[21] His once-ironic use of "betters" as a word for the rich *(Covent-Garden Journal* #27, for example) now becomes an earnest call for the "regulation of the mob by their betters."[22] The once-earnest use of "liberty" ("I am at liberty to make what laws I please. . . .") becomes derogatory: "The only one . . . who is possessed of abso-lute liberty, is the lowest member of society" (84).

Thus language in the *Journal* demonstrates how Fielding's claims of "true history" break down under the demands of his emotional or personal history. He begins with confident asser-tions that the truth can be told simply and understood com-pletely, but quickly he is drawn into a condition of doubt. He lacks confidence in the reader and in the efficacy of words; the narrative pauses to lament "the vague and uncertain use of a word." In the novels, lack of precision and stability in language becomes an opportunity for the pleasures of irony or for self-reflexivity (such as the fight in *Joseph Andrews,* concluding "in short, that he was dead"). Now Fielding is more querulous that "it is not easy to set any bounds to the use of the word." Uncer-tain meaning in words like "liberty," "pitiful," "usual and accus-tomed wages," are specifically decried as sources of "evil," and as "words without any force or meaning." He lingers over Mrs.

Francis's misspelling of "wine" as "wind." The introduction of Captain Veal into the narrative sends Fielding on a digression about language:

> [H]e is called captain; a word of such various use and uncertain signification, that it seems very difficult to fix any positive idea to it: if indeed there be any general meaning which may comprehend all its different uses. . . .
>
> (51)

Critics have seen Fielding's career moving toward a more secure sense of meaning through language, so that by the time he writes *Amelia,* he "demands nothing less than the right he has earned in his earlier writings to use language directly and literally."[23] But the *Journal* does not follow this development. Sometimes direct, at other times ironic, or even sarcastic, it acknowledges to its reader its own potential for obfuscation and subterfuge. These snares for the reader draw our attention to examples of misreading (and miswriting) within the text. For so short a work, Fielding mentions a surprising number of verbal misadventures. He includes travel literature that bores its readers and exposes the vanity of its authors and romances that "pervert and confuse," "impose, and lie." Bills cheat and distort the truth. An entire library worth 500 pounds is comprised of hundreds of duplications of the same text under different titles. A misunderstood treatise on tar-water by Bishop Berkeley prolongs suffering and illness. The nephew's exaggerated story, like bait thrown to credulous fish, becomes a "whole narrative [to be] gulped down" by some of the voyagers. The "strange story" of Circe in the *Odyssey,* Fielding claims had been misinterpreted until he provided the "key . . . for unlocking the whole mystery." These are troubling reading paradigms. Doubts about the consequences of creating texts of any kind impede the action of the voyage. Unlike the "partial magic" of the novels, Fielding here seems to desire no magic at all. And yet he acknowledges the inexplicable and uncontrollable aspects of reading. The texts-within-the-text fail to make that journey through language that is associated with the central trope of the impeded voyage.

Finally, we should recall the rejection of Homer as a romancer who perverts and confuses and whose *Odyssey* is "the confounder and corruptor" of "voyage-writing." "For my own part," Fielding writes, "I must confess, I should have honoured and loved Homer more had he written a true history of his own times in humble prose" (26). Why is he so shrill about "stupid, senseless, incredible lies" and "monstrous improbabilities and absurdities"? Fielding's sense of entrapment does much to explain the substitution of epic voyage by utilitarian travel-narrative. There is no wide-ranging imagination, for this is no journey to gain wisdom.[24] Fielding's unheroic self-representation contrasts with a figure like Odysseus who guides his ship (unlike Fielding trapped below deck), who successfully asserts his will over circumstance, who eventually can go home. Unlike the comic heroes of his novels, Fielding is acutely aware of the conflict between his former "ideal motives and the resistant reality of the world."[25]

The journal is not all gloom. Neither is it an example of cheerful resignation to things as they are. The narrative contains a divided impulse to entertain and to blame. In order for a writer to create a textual self, the reader must become "an active participant in the creative act." Sometimes the discovery of autobiographical strategies of concealment (the writer's self-defenses) make the reader feel closer to the writer, as in the case of James Boswell. Fielding makes this process as difficult as the movement from England to Portugal. He records, recreates, and forces the reader to re-enact the frustration of human effort to arrive safely at a meaningful end. Life is not imitated as a providential journey down a solitary road. We are rather windbound on an open sea or in a strange port—places full of signs that sometimes are as empty, and waiting to be filled, as the sails of a ship.

NOTES

1. Henry Fielding, *The Journal of a Voyage to Lisbon,* ed. Harold E. Pagliaro (New York: Random House, 1963). All references are to this edition.
2. *The Monthly Review* (March 1755, xii. 234–35).
3. Pagliaro comments on the *Journal*'s unlikely qualities as travel-literature, concluding that it "is a work showing so much disrespect for voyage literature that it all but disqualifies itself from the tradition" (8).

4. Robert W. Uphaus, *The Impossible Observor: Reason and the Reader in Eighteenth-Century Prose* (Lexington: University of Kentucky Press, 1979), 7. Uphaus discusses eighteenth-century works that force the abandonment of reason and critical objectivity in the face of a strong emotional appeal. He does not discuss the *Journal,* although he feels that in the novels, Fielding solves moral predicaments for the reader, allowing the reader to remain an external observer, rather than a participant in determining the text.
5. See, for example, Pagliaro, 17.
6. Letter to Richard Bentley in *Letters of Horace Walpole,* ed. Paget Toynbee (1903), iii. 294.
7. Thomas Edwards, letter to Samuel Richardson (May 28, 1755), quoted in A. D. McKillop, *Samuel Richardson* (1906), 176.
8. Letter to Lady Bute, quoted in *Henry Fielding: The Critical Heritage,* ed. Ronald Paulson (London: Routledge and Kegan Paul, 1969), 395.
9. Thomas Edwards, letter to Samuel Richardson (28 May 1755) in A. D. McKillop, *Samuel Richardson* (New York, 1936), 176.
10. C. J. Rawson, *Henry Fielding and the Augustan Ideal Under Stress* (London: Routledge and Kegan Paul, 1972) and Patricia Meyer Spacks, *Imagining a Self: Autobiography and Novel in Eighteenth-Century England* (Cambridge: Harvard University Press, 1976). Rawson begins with the *Journal* as exemplary of traditional beliefs "under stress" during Fielding's career. Spacks compares James Boswell's journals with Fielding's novels (and with their autobiographical qualities) but does not draw on Fielding's autobiographical journal.
11. Pat Rogers, *Henry Fielding: A Biography* (New York: Charles Scribner's Sons, 1979), 214; Richard J. Dircks, *Henry Fielding* (Boston: Twayne Publishers, 1983), 126.
12. Hugh Amory, "Fielding's Lisbon Letters," *Huntington Library Quarterly* 35 (1971), 65–83.
13. The authorship of this letter is discussed and its text quoted in *Henry Fielding: The Critical Heritage,* 394–35.
14. As Pagliaro states, in Act II. iv of George Villiers's *The Rehearsal* (1671), "Gentleman-Usher and Physician effect a revolution by drawing their swords and sitting down in two great chairs" (136).
15. Henry Fielding, *The Covent-Garden Journal and A Plan of the Universal Register-Office,* ed. Bertrand A. Goldgar (Middletown, Connecticut: Wesleyan University Press, 1988).
16. Angela J. Smallwood, *Fielding and the Woman Question: The Novels of Henry Fielding and Feminist Debate 1700–1750* (New York: St. Martin's Press, 1989). Smallwood cites the phrase "Man among Men" from William Ernest Henley, editor of *The Complete Works of Henry Fielding, Esq.* (London: Heinemann, 1903). Her reading of the characters of Sophia and Amelia is both feminist and historicist. See especially pages 64–72 and 144–71.
17. Ronald Paulson, ed., *Fielding: A Collection of Critical Essays* (Englewood Cliffs, N.J.: Prentice-Hall, 1962), 58.
18. Henry Fielding, *Joseph Andrews* and *Shamela,* ed. Martin C. Battestin (Boston: Houghton Mifflin Co., 1961), 11.
19. C. J. Rawson explores in detail the sources for Mrs. Francis, including a comparison of her with Richardson's Mrs. Jewkes in *Pamela.* See *Henry*

Fielding and the Augustan Ideal Under Stress, 56–61. A comparison also may be made to Fielding's own Mrs. Tow-wouse in *Joseph Andrews.* See, for example, the descriptions of their physiognomies, of which that of Mrs. Francis is more grotesque.

20. Battestin describes Fielding's narrator in the Introduction to *Joseph Andrews,* xix.

21. Henry Fielding, *The Covent-Garden Journal,* ed. Bertrand A. Goldgar, 86. Here spurious history is treated indulgently: "We frequently meet with lies in history, when the writer . . . did not deserve the opprobrious name of a liar." Or, "[W]e shall not always conclude that the writer intended to impose a falsehood on us when we reject his narrative as incredible."

22. In *Covent-Garden Journal* #27 he writes, "[Betters is] an appellation which all the rich usurp to themselves and shamelessly use. . . . [This] hath produced a very great mischief in society" (171–72).

23. For example, Glen W. Hatfield, *Henry Fielding and the Language of Irony* (Chicago: University of Chicago Press, 1968), 220.

24. J. Paul Hunter, *Occasional Form* (Baltimore: The Johns Hopkins University Press, 1975), 219. Hunter, with particular reference to *Tom Jones,* suggests the potential affinity between "travels" and "epic journey" as paths to wisdom.

25. Stuart Tave, *The Amiable Humorist: A Study of the Comic Theory of the 18th and 19th Centuries* (Chicago: University of Chicago Press, 1961), 141.

Selective Bibliography:
Reader Entrapment

Carl R. Kropf

Adams, Robert M. *Strains of Discord: Studies in Literary Openness*. Ithaca: Cornell University Press, 1958.

Berger, John. *Ways of Seeing*. New York: Viking Press, 1973.

England, A. B. "World Without Order: Some thoughts on the Poetry of Swift." *Essays in Criticism,* 16 (1966), 32–43.

Fish, Stanley. *Is There a Text in This Class? The Authority of Interpretative Communities*. Cambridge, Mass. and London: Harvard University Press, 1980.

Goodman, Kenneth S. "Reading: A Psycholinguistic Guessing Game." *Journal of the Reading Specialist,* 6 (1967), 126–35.

Girard, René. " 'To Entrap the Wisest': A Reading of *The Merchant of Venice*," in *Literature and Society*. Edward W. Said, ed. (Baltimore and London: Johns Hopkins University Press, 1980), 100–19.

Iser, Wolfgang. *The Act of Reading: A Theory of Aesthetic Response*. Baltimore: John Hopkins University Press, 1980.

———. *The Implied Reader*. Baltimore: Johns Hopkins University Press, 1974.

Jaffe, Nora Crowe. *The Poet Swift*. Hanover, NH: University Press of New England, 1977.

Kenshur, Oscar S. "Fragments and Order: Two Modern Theories of Discontinuous Form." *PPL,* 17 (1981), 227–44.

Leavis, F. R. *The Common Pursuit*. New York: New York University Press, 1962.

Lenderman, Deborah. "Self-Transforming Ironies in Swift's *Tale of a Tub.*" *Comparative Literature Studies,* 16 (March 1979), 69–78.

McCrea, Brian. "Surprised by Swift: Entrapment and Escape in *A Tale of a Tub.*" *PLL,* 18 (1982), 234–44.

Mell, Donald C., Jr., "Irony, Poetry, and Swift: Entrapment in 'On Poetry: A Rapsody.'" *PLL,* 18 (1982), 310–24.

Nelson, Daniel N. "Readers in Texts." *PMLA,* 96 (1981), 848–63.

O'Neill, John H. "The Experience of Error: Ironic Entrapment in Augustan Narrative Satire." *PLL,* 18 (1982), 278–90.

Ong, Walter J. "The Writer's Audience Is Always a Fiction." *PMLA,* 90 (1975), 9–21.

Preston, John. *The Created Self: The Reader's Role in Eighteenth-Century Fiction.* New York: Barnes & Noble, 1970.

Rawson, C. J. *Gulliver and the Gentle Reader.* London: Routledge and Kegan Paul, 1973.

Richter, David H., ed. *The Critical Tradition.* New York: St. Martin's Press, 1989.

Rodino, Richard H. "Varieties of Vexatious Experience in Swift and Others." *PLL,* 18 (1982), 325–47.

Sams, Henry W. "Swift's Satire of the Second Person." *ELH,* 26 (1959), 36–44.

Schaeffer, Neil. " 'Them that Speak, and Them That Hear': The Audience as Target in Swift's *Tale of a Tub.*" *Enlightenment Essays,* 4 (1973), 25–35.

Stephanson, Raymond. "The Education of the Reader in Fielding's *Joseph Andrews.*" *PQ,* 61 (1982), 243–58.

Suleiman, Susan R. and Inge Crosman, eds. *The Reader in the Text: Essays on Audience and Interpretation.* Princeton: Princeton University Press, 1980.

Tompkins, Jane P., ed. *Reader-Response Criticism: From Formalism to Post-Structuralism.* Baltimore: Johns Hopkins University Press, 1980.

Uphaus, Robert W. *"Gulliver's Travels, A Modest Proposal,* and the Problematic Nature of Meaning." *PLL,* 10 (1974), 268–78.

Vickers, Brian, ed. *The World of Jonathan Swift: Essays for the Tercentenary.* Oxford: Basil Blackwell, 1968.

Veith, David M. "Entrapment in Restoration and early Eighteenth-Century English Literature." *PLL,* 18 (1982), 227–33.

———. " 'Pleased with the Contradiction and the Sin': The Perverse Artistry of Rochester's Lyrics." *Tennessee Studies in Literature,* 25 (1980), 35–56.

Index